FAMILY STRESSORS

Brunner-Routledge Psychosocial Stress Series
CHARLES R. FIGLEY, PhD, SERIES EDITOR

1. *Stress Disorders Among Vietnam Veterans*, Edited by Charles R. Figley, PhD
2. *Stress and the Family, Vol. 1: Coping with Normative Transitions*, Edited by Hamilton I. McCubbin, PhD, and Charles R. Figley, PhD
3. *Stress and the Family, Vol. 2: Coping with Catastrophe*, Edited by Charles R. Figley, PhD, and Hamilton I. McCubbin, PhD
4. *Trauma and Its Wake: The Study and Treatment of Post-Traumatic Stress Disorder*, Edited by Charles R. Figley, PhD
5. *Post-Traumatic Stress Disorder and the War Veteran Patient*, Edited by William E. Kelly, MD
6. *The Crime Victim's Book, Second Edition*, By Morton Bard, PhD, and Dawn Sangrey.
7. *Stress and Coping in Time of War: Generalizations from the Israeli Experience*, Edited by Norman A. Milgram, PhD
8. *Trauma and Its Wake, Vol. 2: Traumatic Stress Theory, Research, and Intervention*, Edited by Charles R. Figley, PhD
9. *Stress and Addiction*, Edited by Edward Gottheil, MD, PhD, Keith A. Druley, PhD, Steven Pashko, PhD, and Stephen P. Weinsteinn, PhD
10. *Vietnam: A Casebook*, By Jacob D. Lindy, MD, in collaboration with Bonnie L. Green, PhD, Mary C. Grace, MEd, MS, John A. MacLeod, MD, and Louis Spitz, MD
11. *Post-Traumatic Therapy and Victims of Violence*, Edited by Frank M. Ochberg, MD
12. *Mental Health Response to Mass Emergencies: Theory and Practice*, Edited by Mary Lystad, PhD
13. *Treating Stress in Families*, Edited by Charles R. Figley, PhD
14. *Trauma, Transformation, and Healing: An Integrative Approach to Theory, Research, and Post-Traumatic Therapy*, By John P. Wilson, PhD
15. *Systemic Treatment of Incest: A Therapeutic Handbook*, By Terry Trepper, PhD, and Mary Jo Barrett, MSW
16. *The Crisis of Competence: Transitional Stress and the Displaced Worker*, Edited by Carl A. Maida, PhD, Norma S. Gordon, MA, and Norman L. Farberow, PhD
17. *Stress Management: An Integrated Approach to Therapy*, By Dorothy H. G. Cotton, PhD
18. *Trauma and the Vietnam War Generation: Report of the Findings from the National Vietnam Veterans Readjustment Study*, By Richard A. Kulka, PhD, William E. Schlenger, PhD, John A. Fairbank, PhD, Richard L. Hough, PhD, Kathleen Jordan, PhD, Charles R. Marmar, MD, Daniel S. Weiss, PhD, and David A. Grady, PsyD
19. *Strangers at Home: Vietnam Veterans Since the War*, Edited by Charles R. Figley, PhD, and Seymour Leventman, PhD
20. *The National Vietnam Veterans Readjustment Study: Tables of Findings and Technical Appendices*, By Richard A. Kulka, PhD, Kathleen Jordan, PhD, Charles R. Marmar, MD, and Daniel S. Weiss, PhD
21. *Psychological Trauma and the Adult Survivor: Theory, Therapy, and Transformation*, By I. Lisa McCann, PhD, and Laurie Anne Pearlman, PhD
22. *Coping with Infant or Fetal Loss: The Couple's Healing Process*, By Kathleen R. Gilbert, PhD, and Laura S. Smart, PhD
23. *Compassion Fatigue: Coping with Secondary Traumatic Stress Disorder in Those Who Treat the Traumatized*, Edited by Charles R. Figley, PhD
24. *Treating Compassion Fatigue*, Edited by Charles R. Figley, PhD
25. *Handbook of Stress, Trauma and the Family*, Edited by Don R. Catherall, PhD
26. *Disaster Mental Health Services: A Primer for Practitioners*, By Diane Myers, RN, MSN, and David Wee, MSSW
27. *The Pain of Helping: Psychological Injury of Helping Professionals,* By Patrick J. Morrissette, PhD, RMFT, NCC, CCC
28. *Empathy in the Treatment of Trauma and PTSD*, By John P. Wilson, PhD, and Rhiannon B. Thomas, PhD

FAMILY STRESSORS

INTERVENTIONS FOR STRESS AND TRAUMA

EDITED BY DON R. CATHERALL, Ph.D.

Brunner-Routledge
Taylor & Francis Group
NEW YORK AND HOVE

Published in 2005 by
Brunner-Routledge
270 Madison Avenue
New York, NY 10016
www.brunner-routledge.com

Published in Great Britain by
Brunner-Routledge
27 Church Road
Hove, East Sussex
BN3 2FA U.K.
www.brunner-routledge.co.uk

Cover photo: © PICIMPACT/CORBIS
Cover design: Elise Weinger

Brunner-Routledge is an imprint of the Taylor & Francis Group.

Printed in the United States of America on acid-free paper.

10 9 8 7 6 5 4 3 2 1

Library of Congress Cataloging-in-Publication Data

Family stressors : interventions for stress and trauma / edited by
    Don R. Catherall.
        p. ; cm.. — (Brunner-Rutledge psychosocial stress series ;
no. 29)
    Includes bibliographical references and index.
    ISBN 0-415-94963-7 (pbk. : alk. paper)
    1. Post-traumatic stress disorder—Patients—Family relationships.
2. Family—Psychological aspects. 3. Psychic trauma—Patients
—Family relationships. 4. Family therapy. I. Catherall, Donald
Roy, 1946- . II. Stress
    [DNLM: 1. Family—psychology. 2. Stress, Psychological
Traumatic—therapy.   WM 172 F1985 2004]
RC552.P67F365 2004
616.85'21—dc22
 2004011633

Contents

About the Editor

Don R. Catherall, PhD, is Clinical Associate Professor, Feinberg School of Medicine, Northwestern University, and former Executive Director of the Phoenix Institute. Dr. Catherall has specialized in the areas of relationship problems and traumatization for more than two decades. He is the editor of the *Handbook of Stress, Trauma, and the Family* and author of *Back from the Brink: A Family Guide to Overcoming Traumatic Stress*, as well as numerous articles on families and traumatic stress.

Contributors

Marilyn Peterson Armour, PhD
University of Texas at Austin

Michael F. Barnes, PhD, LMHC
Sarasota Memorial Health Care System
Sarasota, Florida

Christine A. Courtois, PhD
The CENTER: Posttraumatic Disorders Program
The Psychiatric Institute of Washington, DC

Freda B. Friedman, MSW, PhD
Private Practice
Chicago, Illinois

Kathleen R. Gilbert, PhD
Department of Applied Health Science
Indiana University
Bloomington, Indiana

Bryn W. Jessup, PhD
Feinberg School of Medicine
Northwestern University
Evanston, Illinois

Mary Beth Williams, PhD
Trauma Recovery Education & Counseling Center
Warringtonn, Virginia

Introduction

DON R. CATHERALL

Every family deals with stress. For many families, the stress is just an inevitable accompaniment to modern life, a background source of white noise that ebbs and flows with schedules, special events, and the nodal points of the family life cycle. Even losses are part of that normal cycle when they arrive as expected—at the end of life. But for many other couples and families, extraordinary stressors enter their lives. These stressors are unanticipated events that disrupt family life and can potentially damage individuals and their relationships.

Every couple and/or family therapist encounters clients struggling to cope with unexpected stressors. Therapists who work with traumatized couples and families have long observed how the impact of traumatic stressors filters through the relationships in intimate systems. The event may initially strike one individual or subsystem, but sooner or later the entire system is affected. Yet despite the observation that all systems are eventually affected, it is also true that each couple and family is different and every stressor is unique. The best we can do as therapists is to know as much as possible about (a) the common patterns of family structure and functioning and (b) the common elements that contribute to the unique impact of different types of stressor events.

This book identifies eight distinctly different stressors that are encountered by couples and families. All are extrafamilial stressors; intrafamilial stressors such as child abuse, domestic violence, or suicide are not addressed in this volume. Instead, the focus is on events or conditions that are experienced as originating from a source that is beyond the couple's or family's control. Stressor events covered in this volume range from high magnitude traumatic events, such as the death of a child or homicide of a family member, to conditions that have only recently been recognized as significant stressors. These latter conditions were either infrequent (e.g., a couple's infertility or the need for adults to provide care for aging parents), hidden from public view (e.g., the childhood sexual abuse of a

1

spouse), or literally not a part of life as we knew it (e.g., the threat of terrorist attack).

All of the specific stressors in the volume were chosen because of the likelihood that therapists will encounter them in working with modern couples and families. All have the potential to disrupt family life and damage individuals and relationships. The specific stressors covered in this volume include death of a child, homicide of a family member, traumatization of a parent, traumatization of a child, (preexisting) sexual abuse of a partner, infertility of a couple, dysfunction of an aging parent, and the threat of terrorism.

The goal of the authors in this book was to identify the common issues, themes, and idiosyncratic aspects of each of the stressors presented here and to provide the reader with tools for intervening with couples and families coping with these stressors. Each case still has to be understood in its own context, with its own unique combination of individual, systemic, and stressor factors. But the more we know in general, the better we are prepared to deal with the specifics. These chapters provide a general knowledge about specific stressors and specific help in applying this knowledge to treat couples and families.

The publication of this book follows the larger *Handbook of Stress, Trauma, and the Family*, which brings together the latest theory, research, assessment, and treatment models in this area. This volume complements the handbook by describing interventions with specific stressor events. Each volume stands alone, but between the two, students and practitioners will be well prepared to help couples and families cope with the vast array of stressful and traumatic events that impinge on family life. Unfortunately, it appears that our field has never had greater need of this kind of preparation.

DESCRIPTION OF THE CHAPTERS

In chapter 1, Kathleen R. Gilbert focuses on what is commonly regarded as the most difficult kind of loss, the loss of a child. She notes how spouses have different relationships with the child and different grief experiences. Gilbert emphasizes that understanding the issues stemming from these differences is key to effectively intervening with these couples.

In chapter 2, Marilyn Peterson Armour examines the immense impact on the family when a family member is murdered. Armour identifies six core constructs that every family encounters in this situation. Understanding these unavoidable questions and experiences provides the clinician with a grasp of the family's experience so that he or she can help the family anticipate and negotiate these fundamental elements of traumatic grief.

In chapter 3, Mary Beth Williams discusses the impact of parental trauma on children. Williams outlines the reactions of children according to developmental stage and offers guidance for supporting children according to those stages. Williams emphasizes the role of attachment security in thinking about how to intervene with children affected by parental traumatization.

In chapter 4, Michael F. Barnes focuses on the impact on parents when a child has been traumatized. Barnes reviews the literature and derives six axioms that capture the changes in the family structure as the family reacts to the trauma. The traumatized child becomes the focus of the family, but the parents' perceptions determine the impact of that change.

In chapter 5, Christine A. Courtois discusses the treatment of individuals who were sexually abused. Traditional treatment of this population has been individually focused, and Courtois argues the importance of the partner's role in therapy. She approaches treatment with the goal of strengthening attachment bonds and increasing security within the relationship to reverse the interpersonal effects of the traumatic past.

In chapter 6, Bryn W. Jessup examines the stressful experience of couples who are infertile. He emphasizes how this non-life-threatening experience nevertheless produces many of the effects of traumatic stress and ambiguous loss. Jessup's approach to treatment relies on restoring meaning, a sense of agency, and an improved connection between the partners.

In chapter 7, Freda B. Friedman discusses a source of stress that is increasing in parallel with the expanding age span of the elderly—the impact on adult children when their aging parents develop disabilities and require care. New roles are required of family members, and these changes affect both the system and the relationships between members, often reviving dormant issues. Friedman emphasizes engaging the entire system and unlocking conflicts that interfere with effective task resolution.

In chapter 8, Don R. Catherall considers a different type of external stressor—the threat of potential terrorist attack. He explains how anxiety can increase when family members differ in their appraisals of danger or their preferences for how the family should cope. He also notes the difference between anxiety and fear, and offers guidelines for dealing with each. His emphasis is on interventions that preserve the connection between family members.

The kinds of stressors discussed in these chapters cannot be eliminated from the lives of modern families. Some couples and families negotiate these stressors without help, whereas others cannot adapt on their own and require assistance with unexpected difficulties. From the opening chapter on the kind of loss that is widely regarded as the most painful of all to the final chapter on the nebulous fears associated with an unsafe environment, the authors assembled here offer specific advice to help clinicians provide that assistance.

1

When a Couple Loses a Child

KATHLEEN R. GILBERT

It is difficult to conceive of a loss that is more painful and overwhelming than the death of a child. The death of one's child has been described as fundamentally different from any other loss (Kagan Klein, 1998), the worst loss that one can experience in adulthood (Rando, 1986; Sanders, 1980), and one of the losses most likely to lead to profoundly overwhelming and life-changing grief (Rosenblatt & Burns, 1986; Walsh & McGoldrick, 1991). Compared to other adulthood losses, the death of a child produces the most intense grief and the widest range of emotions (Sanders, 1980). With the death of one's child "a significant portion of the parent's life energy can effectively die with the child" (Rubin & Malkinson, 2001, p. 219). Deeply held beliefs are confronted with a child's death: Children should outlive their parents and serve as a bridge to the future. Parents should be able to guide, protect, and keep their children from harm, and their inability to do so is devastating. Children are part of their parents, who sometimes use metaphors of amputation to describe the impact such a loss has on them (Gilbert & Smart, 1992).

The bereaved couple is defined broadly in this chapter as two individuals who have maintained a committed, intimate relationship and are the parents of a child who has died. Much of the literature cited here is based on studies of married couples. Little research has been conducted on unmarried heterosexual couples who have lost a child and even less on same-sex bereaved parents. Because marital status is not essential to the experience of couple bereavement, the terms *spouse* and *partner* will be used interchangeably, and, for the most part, marital status will not be assumed.

PARENTAL GRIEF: RESPONSE TO A DEVASTATING LOSS

Grief has been defined in many different ways. For purposes of this chapter, grief is seen as an internal process in which a person progressively reconciles him- or herself from a reality in which a loved one was a living part of his or her life to a reality in which that person can only exist as a concept or memory. This process is progressive but not linear, particularly when the desire to return to the earlier, more desirable reality is triggered. For parents, this often occurs at life events that they had long anticipated. For example, triggers might involve other children reaching significant milestones, such as 16th birthdays, graduations, first dates, proms, and weddings.

This process of grief is evidenced outwardly by a variety of somatic, psychological, social, and behavioral phenomena typically recognized as grief. Inwardly, the process is a progressive reconciliation to the revised reality. For parents, the cause of this grief can range from the death of an adult child to the progressive death of hope for a couple who is struggling to conceive. This process is ongoing, and the elements of the reality that is being constructed are changeable and "fuzzy" (Hagemeister & Rosenblatt, 1997). As Attig (1990) noted, grief involves a type of "relearning of the world." For parents, this involves piecing together a world that has some coherence in which their child is no longer a living, breathing individual (in the case of the death of a living child) or the loss of a dream (where the loss is related to fertility).

The death of a child precipitates a severe crisis of meaning and a related search for meaning (Wheeler, 2001). If the child's death is sudden and unanticipated with little or no time for parents to prepare, the impact of the loss is especially intense (Figley, 1989), and bereaved parents feel out of control, helpless, and confused (DeFrain, 1991; Gilbert & Smart, 1992). The death of a child results in disruption of the normal order of things (Shapiro, 1994); bereaved parents report feeling out of sync with normal life (Gilbert & Smart, 1992), almost as if real life is taking place in a parallel reality as they struggle, sometimes for the rest of their lives, to come to terms with the fact that they have survived their child.

To lose one's child is traumatic regardless of the age of the child (Shapiro, 1994; Rando, 1986) and will result in a loss that is difficult to come to terms with and to resolve (Rubin & Malkinson, 2001). Because the death is out of sequence, it is accompanied by a sense of untimeliness and a perception of injustice that such a thing happened (Janoff-Bulman, 1992).

Bereaved parents may question their competency as parents and the legitimacy of their right to that identity (Gilbert, 1997; Rubin & Malkinson, 2001). They typically report a strong sense of guilt for their inability to protect and nurture their child (Sanders, 1980; Rando, 1986). Questions about their responsibility for the child's death and about their personal identity as parents commonly follow the death of a child (Rosenblatt, 2000).

Normality of Parental Grief

In parenting, important aspects of the parents' selves are invested in their children, thus what are considered to be normal bereavement processes, such as relinquishing the tie to the deceased, are not realistic for parents (Shapiro, 1994). These are people who are now the parents of a child who has died—abandoning that parental role and the parent-child relationship will be difficult, if not impossible. The common expectation that the bereaved will let go and move on will not be a realistic one for many parents. What looks like pathology for other forms of loss may be normal for bereaved parents, and the use of such models of bereavement as spousal bereavement for understanding and predicting parental bereavement may produce a diagnosis of pathology where none exists (Kagan Klein; 1998; Rando, 1986).

Conflicting Inner Realities

Children are as much a conceptual reality as a physical reality in their parents' lives, and parental bereavement reflects this. In the two-track model of parental grieving (Rubin & Malkinson, 2001), parents are seen as conceptualizing and remembering their deceased children both in terms of (a) their actual deaths and (b) what they would have become had they lived. Parents are seen as grieving simultaneously along two tracks. The first track is a more external track that involves "how people function naturally and how this functioning is affected by the cataclysmic life experience that loss may entail" (Rubin & Malkinson, p. 223). This track takes into account the classic, observable characteristics associated with grief. The second involves how people go about "maintaining and changing their relationships with the memories and mental representations of the deceased" (Rubin & Malkinson, p. 223). This track is tied to the unique, idiosyncratic features of the relationship the bereaved parent had with the deceased child. These sometimes conflicting tracks involve what Klass (1993) called the "inner representation of the child," that is, (a) the image of the child that is the concrete representation of the child at the time of death and (b) the imagined child, growing and aging with time.

In a private conversation, a bereaved mother whose daughter died as an infant told me, "I find myself reacting to kids who would be her age. So, babies don't bother me anymore. It's the kids who are the age she would have been. She'd be learning to drive now and I hate the parents who complain about teaching their kids to drive. I want to shout, 'at least you have them to teach. Be glad for what you have.' But it's funny. I still picture her as a baby."

The Readjustment Model of Parental Bereavement: Inward and Outward Steps (Kagan Klein, 1998) focuses on an ongoing process of dealing with the loss. "*Inward steps* originate and are acted on only in reference to one's self. *Outward steps* originate with the self but are intended and taken toward some component of the outside world" (p. 126). Inward steps can only be assumed by others, and when the parent is focusing on inward steps, he or she may appear to be withdrawn, even catatonic. Outward steps are much like the first track in Rubin and Malkinson's model, while in this model inward steps may involve internal images of the child but may also include internally directed self-work.

Although these models differ, what is clear is that bereaved parents are, at any point, working on their grief in observable and unobservable ways, and this grief may be a lifelong process of reevaluating and reconstructing their view of reality as it relates to their deceased child. What also is apparent is that the couple probably will not be at the same place in their grief, and spouses may not have the internal resources to be available to each other, wherever the other may be in the grief process.

The Assumptive World

The grief response of parents is an active, dynamic process that is centered on regaining control and predictability in their lives while also working to make sense of the loss and integrate it into their interpretive structures (Attig, 1996; Gilbert & Smart, 1992). These interpretive structures are a generalized set of beliefs within which one operates on a day-to-day basis, allowing the individual to organize information encountered in the environment and to reasonably anticipate future events, and will be referred to as the *assumptive world* (Janoff-Bulman, 1992; Parkes, 1972). Such basic beliefs as personal invulnerability, a positive view of oneself, and an orderly and predictable world (Janoff-Bulman, 1992) are affected by a significant loss. Due to the nature of the parent-child relationship, similar beliefs are extended to one's child or one's wished-for child (Davidson, 1979). Many other beliefs are also affected and include the sense of who and what they have lost, the idea that innocence will protect the young, and the view parents hold of themselves as individuals and as partners (Gilbert & Smart). In order to make sense of the death of their child, parents must consider and reconsider these and other beliefs. This process of questioning results in psychological upheaval for parents (Janoff-Bulman, 1992) and can lead to disruption of the dyadic grief processes.

In the time immediately surrounding their child's death, parents are faced with a senseless event and feel a strong need to attribute meaning to what has happened and reconcile the effects on the assumptive world (Gilbert, 1998; Janoff-Bulman, 1992; Wheeler, 2001). Grief for them is "a form of psychic energy . . . results from the tension created by the individual's strong desire to (a) maintain their assumptive world . . . as it was before their loss, (b) accommodate themselves to a newly emerging reality resulting from their loss, and (c) incorporating this new reality into their assumptive world" (Martin & Doka, 1998, p. 134). In a process of meaning making and reality construction, the bereaved parents may adjust their view of the loss so that it becomes consistent with existing assumptions or they may modify existing assumptions to accommodate to their new view of the world in which children die before their parents and there is nothing that parents can do to stop it (Fowlkes, 1991; Janoff-Bulman, 1992; Parkes, 1972).

In order to reconcile oneself to a loss, meaning must be attributed and some sort of explanation—a personal or healing theory (Figley, 1983, 1985) or personal loss narrative (Rosenblatt, 2000) —must be developed. By constructing such a narrative, bereaved parents modify their assumptive world to incorporate the loss, thereby achieving a new sense of normalcy and purpose. In this way, they are able to reestablish some of the sense of control and predictability felt prior to the death of their child, to find some sort of understanding, and to gain a sense of mastery with regard to the death and surrounding events (Rosenblatt). After a loss, bereaved parents report commonly being told to get on with their lives or to get back to normal. They typically perceive this as a demand that they abandon the memory of their child. Their lives have become, in a very real sense, meaningless, and there is nothing they can call normal to which they can return (Gilbert & Smart, 1992). Pressured to stop grieving, they may "go underground" with their grief, hiding it from all but a select few (Dyregrov & Dyregrov, 1999). This pressure can also add a layer of complexity to their grief, disenfranchising them and isolating them from support (Doka, 1989).

GRIEF AS A DYADIC PROCESS

The couple serves as the basic building block of the family, the basic unit of reproduction, intimacy, and love (Blumstein & Schwartz, 1983), and partners are in a unique position to provide support and affirm each other's beliefs and perceptions (Berger & Kellner, 1964). Bowlby (1980) has identified the spousal relationship as critical to overall grief resolution following the death of a child within the family:

> How well or badly mourning proceeds . . . turns in great degree on the parents' own relationship. When they can mourn together, keep in step from one phase to the next, each deriving comfort and support from the other, the outcome of their mourning is favorable. When, by contrast, the parents are in conflict and mutual support absent, the family may break up and/or individual family members become psychiatric casualties. (pp. 120–121)

The relationship the couple shares can be an important resource after the death of a child, but the loss can also leave the partners profoundly estranged (Shapiro, 1994). The loss of a child results in what Klass (1988) has called a paradoxical bond between parents in which each partner simultaneously experiences his or her own loss while also sensing that the spouse may be experiencing the loss in very different ways. As bereaved parents, they struggle with their own pain, confusion, and anger; at the same time, they must also cope with the impact of the loss on their relationship. Their roles as parents and as spouses are forever changed by the death (Raphael, 1983). The death of their child affects them in so many ways: Each is a parent who has lost a child, their spouse may no longer seem to be the same person, and the comfortable relationship they once shared with their spouse may now be strained (Gilbert, 1996, 1997, 1998). Bowlby's view may be overly optimistic, as couples frequently find themselves unable to support each other and vary widely in their response to the loss.

Individual and Relational Concerns

The couple is an interactive grieving system in which partners cope with individual and relational concerns that result from the death of their child. Each partner exists as a part of the couple system, reacting to relational pressures, but also as an individual responding idiosyncratically to the loss (Broderick, 1993; Nichols & Schwartz, 1998). These simultaneous self and partner identities are particularly important, especially in light of the effects of the loss on the assumptions, perceptions, and beliefs of bereaved couples (Broderick).

Relational as well as personal assumptions are affected by the trauma (Gilbert & Smart, 1992). Partners may find that in trying to make sense of their spouse's experience, interactional patterns that facilitated their relationship in the past no longer can fulfill this function. Areas of conflict that

had relatively little effect in the past may become overwhelmingly difficult to manage after the loss. At the same time, abilities that were ignored
or derided in the past may come to be seen as strengths, both personally
and relationally. The partners' assumptions about their relationship and
related role behavior can be destabilized or can be reinforced by their interactions after their child's death.

Constructing a Loss Narrative

As they work to make sense of their loss and construct a personal loss
narrative, bereaved parents turn to others around them for help. By confirming the subjective views of the bereaved parents, these views come to
be seen as taking on an objective reality (Berger & Luckman, 1966). However, if partners do not receive confirming external views, they question
their own or each other's perceptions, and the formation of an objective
reality is made more difficult.

Spouses serve as the primary source of support in this narrative formation, functioning in a role Rosenblatt (2000) called the *primary conversation partner*. As he found, even when couples engage in little or no talk,
there is some consistency in their grief narratives, and even when couples
talk a great deal, there can be disagreement. But serving as primary conversation partner may be overwhelming. Both partners have lost the same
child, and their shared lives, with their common history and established
pattern of interaction, are seen as natural resources in facilitating understanding. Unfortunately, the emotional baggage of negative elements in
their shared history, combined with the overwhelming nature of the death
of a child, may prevent them from being available to each other (Gilbert &
Smart, 1992). If partners do not get direct feedback from each other, they
each may resort to interpretation of the other's behavior, leading to
greater confusion (Israelstam, 1989). The behavior of one's spouse may
not be interpreted in the same way it was intended. For example, a husband might avoid showing strong emotion in order to keep his wife from
being upset by his tears. Rather than perceiving this as helpful, she might
see it as evidence of his cold and uncaring nature, resulting in avoidance
and isolation for the couple (Gilbert & Smart).

Clashes in Coping Style

Another area of conflict for couples centers around the need for a continuing bond between the bereaved and the deceased (Klass, Silverman,
& Nickman, 1996). In a study of the use of photographs by bereaved parents, Riches & Dawson (1998) found that artifacts that represent the reality of the child's existence brought great comfort to some parents, while

not to others. Consider the impact of one parent finding great comfort in such physical reminders while the other might find them to be too overwhelming to bear. These artifacts can contribute to the development of shared meaning, or they can serve to push the partners farther apart as one partner works to manage the secondary effects of his or her grief being triggered by items that bring comfort and make the grief of the spouse more manageable.

According to Wheeler (2001), meaning for bereaved parents comes from their connection with others, activities in which they are involved, their personal beliefs and values, personal growth, and continued involvement with their child. Marital partners are able to develop a shared view of their loss by reducing their ambiguity and uncertainty about who and what has been lost, how they are to cope with that loss, and how they are to go on with their lives (Gilbert, 1996, 1997; Gilbert & Smart, 1992). By validating each other's subjective views of the loss, these views come to be seen as more real (Gilbert, 1996; Fowlkes, 1991).

The loss of a child will have a ripple effect through aspects of parents' lives that extend beyond the death and its immediate effects. Couples may find themselves questioning the nature of their marriage as a whole. They may need to reassess their roles and the way in which they view each other (Raphael, 1983). Thus, the loss of their child can result in spouses questioning their marriage and their view of themselves and each other in such roles as parents, partners, nurturers, caregivers, and protectors (Gilbert, 1997).

The Dyadic System of Beliefs

In his discussion of the family's construction of reality, Reiss (1981) referred to fundamental beliefs, assumptions, and orientations shared by family members as their family paradigm. Reiss conceptualized this as a system-level phenomenon in which "assumptions are shared by all family members, despite the disagreements, conflicts, and differences that exist in the family" (p. 1). The dilemma faced here is that this view assumes a shared set of beliefs that can be so basic to all family interaction as to be hidden from family members, making this unverifiable. The view taken here is consistent with that of Broderick (1993), who wrote, "only an individual can have a belief or value or world view or an understanding of something" (p. 186). Partners are hampered by the fact that they cannot know, absolutely, what their spouse is thinking. Yet, even though they may not share a reality in the sense that their views are identical, the need to believe that the loss has comparable meaning for both of them appears to be strong. This need to believe in a shared perspective is borne out by the tremendous difficulty parents have with accepting that each spouse views their child's loss and grieves differently (Gilbert, 1996; Gilbert & Smart, 1992; Peppers & Knapp, 1980).

Couples exist in an interactive system of confirmation and disconfirmation of beliefs expressed by each partner. Through this interactive system, each partner constructs a contextualized view that is experienced as his or her dyadic paradigm. Each partner functions as if they both hold a consistent view of the world, especially in matters of extreme importance. This *as if* quality in their observations and interactions allows them to function as if they both agree (or agree to disagree) on the meaning of the loss. Behaviors and other aspects of the loss are interpreted and comments are assessed all within the context of each partner's assumptions about how their marriage should progress. In my discussions with parents, the recognition that they do not share the same view is cited as one of the most disheartening and frustrating recognitions following their child's death (Gilbert, 1996; Gilbert & Smart, 1992). "I never thought he (or she) felt so differently than I did on this. It was so hard to recognize that we didn't share the same view" has been a common theme throughout my interviews.

It is within the context of this dyadic view that marital partners recognize the loss as a couple, reorganize the way in which they function as a system, and reinvest themselves toward the future (Jordan, 1990; Walsh & McGoldrick, 1991). This dyadic paradigm is more complex than the individual's assumptive world; it encompasses each partner's perceptions of the loss as well as their expectations and perceptions of each other and themselves as spouses. The emphasis is on the consistency of the partners' expressed views of the situation and their ability to work together to reestablish a stable sense of meaning as a couple.

Differential Grief and the Marital Dyad

Bereaved parents, focused on their own struggle, may find it difficult, if not impossible, to provide each other with mutual validation and support (Frantz, 1984; Peppers & Knapp, 1980; Rando, 1983, 1984). Just because two people experience a mutual loss does not make it safe to assume that they can provide support for each other. It is more likely that they would be less able to do this than at other times (Rosenblatt et al., 1991). Rather than helping them to grieve together, the baggage of their relationship with each other impedes mutual grief resolution. Indeed, parents have said that in addition to losing the child, it seemed as though they had lost their spouse for a time (Rando, 1983), or that their spouse was the least helpful person in coping with the death (Frantz, 1984). The interaction of their differences and other conflicts may come together to place tremendous strain on the couple (Miles, 1984). Even though the loss is a mutual one, each parent is directly affected by the loss and may be unable to provide much support to the other (Bugan, 1983; Rosenblatt et al., 1991). Partners only have each other's behavior and imperfectly communicated information on which to base their interpretation of the other's grief state —thus, it is not surprising that conflict occurs.

When spouses are unable to affirm each other's expectations, they feel less stability and control, and are less satisfied with their communication (Fowlkes, 1991). Spouses grieve differently but may be unavailable to each other to work through the grief of their loss if they cannot accept these differences (Gilbert, 1996). The lack of willingness on the part of one spouse to talk meaningfully with the other can lead to a crisis of meaning for one or both of the partners and further complicate creation of their loss narrative (Riches & Dawson, 1998).

Different losses produce different grief. Each spouse must struggle with a unique loss while attempting to cope with changes in his or her partner and in their relationship. As noted previously, this is because the spouses likely will experience different subjective losses. In a sense, they will not have lost the same child; each will have had a different relationship with their child and it will be the loss of that relationship, that connection, that they will feel most keenly. As Rando (1984) has suggested, this relationship need *not* have been a warm, loving one; one high in conflict may result in a more complex pattern of grief with an additional component related to the loss of any opportunity to resolve their differences.

The interaction of their differences and related conflicts place tremendous strain on the couple (Miles, 1984). Given that partners have only each other's behavior and imperfectly communicated information on which to base their interpretation of each other's grief states, it is not surprising that such conflicts occur. Even if one spouse attempts to be supportive of the other, the interpretation by the other spouse may be negative (Gilbert & Smart, 1992).

The common view is that the partners will have the same grief and will be able to reach out to each other better than anyone else (Gilbert, 1996). The reality is that *differential grief* (Gilbert, 1996) is far more common, as each spouse copes idiosyncratically with the loss. This can be experienced as incongruent or out-of-sync (Peppers & Knapp, 1980) if the emphasis is placed on the differences. It can also be viewed in a positive way if the couple sees it as a source of strength. Most often, at least initially, it is seen as a source of stress and weakness.

Assessing Spousal Grieving

Several dimensions of the loss experience, the individuals, and their relationships (both between spouses and between each parent and the lost child) influence the nature of the grieving experience between the two parents. The professional helper can seek to answer the following questions in order to determine how to best intervene.

What is each parent's unique style of grieving? As they attempt to come to terms with the death of their child, each parent will implement behaviors to cope with the loss; these combine to form a unique and idiosyncratic approach toward coping with grief. Each individual also brings different ideas from a variety of sources about the best way to respond to the loss. A triggering agent (e.g., event or sensory input) might cause a recurrence of the pain of grief for one spouse, accompanied by an increase of grieving behavior (Horowitz, 1986) and possibly even symptoms of posttraumatic stress disorder (Rinear, 1988). Such behavior could be seen as frustrating and counterproductive on the part of the other spouse.

Partners may avoid sharing feelings and thoughts because of role expectations about appropriate behavior (Cook, 1988; Gilbert & Smart, 1992) or as an effort to protect each other. They may also avoid each other, or use hurtful comments to create distance, because they feel overwhelmed by their own grief and unable to provide support (Gilbert, 1998) or because the other person's grief triggers their own (Cornwell, Nurcombe, & Stevens, 1977; Gilbert & Smart, 1992). This is especially true when one partner feels that he or she has moved on; that spouse may not want to be pulled back into his or her grief, and the other spouse may resent his or her abandonment of grief (Gilbert & Smart). The inability of the partners to talk about the loss (and validate their growing healing theories with each other) inhibits reconstruction.

One aspect of grief that may cause conflict between partners is the need of one partner (often male) to be alone. This can contribute to a feeling on the part of the other spouse of being rejected and left alone in his or her grief. It is important to remember that the spouse who wishes to be alone does not always need to physically leave. Sometimes, he or she will remain present but will mentally isolate himself or herself. This can cause problems if the other spouse wants the two of them to be together and to talk about the loss.

What are the unique experiences of each parent that are tied directly to the loss? Each parent is likely to go through some experiences that will be highly specific; this often contributes to a feeling of estrangement (Silver & Wortman, 1980). Examples include (a) one parent identifying their child's body whereas the other spouse is unable or unwilling to do so, (b) making the decision about terminating life support, and (c) going alone to the mortuary to make funeral arrangements. As a result, each parent deals with at least some memories that are unique. These are likely to result in individualized triggers of recurrences of grief for each parent (Green, Wilson, & Lindy, 1985) and can contribute to the feeling that the spouse does not understand, leading to isolation (Horowitz, 1986).

What are each parent's unique experiences with death prior to the death of their child? Disparate experiences with death and other losses prior to the death of their child also contribute to dysynchronous expectations in the couple (Silver & Wortman, 1980). For example, one spouse may have experienced the death of a sibling during childhood whereas her partner has had no direct exposure to death. Or perhaps both went through childhood losses but one's family dealt with the deaths in an open way while the other's family refused to talk about the death.

What was the character of the relationship each parent had with the deceased child at the time of the death? Grief appears to be related to such factors as the closeness of the relationship with the deceased and the perception of pre-ventability of the death (Bugan, 1983; Wortman & Silver, 1989). This rela-tionship need not be a warm, loving one. Indeed, Rando (1984) has suggested that a conflict-laden relationship may result in a more compli-cated pattern of grief. For example, the mother who had a close but con-flictual relationship with her teenaged son may have more trigger points and guilt than the father whose relationship was less intense.

Each parent has a unique relationship with a child; thus if that child dies, the loss will have special meaning for each parent, and the impact of the loss will be distinctive to each parent. The specific assumptions, the tenacity with which each parent holds them, and the fact that these as-sumptions must be faced over and over again after their child's death can have an effect on the dyadic grief process (Gilbert & Smart, 1992; Janoff-Bulman, 1992; Peppers & Knapp, 1980; Rosenblatt & Burns, 1986). Although both parents have experienced the same objective loss of a child, each loses a different symbolic child. This then leads to different grief experiences, and possibly to dyadic conflict (Gilbert, 1998; Rando, 1984).

Spouses often expect they will support each other, yet they may find that they are unable to provide this support. Because of their unique rela-tionships with the child and their idiosyncratic coping styles, each spouse will deal with the loss in his or her own way. For example, one spouse may not wish to dwell on the death, whereas the other wishes to discuss noth-ing else. It is also possible that one spouse may not experience the loss to be as painful as the other has. Just as they each had a different past with their child, partners may be surprised to discover that they do not share the same imagined future for their child, creating discrepancies in what each spouse must resolve in the grieving process (Klauss & Kennel, 1976).

To what degree was each parent able to anticipate the loss? The unique char-acter of anticipatory grief is that it involves a period of preparation for grief that provides the bereaved parent with opportunities to rehearse the loss of a wished-for future with the dying individual (Rando, 1986). It may be that one parent has begun to anticipate the death of the child, say from terminal cancer, while the other refuses to accept the possibility that the cancer will not be cured. If this is the case, when the child dies, the first parent will have gone through some preliminary grief work (Lindemann, 1944), and the other parent may feel abandoned in her or his pain.

Alternatively, the parent who began to emotionally disengage while the child was still alive and came to see the child as dead before he or she was physically no longer living may come to see him- or herself as having abandoned the child and may deal with issues later.

To what degree has each parent experienced the loss as traumatic? Losses are more likely to be experienced as traumatic in the case of sudden and unanticipated death, when the bereaved have little or no time to prepare, and when survivors have had little or no previous experience with loss. The impact of traumatic loss is intense. Following such a loss, survivors feel out of control, helpless, and confused. This is accompanied by a sense of untimeliness to the death as well as a perception of injustice that such a thing could have happened (Gilbert, 1998). For many, examples that immediately come to mind when thinking of traumatic loss include the loss of a child to suicide or homicide, although the death of one's child confronts so many basic beliefs about life that any form of death is liable to be traumatic (Gilbert, 1998).

How ambiguous is the loss? Ambiguous losses involve at least some uncertainty and are not easily resolved. Because of the uncertainty and the differences in parental approach to the death, couples may struggle not just with the death, but also with their disparate responses to the death. For example, perhaps a child at college died mysteriously, leaving the parents with no way to determine exactly how the death occurred. Each parent's response is then heavily influenced by assumptions and fears about what is not known. The father, sure there is a guilty party who can be made to suffer for his son's death, may want to initiate an investigation, whatever the cost. The mother, on the other hand, might fear that it was her son's own wild temperament that caused his death and that further investigation will reveal this shameful fact.

In the case of such ambiguous losses as fetal and infant deaths, there is uncertainty as to what or who exactly has been lost. One parent may experience a pregnancy loss as a disappointment or even a relief, whereas the other may experience it as the devastating loss of a baby. The ambiguity extends beyond the spouses, and parents may find their social network to be highly unsupportive.

A unique form of ambiguous loss that seems to be never ending is interminable loss, as in the case of infertility. In this form of loss, the uncertainty of an ambiguous loss is combined with the lack of control and helplessness of a traumatic loss. There may not even be any person to whom their sense of loss can be tied. For couples who are infertile, each month and each treatment brings a new sense of loss, yet there is no public event to mark their loss and only limited support for their grief.

Is there disenfranchised grief or a stigmatized loss? Disenfranchised grief occurs when a person or a group of persons experiences a loss but is not seen as having "a socially recognized right, role, or capacity to grieve" (Doka, 1989, p. 3). Although they have suffered a loss, they are unable to mourn publicly. This may be seen in the hidden grief of grandparents when they experience a loss of a grandchild but then must be strong for their child, the bereaved parent. In many cases, men also experience a disenfranchisement of their grief because of gender expectations regarding appropriate male behavior after a loss.

Stigmatized losses, such as loss of a child through suicide (Bouvard, 1988) or to AIDS (Colburn & Malena, 1989), may serve to isolate parents from others outside the family. They may also become isolated from each other, especially if they resort to blame as an explanation for the loss. Generally, men experience a unique form of stigmatization of grief (Cook, 1988). Cook found that men are caught in a double bind; they are taught to contain their emotions and "act like a man," yet they are expected to express their emotions after a loss "like a woman." Regardless of how they respond to the loss, they will experience some form of censure for acting inappropriately. Surprisingly, even such losses as the death of a child to illness (Arnold & Gemma, 1983; Frantz, 1984; Getzel & Masters, 1984) result in some level of stigmatization. Most parents express at least some sense that their grief has been stigmatized (Arnold & Gemma, 1983; Frantz, 1984; Getzel & Masters, 1984; Helmrath & Steinitz, 1978). It may be that the death of a child is so frightening, and the intense and long-lasting parental grief so disturbing, that people who would ordinarily be supportive simply can not bring themselves to reach out to grieving parents. By exerting social pressure, either through direct encouragement to get on with life or through indirect shunning, others may be able to convince the grieving parent to abandon his or her public expression of grief (Stephenson, 1985).

How does each partner's gender affect his or her grieving? Significant gender differences in grief approach contribute to conflict in parental grief (Cook, 1988; Rando, 1986). Self-reports of parents in my research indicate that they think gender differences in grief are a major, if not the major, contributor to spousal conflict following the death of a child.

Men tend to grieve differently from the traditional expectation of emotionally expressive, social grief. This traditional image of healthy grief was based on early grief studies, which utilized the most willing and available grievers—widows and mothers (Cook, 1988). Thus, the social, emotional grief—which Cook has called women's grief and Martin and Doka (1998) have called conventional grief—has come to be viewed as normal and healthy. The cognitive, solitary grief that predominates among men has been seen as unhealthy and counterproductive to grief resolution. Activities like spending time alone or working out at the gym are generally not seen as a healthy approach to grief, yet our growing understanding of men's grief suggests that such activities can be extremely healthy (Doka & Martin, 2001).

Martin and Doka (1998) identified men as moderating their feelings in masculine grief. Their feelings were muted, and emphasis was placed on self-control and mastery of feelings. Martin and Doka suggested that men may be unable to experience extreme feelings and may simply be more oriented toward rational thinking than emotional expression. Men felt the same emotions as conventional grievers, but they felt them at a lower level and did not necessarily need to express them. Masculine grievers were focused on thinking, and most dealt cognitively with grief. Masculine grievers associated their emotions with specific thoughts and thus were better at controlling their emotions by using cognitive techniques. They were goal oriented rather than emotion expression focused. Masculine grievers focused on problem solving. They had a strong desire for solitude and were reluctant to share grief, especially in group settings.

Studies of gender differences in the grief of bereaved parents support these basic differences: Dyregrov and Dyregrov (1999) found that parents reacted differently, especially during the first year. Mothers had more intense grief with stronger and longer lasting reactions. Fathers hid tears with the intent of being strong and protecting their wives. Differences resulted in misunderstandings and blaming; innocent remarks triggered guilt. Both partners reported misinterpretations and overinterpretation about each other's behavior. Men used hobbies to distract themselves from their grief. Smart (1992) found that fathers feel an obligation to act the strong role for their wives and cannot allow themselves to break down and cry.

Rosenblatt (2000) found that "typically, women grieve more, grieve more openly, express feelings verbally, or seem less controlled" (p. 145). "Typically, it was the man who felt put upon, to feel, relate, and act in ways that did not fit for him, and typically it was the woman who felt emotionally abandoned and that she had to fight to have her feelings acknowledged and respected." (p. 147). Even with all their struggles, couples felt they became a stronger unit following their child's death.

Is there a resonating grief process? A type of emotional triggering has been seen in the mutual reaction between spouses when both partners have experienced the same trauma, the death of their child (Gilbert, 1998). Through repeated exposure to each other's actions, the behaviors of each spouse come to serve as a trigger for the other. Simple exposure to a spouse exhibiting strong emotion sets off the same response in the observing spouse. Unfortunately, the end result of this may be that both spouses hide their emotions, hoping that this will make the loss easier for their partner. If, on the other hand, resonating grief goes on, the spouse being triggered may avoid the other, contributing to their mutual sense of isolation.

Similarly, Cornwell et al. (1977) described a type of resonating grief in which spouses influence each other's emotional state. In this process, partners are emotionally sympathetic; their emotions are close to the surface and they easily set each other off.

What is the character of the spousal relationship? The remaining area to assess is simply the overall quality of the partners' relationship and the way in which they deal with stress in general, both individually and as a couple. This includes their respective expectations of themselves and each other as well as their behavior both premorbidly and since the loss.

FINDING STRENGTH AS A COUPLE—COUPLE COPING

Though most couples struggle through a difficult period following their loss, many survive the loss and its effects on themselves and their marriage and even describe their relationship as stronger than ever (Rosenblatt, 2000). In interviewing intact, married couples who had survived child loss, we found a strong commitment among participants to maintain their marital relationship (Gilbert & Smart, 1992). Participants expressed a commitment to marriage, either as an institution or as a central relationship in their life, and had worked to find ways of maintaining their marriage. This section addresses *couple coping* (Gilbert, 1997), the ways in which couples resolve differences and work together to strengthen their marriage.

Spousal Communication

The ability to engage in open and honest communication has been identified as essential to recovery from loss, and this is especially important for couples (Gilbert & Smart, 1992; Raphael, 1983; Rando, 1984). Because couples are essentially a system, they must exchange information to continue to exist and function as a couple. A part of that "coupleness" is to develop a shared narrative, a difficult task at best. Supportive couple communication facilitates discussion of emotions and the development of the shared narrative, increasing the likelihood of a shared understanding of each other's experience and the willingness to be supportive of each other (Walsh & McGoldrick, 1991). Partners are able to co-mingle their separate realities through communication (Broderick, 1993). This then facilitates the couple's adjustment after experiencing the loss (Raphael, 1983).

The Willingness to Communicate

Marital communication, even attempts at communicating, has been cited as the most helpful aspect of their relationship (Gilbert & Smart, 1992). "He listened to me even when he wasn't listening." This ability to communicate with one another helps buffer the stigmatization felt from others. Their willingness to talk with one another can give them a sense of being connected and allow them to test and confirm their developing narratives. Even people—both men and women—who were relatively un-communicative agreed that communication was essential.

One of the principal ways in which parents increase a sense of mutuality, understanding, and shared concern is through information sharing. This might be information about the death, resources in the community, how they are feeling, or anything they might feel would be useful to their spouse. Because each parent grieves the loss of a unique relationship with the child, sharing information about their child, as well as their hopes for the future, can give each partner new insights about both the child and his or her spouse.

Emotional Expression

As Helmrath and Steinitz (1978) suggested, the ability to cry together and display deep emotions in each other's company is frequently seen as helpful. These emotions can be surprising, even frightening, but sharing feelings can provide additional insights between partners. This can be particularly difficult for men, who often feel the need to protect their wives from such sights. Interestingly, wives have reported this to be the least helpful thing their husbands did in response to the death of their child (Gilbert & Smart, 1992). Based on our new understanding of men's grief, this likely is one of the more challenging aspects of dealing with dyadic grief and may need to be dealt with in a structured way. The couple might take advantage of mixed-sex support groups, if they are available, and take into account the reality of men's grief. They might also make use of agreed-upon rituals that allow both parents to express their feelings in a non-threatening environment (Bowen, 1991; Imber-Black, 1991).

Listening

An essential component of any communication system is the quality of listening—are the partners truly hearing each other? It is important that the listening be nonjudgmental; this is a particular challenge for men, whose problem solving orientation can seem judgmental. Women seem to find their need to talk about the child and the loss to be almost compulsive (Peppers & Knapp, 1980). Listening to one's spouse express strong and painful emotions can be a challenge and can lead to elevated levels of emotion for the listener, especially if the result is conflicted feelings or a conclusion that the problem cannot be solved (Cornwall et al., 1977; Gilbert, 1996, 1998). Yet, despite increased personal stress, listeners often persist because they feel they are helping their spouse to come to terms with the loss. The spouse's willingness to listen can help validate the legitimacy of feelings and build acceptance of their differences. This can have particular value when the personal relationships with the child were extremely different. Listening also affords opportunities for the couple to clarify things and resolve any differences.

Nonverbal Communication

Even with all their efforts, spouses sometimes find it difficult to express their thoughts and emotions to one another. At these times, nonverbal means of communicating can be useful. Nonverbal communication that is consistent with verbal messages can be used to supplement and clarify them. A touch or a glance, when based on a dyadic history, can carry a great deal of information. The same is true for notes and the use of visual artifacts that communicate an intended message. The only risk with nonverbal communication is that it is subject to misinterpretation, so it is most effective when used in concert with other, more direct, forms of communication. Parents may also wish to use code words and signals as forms of verbal and nonverbal shorthand. These can be used to reinforce previously shared information

A Positive View

One of the most distinctive characteristics of couples who report very little conflict is the positive view they hold of each other and their relationship (Gilbert & Smart, 1992). The degree to which a couple had moved to a positive view seemed to be a key to determining the depth of their continued grieving and its impact on their relationship. It also appears that an optimistic view predisposes the parents to seeing positive aspects of their relationship and of each other's behavior, thus allowing them to build positive on positive. This may follow a period of bottoming out for one or both spouses; it may be a gradual improvement; or it may be a consistent view held by the couple.

For many couples, the shift from a negative to a more positive view involves reframing their negative view to a more positive one. The result is a change in the meaning attributed to the spouse's behavior without him or her actually changing (Watzlawick, Weakland, & Fisch, 1974). By positively reframing their spouse's behavior, individual partners can then alter their general perception of their spouses' behavior. This is a natural and automatic process for some couples (Gilbert & Smart, 1992). The urge to put their spouse's behavior in a positive frame can be quite strong, occurring spontaneously as spouses review each other's behavior. By putting a positive frame on the aspects of their spouse's behavior that are contrary to expectations, the reframing spouse can move past disagreements and rebuild the marital relationship.

Sharing the Loss

The strong desire on the part of spouses to have a shared narrative regarding the loss has been noted. The ability to create a shared narrative, or at least to have some of the narrative shared, is important to stress resolution (Reiss, 1981), particularly traumatic stress (Figley, 1989). When marital partners are able to see the loss as shared, not necessarily as the same experience but one in which they feel they have been and are available to each other, they experience a greater sense of connection.

Couples who grieve together are physically available to each other—hugging, touching and occasionally talking—as they increase their sense of the loss as something they share. Grieving together does not mean that partners are at an identical point in their grief resolution, but that they grieve in each other's company. This facilitates communication because being together exposes them to more information about each other's grief and provides a stronger contextual base for interpreting each other's experience. Thus, grieving together increases the likelihood that spouses will accurately interpret each other's behavior.

In addition to grieving together, simply spending time with each other without other obligations is helpful, especially in the days or weeks immediately following or surrounding the death. This may involve taking a trip together or engaging in some leisure activity together. Parents have talked about the satisfaction of going bowling together and coparticipating in other sports that involve elaborate movements and exertion. Activities that did not involve exertion were not seen as helpful nor were activities that involved maintaining conversations with others.

It is important to be aware that an extended period of isolation is not helpful. Spending time alone at first, however, can allow couples the opportunity to establish the loss as their own and to reestablish their sense of what it meant to be a couple.

In addition to reestablishing themselves as a couple, maintaining an external focus allows partners to work as a team, to concentrate on something other than themselves, and to emphasize their identity as a couple. A shared focus on the surviving children is very helpful for many couples, as is helping other family members with their grief, especially bereaved grandparents and siblings of the child who has died. Working together to help other bereaved parents or to prevent other children from dying in a similar fashion to their child also may be useful.

Couples often build a shared focus within their marriage. This shared focus might include joint rituals (Broderick, 1993; Imber-Black, 1991), such as regularly visiting the grave, which can provide a socially approved location to express their grief. Private rituals serve many valuable functions for couples, such as validating the reality of their child, legitimizing their continued relationship with the child, and reaffirming their relationship. Of course, rituals should be meaningful to both parties to serve these purposes.

Sharing Goals and Values

Another way couples can pull together as a unit is by directing their efforts toward some common goal. Initially, the effort to identify a common goal may produce conflict; one partner may identify a goal with which the other is not comfortable. However, if both partners feel committed to the goal, it can reduce strain on the relationship. Common values, especially religious values, are also important for couples. Religious beliefs may serve as the basis for much of their organization of reality. Given that religious beliefs frequently are used to explain new and confusing phenomena, the couple's shared religious values can shape their perception of the loss. The nature of the specific beliefs is not as critical for the marital relationship as the commonality of those beliefs. Consistency between the partners' beliefs about the religious meaning of the loss can reduce marital strain.

An important shared belief that is unique to married couples is the conviction that marriage is important, either as an institution or as a relationship. For participant couples in the Gilbert and Smart (1992) study, at least one person in each couple spoke with great emotion about the importance of marriage. It may be that there are beliefs and values associated with nonmarital couples that are equally important, but the paucity of research on nonmarital couples precludes our knowing what those variables might be.

Flexibility

Flexibility is the ability to change in response to need or to accept some type of information that contradicts previously held beliefs. This information can come from observing or interacting with the partner. As indicated previously, negative interpretations of differential grieving is common among bereaved couples. After time, however, if couples become aware of the bases for these differences, they may learn to be more tolerant of one another.

This realization may come very early in the grieving process for some couples; other couples may slowly move toward acceptance of each other; still others may need to bottom out before they can do so. Partners might feel it is necessary to grieve separately, even though their grief experience is a shared one. Because it is normal and healthy for men to need time alone, female partners can reduce marital stress by accepting this as an appropriate way to grieve and providing their partners with time alone. Even when spouses experience different emotions and have contradictory views of the loss, having the differences acknowledged and accepted by each other is helpful. This acceptance reduces strain between them and allows each to stop feeling guilty over how he or she is grieving.

Role flexibility, the easy ability to shift role performance between partners, allows them to take turns and provide each other with the opportunity to take a break from responsibilities. If this was a normal part of their relationship prior to their child's death, the shift is easier and the couple can reorganize more easily (Jordan, 1990).

Sensitivity to Each Other's Needs

Another way in which partners try to reduce marital strain is by watching for cues that might indicate what their spouse needs from them. This can be challenging in the early period after the loss when both partners are feeling overwhelmed, but many speak with emotion about how much they appreciated simple, basic things that their spouses did for them (Gilbert & Smart, 1992). These small acts can also serve the purpose of validating and legitimizing the parents' continued emotional connection to the deceased child.

Sometimes, these efforts are done to reduce tension in the home. Helping one's spouse and focusing on meeting his or her needs can also benefit the person doing the helping. Focusing on the other spouse can serve as a distraction for the helper, while the spouse that is being helped also may learn new coping strategies by observing the helping spouse. The helping spouse may feel increased self-efficacy because he or she is able to help another person rather than only needing to be helped.

In addition to being aware of one's spouse's needs, accepting one's own limitations, recognizing one's own needs, and not trying to be everything to the spouse can benefit both partners. Rather than try to exceed their abilities, partners can encourage their spouses to go to appropriate resources outside the marriage, such as a friend, a clergy member, a therapist or counselor, or a support group.

CONCLUSION

The death of a child can be devastating to parents, both in its impact on them as individuals and in its impact on their relationship. Couples may feel as though they are out of sync when their child dies, believing that they should grieve in similar ways because they have lost the same child. Parents, and those around them, may need to be helped to see that they have had different subjective losses and are likely to grieve in unique ways. Indeed, this differential grief is the norm for parents who have lost a child; the experience of matching grief styles is the exception.

As grieving parents work (a) separately to rebuild their assumptive worlds and (b) together to rebuild their dyadic paradigm, there are a number of things they can do to enhance their ability to survive the loss as a couple (Gilbert, 1997). These points can be incorporated into therapeutic interventions with marital couples.

- The death of one's child is one of the most difficult losses to cope with and is likely to result in complicated grief. For many parents, it results in lifelong grief. This does not mean that the grief will be overwhelming, but that it will recur and affect them throughout their lives.
- When their child dies, marital partners do not experience the same subjective loss. Each will have specific issues to be worked through that are related to a variety of unique personal issues related to the loss.
- Some of the unique issues that influence parental grief include their idiosyncratic approach to overwhelming stress, the unique experiences of each parent at the time of the loss, prior experience with death, their relationship with the child, their ability to anticipate the loss, the degree to which they experienced the loss as traumatic, the amount of ambiguity of the loss, the degree to which the loss is stigmatized and the grief is disenfranchised, their gender, and the nature of their couple relationship.
- The norm for parents is that they will grieve differently from each other. In addition, they will progress through various aspects of their grief at different speeds. Such differences can be painful to acknowledge as so much implicit information is attributed to the behavior of one's spouse. Yet, if they are able to reframe this differential grief from "incongruent" to perceived strengths, partners may be able to learn from each other.
- Underlying everything else they will do is a need for the couple to build and maintain open lines of communication, both within the relationship and with others outside the relationship. Without this communication, partners may end up "running along parallel tracks" rather than actually being available to each other.
- Partners benefit from holding or developing a positive view of themselves and their relationship. For those who are married, this may include a positive view of the institution of marriage (Gilbert & Smart, 1992). Reframing (Figley, 1989) is a useful tool in moving to this positive view.
- The ability to build a shared view, even the view that they will agree to disagree and will not argue about differences, is important for the couple. One of the most difficult challenges to maintaining their sense of being a couple comes when the partners recognize that they have conflicting views. Finding points of similarity in their personal loss narratives can moderate the impact of conflicting views.

- Participation in activities together facilitates the partners' sense of being a couple. This may involve simply being together and going for walks, working on tasks or hobbies together, or caring for surviving children. Leisure activities that involve an expenditure of energy may also be helpful. As they reassess their roles and their relationship with each other, shared time and shared activities can allow partners to negotiate how these new or modified roles will be carried out.

- Partners need to strive for flexibility in their relationship and sensitivity to each other's needs. As each of them has experienced a different loss, and because each has a different style of grieving, each will have his or her own issues to work out. It may be necessary for one or both of them to have some time to be alone. One partner may need outside resources (e.g., support groups or individual therapy) more than the other.

Bereaved couples often find the death of their child to be initially overwhelming and beyond belief; their relationship bonds are sorely tested by the aftermath of their loss. However, as difficult as it seems at first, both Gilbert and Smart (1992) and Rosenblatt (2000) affirmed that couples can come through the death of their child with their couple relationship strengthened.

REFERENCES

Arnold, J. H., & Gemma, P. G. (1983). *A child dies: A portrait of family grief*. Rockville, MD: Aspen.

Attig, T. (1990). Relearning the world: On the phenomenology of grieving. *Journal of the British Society for Phenomenology, 21*, 53–66.

Attig, T. (1996). *How we grieve*. New York: Oxford University Press.

Berger, P., & Kellner, H. (1964). Marriage and the construction of reality: An exercise in the microsociology of knowledge. *Diogenes, 46*, 1–25.

Berger, P., & Luckman, T. (1966). *The social construction of reality*. New York: Doubleday.

Blumstein, P., & Schwartz, P. (1983). *American couples*. New York: William Morrow and Co.

Bouvard, M. (1988). *The path through grief: A practical guide*. Portland, OR: Brietenbush Books.

Bowen, M. (1991). Family reactions to death. In F. Walsh & M. McGoldrick (Eds.), *Living beyond loss: Death in the family* (pp. 79–92). New York: W. W. Norton & Co.

Bowlby, J. (1980). *Attachment and loss (Vol. 3)*. New York: Basic.

Broderick, C. (1993). *Understanding family process: Basics of family systems theory*. Newbury Park: Sage.

Bugan, L. A. (1983). Childhood bereavement: Preventability and the coping process. In J. E. Schowalter, P. R. Patterson, M. Tallmer, A. H. Kutscher, S. V. Gallo, & D. Peretz (Eds.), *The child and death* (pp. 357–366). New York: Columbia University Press.

Colburn, K., & Malena, D. (1989). Bereavement issues for survivors of persons with AIDS: Coping with society's pressures. *Advances in Thanatology, 1*, 126–131.

Cook, J. A. (1988). Dads' double binds: Rethinking fathers' bereavement from a men's studies perspective. *Journal of Contemporary Ethnography, 17, 285–308.*

Cornwell, J., Nurcombe, B., & Stevens, L. (1977). Family response to the loss of a child by Sudden Infant Death Syndrome. *Medical Journal of Australia, 1, 656–658.*

Davidson, G. W. (1979). *Understanding the death of the wished-for child.* Springfield, IL: ORG Service Corp.

DeFrain, J. (1991). Learning about grief from normal families: SIDS, stillbirth, and miscarriage. *Journal of Marital and Family Therapy, 17, 215–232.*

Doka, K. (1989). *Disenfranchised grief: Recognizing hidden sorrow.* Lexington, MA: Lexington Books.

Doka, K. D., & Martin, T. (2001). Take it like a man: Masculine response to loss. In D. A. Lund (Ed.), *Men coping with grief (pp. 37–48).* Amityville, NY: Baywood Publishing.

Dyregrov, A., & Dyregrov, K. (1999). Long-term impact of sudden infant death: A 12- to 15-year follow up. *Death Studies, 23, 635–661.*

Figley, C. R. (1983). Catastrophes: An overview of family reactions. In C. R. Figley & H. I. McCubbin (Eds.), *Stress and the family. Vol. II: Coping with catastrophe (pp. 3–20).* New York: Brunner/Mazel.

Figley, C. R. (1985). From victim to survivor: Social responsibility in the wake of a catastrophe. In C. R. Figley (Ed.), *Trauma and its wake: The study and treatment of posttraumatic stress disorder (pp. 398–417).* New York: Brunner/Mazel.

Figley, C. R. (1989). Posttraumatic family therapy. In F. Ochberg (Ed.), *Posttraumatic therapy (pp. 83–109).* New York: Brunner/Mazel.

Fowlkes, M. R. (1991). The morality of loss: The social construction of mourning and melancholia. *Contemporary Psychoanalysis, 27, 529–551.*

Frantz, T. T. (1984). Helping parents whose child has died. In T. T. Frantz (Ed.), *Death and grief in the family (pp. 11–26).* Rockville, MD: Aspen Systems Corp.

Getzel, G. S., & Masters, R. (1984). Serving families who survive homicide victims. *Journal of Contemporary Social Work, 65,* 138–144.

Gilbert, K. R. (1996). 'We've had the same loss, why don't we have the same grief?' Loss and differential grief in families. *Death Studies, 20, 269–283.*

Gilbert, K. R. (1997). Couple coping with the death of a child. In C. R. Figley, N. Mazza, & B. Bride (Eds.), *Death and trauma: The traumatology of surviving (pp. 101–122).* Bristol, PA: Taylor & Francis.

Gilbert, K. R. (1998). Spouses. In C. R. Figley (Ed.), *Burnout in families: Secondary traumatic stress in everyday living (pp. 47–74).* Boca Raton, FL: St. Lucie Press.

Gilbert, K., & Smart, L. (1992). *Coping with fetal or infant loss: The couple's healing process.* New York: Brunner/Mazel.

Green, B. L., Wilson, J. P., & Lindy, J. D. (1985). Conceptualizing posttraumatic stress disorder, a psychosocial framework. In C. R. Figley (Ed.), *Trauma and its wake* (pp. 53–69). New York: Brunner/Mazel.

Hagemeister, A., & Rosenblatt, P. C. (1997). Grief and the sexual relationship of couples who have experienced a child's death. *Death Studies, 21, 231–252.*

Helmrath, T. A., & Steinitz, E. M. (1978). Death of an infant: Parental grieving and the failure of social support. *The Journal of Family Practice, 6, 785–790.*

Horowitz, M. (1986). *Stress response syndrome (2nd ed.)* New York: Jason Aaronson.

Imber-Black, E. (1991). Rituals and the healing process. In F. Walsh & M. McGoldrick (Eds.), *Living beyond loss: Death in the family* (pp. 207–223). New York: Norton.

Israelstam, K.V. (1989). Interacting individual belief systems in marital relationships. *Journal of Marital and Family Therapy, 15, 53–63.*

Janoff-Bulman, R. (1992). *Shattered assumptions: Towards a new psychology of trauma.* New York: Free Press.

Jordan, J. (1990). *Loss and family development: Clinical implications.* Paper presented at the 98th Annual Convention of the American Psychological Association, Boston, MA.

Kagan Klein, H. (1998) *Gili's book: A journey into bereavement for parents and counselors*. New York: Teachers College Press, Columbia University.

Klass, D. (1988). *Parental grief: Solace and resolution*. New York: Springer.

Klass, D. (1993). Solace and immortality: Bereaved parents and their continued bond with their children. *Death Studies, 17, 343–368.*

Klass, D., Silverman, P., & Nickman, S. L. *Continuing bonds: New understandings of grief*. Washington, DC: Taylor & Francis.

Klauss, M. H., & Kennell, J. H. (1976). *Maternal–infant bonding*. St. Louis, MO: Mosby.

Lindemann, E. (1944). Symptomatology and management of acute grief. *American Journal of Psychiatry, 101, 141–148.*

Martin, T. L., & Doka, K. D., (1998). Revisiting masculine grief. In K. J. Doka & J. D. Davidson (Eds.), *Living with grief: Who we are how we grieve (pp. 133–142)*. Washington, DC: Hospice Foundation of America.

Miles, M. S. (1984). Helping adults mourn the death of a child. In H. Wass & C. A. Corr (Eds.), *Childhood and death (pp. 219–239)*. Washington, DC: Hemisphere.

Nichols, M. P., & Schwartz, R. (1998). *Family therapy, concepts and methods (4th ed.)*. New York: Allyn & Bacon.

Parkes, C. M. (1972). *Bereavement: Studies of grief in adult life*. New York: International University Press.

Peppers, L. G., & Knapp, R. J. (1980). *Motherhood and mourning: Perinatal death*. New York: Praeger.

Rando, T. A. (1983). An investigation of grief and adaptation in parents whose children have died from cancer. *Journal of Pediatric Psychology, 8, 3–20.*

Rando, T. A. (1984). *Grief, dying, and death: Clinical interventions for caregivers*. Champaign, IL: Research Press.

Rando, T. A. (1986). A comprehensive analysis of anticipatory grief: Perspectives, processes, promises, and problems. In T. A. Rando (Ed), *Loss and anticipatory grief (pp. 3–38)*. Lexington, MA: Lexington Books.

Raphael, B. (1983). *The anatomy of bereavement*. New York: Basic Books.

Reiss, D. (1981). *The family's construction of reality*. Cambridge, MA: Harvard University Press.

Riches, G., & Dawson, P. (1998). Lost children, living memories: The role of photographs in processes of grief and adjustment. *Death Studies, 22, 121–140.*

Rinear, E. (1984). Parental response to child murder: An exploratory study. Unpublished doctoral dissertation, Temple University.

Rinear, E. E. (1988). Psychosocial aspects of parental response patterns to the death of a child by homicide. *Journal of Traumatic Stress, 1, 305–322.*

Rosenblatt, P. C. (2000). *Parent grief: Narratives of loss and relationship*. New York: Brunner/Mazel.

Rosenblatt, P. G., & Burns, L. H. (1986). Long-term effects of perinatal loss. *Journal of Family Issues, 7, 237–253.*

Rosenblatt, P. C., Spoentgen, P., Karis, T. A., Dahl, C., Karis, T., & Elde, C. (1991). Difficulties in supporting the bereaved, *Omega, 23, 119–128.*

Rubin, S. S., & Malkinson, R. (2001). Parental response to child loss across the life cycle: Clinical and research perspectives. In M. S. Stroebe, R. O. Hansson, W. Stroebe, & H. Schut (Eds.), *Handbook of bereavement research: Consequences, coping, and care (pp. 219–240)*. Washington, DC: American Psychological Association.

Sanders, C. (1980). A comparison of adult bereavement in the death of a spouse, child, and parent. *Omega, 10, 303–322.*

Shapiro, E. R. (1994). *Grief as a family process: A developmental approach to clinical practice*. New York; Guilford.

Silver, R. L., & Wortman, C. B. (1980). Coping with undesirable life events. In J. Garber & M. E. P. Seligman (Eds.), *Human helplessness: Theory and applications, (pp. 279–340)*. New York: Academic.

Smart, L. S. (1992). The marital helping relationship following pregnancy loss and infant death. *Journal of Family Issues, 13, 81–98.*

Stephenson, J. S. (1985). *Death, grief and mourning: Individual and social realities.* New York: Free Press.

Walsh, F., & McGoldrick, M. (1991). Loss and the family: A systemic perspective. In F. Walsh & M. McGoldrick (Eds.), *Living beyond loss: Death in the family (pp. 1–29).* New York: W. W. Norton.

Watzlawick, D., Weakland, J., & Fisch, R. (1974). *Change: Principles of problem formation and problem resolution.* New York: W. W. Norton.

Wheeler, I. (2001). Parental bereavement: The crisis of meaning. *Death Studies, 25, 51–66.*

Wortman, C. B., & Silver, R. C. (1989). The myths of coping with loss, *Journal of Consulting and Clinical Psychology, 57, 349–357.*

2

When a Family Member Is Murdered

MARILYN PETERSON ARMOUR

Approximately 20,000 people are murdered in the United States on an annual basis (Federal Bureau of Investigation, 1999). Although this figure is sizable, the number of family members affected by a homicide is substantially larger. Indeed, a national prevalence study found that 9.3% of the adults sampled had close friends or relatives who had been murdered (Amick-McMullan, Kilpatrick, & Resnick, 1991). Moreover, children are disproportionately affected in certain settings because they may frequently witness the assaults and murders of their peers. A study of 221 low-income African-American youth found that 43.3% had witnessed a murder (Fitzpatrick & Boldizar, 1993). In Los Angeles, 10 to 20% of all homicides are witnessed by children (Larson, 1994).

In contrast to bereavement associated with natural dying, survivors of homicide victims describe the changes to their lives as "lasting" and report there is no "recovery" (Murphy, Johnson, & Lohan, 2002). This lack of closure reflects the mourners' ongoing reactions to the horrific mode of death as well as to the public nature of what is otherwise a private and personal matter marked by sadness. Instead of the solitude necessary for grieving their loss, homicide survivors may find themselves caught up in (or revictimized by) protracted court trials, negative media retrospectives on the victim, and parole hearings for the offender years after the murder.

Because murder is a crime against the state, the social imperative of understanding how the death occurred, apprehending and punishing whomever is responsible, and protecting the public eclipses the needs of family members who become bystanders to the state's process. They may be shunned by friends and family, blamed or slandered for the way the victim died, or even maligned for the way the victim lived. The lack of social validation for their experience uproots survivors from their communities and changes the basis for their belonging.

Homicidal grief has been described as prolonged and extreme (Rando, 1993; Spungen, 1998). Murphy and her associates (2002) found that 5 years after the violent death of their children, 61% of mothers and 62% of fathers met diagnostic criteria for mental distress, and 27.7% of mothers and 12.5% of fathers met diagnostic criteria for posttraumatic stress disorder (PTSD). Moreover, 66 percent of parents whose children died from homicide were unable to find meaning in the death. Personal and family prayer and church attendance did not improve outcomes over time (Murphy, Johnson, Lohan, & Tapper, 2002). Although participation in a support group seemed to make some difference, mutual support did not aid in the reduction of mental distress and PTSD. Another study found that neither antidepressant medication nor interpersonal psychotherapy appeared to relieve traumatic grief symptoms (Reynolds III et al., 1999).

Family members of homicide victims tend to avoid therapists because they quickly discover that most therapists know little about the post-homicide experience. Family members also quickly become sensitized to the reactions of others and easily recognize when therapists shy away from the horrific details or promote medications or other solutions as a way to "fix" the problem. Finally, family members generalize their mistrust as a way to protect themselves from future pain. Consequently, therapists must recognize that they will be on trial until the family is assured that the therapist is a genuine human being who will not abandon them along the way.

Treatment of family members of homicide victims requires both an understanding of traumatic grief symptoms and recognition of the onslaughts from the social milieu. By including both dimensions, clinicians can respond more comprehensively to the totality of the experience, help survivors manage the ongoing crises that accompany murder, and use the dynamic interplay between family members and the larger community to construct meaning-making interventions.

TRAUMATIC GRIEF

Clinicians have long struggled with how to categorize the unique reactions of family members to homicide. Traditional models of grief do not fully encompass the extreme shock that induces a wide array of both physical and emotional reactions, including significant sleep disturbance and exaggerated startle behavior; the shattering of basic assumptions about the world; and the feelings of rage, fear, horror, guilt, and shame (Spungen, 1998). Indeed, when compared to the grief that accompanies "natural" dying, the intensity and duration of these "normal" homicide reactions appear to be atypical or even pathological (Armour, 2002a). The gradual recognition of a trauma response to violent death, however, has begun to move the fields of grief investigation and traumatology closer together. Rynearson, in particular, has asserted that the coexistence of trauma and loss in homicide survivors creates a synergism of delayed recovery, noting that the "disintegratory effects of traumatic imagery and avoidance on cognition, affect and behavior impair the more introspective and reflective demands of acknowledging and adjusting to the loss" (Rynearson & McCreery, 1993, p. 260). Hence, trauma could prolong bereavement, and bereavement could prolong trauma. The duality of the experience has also been recognized by Spungen (1998), who contended that events that reactivate homicide-related trauma might simultaneously trigger a subsequent temporary upsurge of grief (STUG) reaction. Today, there is greater recognition of the co-occurrence of trauma and grief as "normal" responses to homicide death. Mastery of responses to the trauma of how the loved one died is seen as a necessary first step to accessing the deep pain and sadness underneath horrific loss (Rynearson, 1996).

The concept of traumatic grief, therefore, is an emerging diagnostic disorder with two symptom clusters: symptoms of separation distress (Cluster A) and symptoms of traumatic distress (Cluster B) (Prigerson et al., 1999). Symptoms of separation distress are related to the motivation for attachment. Symptoms of traumatic distress are primarily related to the motivation for autonomy and self-protection (Rynearson, 2001). The refined symptom criteria proposed for traumatic grief are listed in Table 2.1. Although the occurrence of these symptoms is considered "normal" for homicide survivors, individuals with marked and persistent symptoms are considered to be distressed and at risk. Studies using independent bereavement samples demonstrate that the symptom criteria for traumatic grief are distinct from symptoms of depression and anxiety (Bierhals, Prigerson, Fasiczka, Frank, & Miller, 1996; Prigerson et al., 1995, 1996). Despite some controversy about the duration of symptomatology necessary for assigning a clinical diagnosis, data from two separate samples suggest that a 6-month assessment is superior to a 2- or 3-month evaluation in predicting numerous mental and physical health impairments (Prigerson et al., 1995, 1996, 1997). Duration criteria are still being tested.

Families of homicide victims are a hidden but sizable population whose numbers are not considered in crime statistics. The movement to standardize criteria for traumatic grief helps validate the arduousness of

Table 2.1
Refined Criteria for Traumatic Grief[1]

Cluster A criteria
1. Person has experienced the death of a significant other
2. Response involves three of the four following symptoms experienced at least sometimes:
    (a) Intrusive thoughts about the deceased
    (b) Subjective sense of numbness, detachment, or absence of emotional responsiveness
    (c) Searching for the deceased
    (d) Loneliness as result of the death

Cluster B criteria
1. Purposelessness or feelings of futility about the future
2. Subjective sense of numbness, detachment, or absence of emotional responsiveness
3. Difficulty acknowledging the death (e.g., disbelief)
4. Feeling that life is empty or meaningless
5. Feeling that part of oneself has died
6. Shattered worldview (e.g., lost sense of security, trust, control)
7. Assumes symptoms or harmful behaviors of or related to the deceased person
8. Excessive irritability, bitterness, or anger related to the death

---

[1]Taken from Prigerson et al. (1999). Consensus criteria for traumatic grief: A preliminary empirical test. *British Journal of Psychiatry, 174*, 67–73.

family members' struggles and recognize their efforts as legitimate and worthy.

RISK ISSUES

Several studies have identified risk factors that increase the likelihood of PTSD and mental distress in homicide survivors. Risk factors may include aspects of individual personality and temperament, family structure and functioning, social contexts, and the interactions between these system levels (Smith & Carlson, 1997). A significant relationship has been found, for example, between grief and pathology and feelings of closeness to the victim (Stevens-Guille, 1999). Mothers, in particular, are at risk because of the intense caregiving attachment, regardless of the age of the child (Murphy et al., 1999). In a study of African-American women, mothers scored higher on posttraumatic stress symptomatology and distress than their respective counterparts if they (a) lived with the victim at the time of the murder, (b) reported a high degree of closeness to the victim, or (c) reported seeing the victim regularly (Thompson, Norris, & Ruback, 1998). Young children are also more prone to difficulties because of their intense dependent attachment to the deceased and possible direct exposure to the dying (Rynearson, Favell, & Saindon, 2002).

Contact with Social Institutions

Risk factors also include negative experiences with social institutions. Family members who are dissatisfied with the criminal justice system are more likely to develop PTSD (Amick-McMullan et al., 1991). Improperly handled death notifications can heighten a family's risk because the messenger and method used become fused with the information itself (Spungen, 1998). A family highlighted their extensive rage in describing how a police chaplain had delivered the news that their father/husband had been killed:

> [He] just told us briefly, very briefly what had happened and then he said, "You know I need to tell you now that as you go through this whole process that you got to think about forgiveness [because] you don't want to be angry." We all wanted to (yelling) plaster the man.

Issues with the Nature of the Death

Issues related to the details of the victim's actual dying and the status of the offender further add to the potential for difficulties. If the offender is not apprehended, the tragedy remains unbuffered by solution, punishment, retribution, or redemption (Rynearson, 1988). Moreover, the motive of the murderer may intensify the family's horror and/or rage (Shapiro, 1996). If death involves violence, mutilation, or the likelihood of intense suffering, family members may be haunted by images, thoughts, and questions about whether the murder victim knew he or she was about to die, whether he or she was afraid, and whether he or she suffered (Davis, Wortman, Lehman, & Silver, 2000).

Issues with Meaning

Homicide shatters the assumptive base about meaning, order, and self-worth. posthomicide experiences can exacerbate the dismantling of this psychological foundation. The stigma associated with murder, for example, frequently results in the severing of external family support along with the disruption of attachment bonds with the deceased. (Murphy et al., 1999). Parents with PTSD have been found to have, among other characteristics, less social support. There is also a relationship between parents' inability to find meaning after a homicide and their mental distress, marital satisfaction, and physical health. In a study of violent death, parents of homicide victims were found to have more difficulty finding meaning than parents of either suicide or accident victims (Murphy, Johnson, &

Lohan, 2003). This same study found the incidence of PTSD among mothers to be three times higher than among women in the Kessler, Sonnega, Bromet, Hughes, & Nelson (1995) national comorbidity study. Fathers reported twice the rate of PTSD as a normal sample of U.S. males.

Mental Illness

The presence of a psychiatric disorder in family members can add additional risk for PTSD and mental distress. Specifically, anxiety, major depression, and substance abuse disorder are associated with prolonged dysfunction (Rynearson, 2001). In a study of violent death, mothers with PTSD appeared to self-medicate with alcohol consumption (Murphy et al., 1999). Indeed, 15% of these mothers consumed more than 20 drinks per week, or three times the amount currently recommended for women (Archer, Grant, & Dawson, 1995).

Family members are likely to have endured post-homicide distress that did not substantially lessen over time (Thompson, Norris, & Ruback, 1998) and are more likely than other direct crime victims to be classified as positive for lifelong PTSD (Freedy, Resnick, Kilpatrick, Dansky, & Tidwell, 1994). These reactions may be manifested in anxiety attacks, existential crises resulting in suicide ideation, phobic avoidance of homicide-related stimuli, and overwhelming rage triggered by trivialities. They also mask, inhibit, and delay the mourning process.

COMMONLY USED INTERVENTIONS

Interventions for homicide survivors have focused on the use of open-ended peer-led self-help support groups followed by individual psychotherapy, psychoeducational and structured brief therapy groups, or adjunctive therapies including medication and eye movement desensitization and reprocessing (EMDR).

Self-Help Groups

Self-help groups such as Parents of Murdered Children, Compassionate Friends, or For the Love of Christi offer family members a community that shares a common experience that facilitates understanding and normalization of intense feelings of anger and rage, vengeance, guilt, anxiety, and profound sadness. Group members give hope to one another through their ability to survive horrific death. Family members also have a setting in which to learn and practice new coping skills. Parents of Murdered Children, in particular, provides a mechanism to channel anger and rage into advocating for victims' rights and more speedy justice

(Peach & Klass, 1987). An effectiveness study of Compassionate Friends found that active participation increased parents' comfort in discussing bereavement with others and reduced parents' self-directed anger (Videka-Sherman & Lieberman, 1985). Psychotherapy did not have these effects. Group members also reported increased self-confidence, sense of control, happiness, and freedom to express feelings and decreased depression, anxiety, guilt, anger, and isolation.

Individual Psychotherapy

Accounts of individual psychotherapy suggest that interventions are focused on intrusive, avoidant, anxious, and depressive symptoms. Family members who seek individual psychotherapy frequently cannot move beyond strong feelings of rage, horrific images, feelings of guilt and self-reproach, and extreme anxiety. Both psychodynamically oriented treatments and behavioral/cognitive treatments have some proven effectiveness (Jacobs & Prigerson, 1999). Behavior therapies, in particular, focus on trauma desensitization through exposure to feared and avoidant bereavement cues. Narrative approaches show promise because they help family members organize and articulate their experience into a coherent whole, thus reducing psychological dissonance (Levy & Wall, 2000; Temple, 1997). Regardless of the theoretical model employed, individual work requires a long-term commitment to attending to the unique circumstances in each case while helping family members to break out of the vicious cycles.

The development of the therapeutic relationship is of the utmost importance. The therapist's capacity to absorb family members' intense feelings is critical not only to providing a sense of safety in which to overcome terror and helplessness, but also to countering family members' fears that no one can tolerate truly hearing the complete and tragic story of what happened. Besides providing guidance and expression of a range of feelings, the therapist needs to respond to all aspects of family members' lives. Specifically, the therapist must be familiar with the high potential for secondary victimization from institutions and have a thorough grasp of survivor-victims' rights, including disability insurance and victims' assistance programs.

Professional Groups

Psychoeducational and structured brief therapy groups have emerged recently as promising interventions for homicide survivors. A 10-week model for adolescent survivors of homicide victims focuses on education about grief and trauma, the facilitation of thoughts and feelings related to grief and trauma, and the reduction of PTSD symptoms (Salloum & Vincent, 1999; Salloum, Avery, & McClain, 2001). A siblings bereavement group has facilitated individual mourning by helping members deal with their feelings of rage by talking about these feelings and recognizing and accepting the awful fact that there is both evil in the world and a lack of fairness in random violence (Moss & Raz, 2001). Rynearson (2001) and Rynearson, Favell, and Saindon (2002) have developed two 10-week group interventions: the criminal death support group and the restorative retelling group. The criminal death support group is an advocacy group that offers support and educates group members about grief, self-care, and the criminal justice system. The restorative retelling group follows a format that first reinforces resilience and commemoration of the victim, then follows with an intervention to moderate internalized and debilitating death imagery that allows a transcendent retelling of the violent death. Regardless of the specific group format, psychoeducational and structured brief therapy groups commonly address issues of guilt for not having prevented the murder, anger, fears of losing one's mind, and fearful and murderous feelings (Miranda, Molina, & MacVane, 2003). Moreover, interaction with others helps activate accommodation to the tragedy, altruism from and toward others, and coherence based on the capacity to find some meaning in the tragedy (Rynearson & Geoffrey, 1999).

A FRAMEWORK FOR FAMILY INTERVENTIONS

A qualitative study of families of homicide victims that employed a hermeneutic phenomenological approach found that six core constructs define the essence of the post-homicide experience (Armour, 2002b; Peterson, 2000). The challenges embedded in each of the core constructs provide clinicians with a therapeutic map to move families toward healing by helping them navigate the labyrinth of crises. Because each family member reacts differently, the clinician must move between the individual, family subsystem, and whole-system levels based on an ongoing assessment of priority and need. Likewise, because the murder of a loved one is a public event, the clinician will likely move between the family and larger community, that is, help family members broker relationships with teachers or employers, assist in redressing the media for defaming a loved one, and so on. Therefore, in many cases, the clinician will use an intersystem approach that moves from the individual to the community while targeting the family's health as the primary frame of reference.

This Is a Nightmare You Don't Wake Up From

Description.   Learning that a loved one has been murdered is a defining moment. It plunges family members into a netherworld from which there is no escape. It leaves an indelible imprint and reduces family members to a primal state. Screaming, howling, banging, and mindless pacing are behaviors normally reserved for lower forms of life. A mother vividly recalled her response after being awakened by police banging at her bedroom window at 3:30 in the morning to tell her of her son's murder: "I walked around the house and around the house, screaming and screaming until daylight. You know, until people came."

The death notification is only one in a succession of sudden and unanticipated onslaughts that thwart the ability of family members to regain a firm footing and leave them feeling defeated. A father described his fall after he later learned that his 14-year-old daughter had also been raped. "Now the only good thing of her dying a virgin is gone. Now I'm mad . . . I mean I've sunk another level lower . . . You're just, you're falling and . . . you can't catch yourself. I'm just—God, I'm drowning."

Family members cannot fathom why someone would take the life of their loved one. The "why" question provokes guilt and leaves family members adrift in an ocean of infinite possibilities. The lack of answers leaves them suspended, preoccupied with the details that surround the homicide, and without a clear target for their rage. A sister went to the courthouse: " . . . I read all the documents. I . . . read every page because I had to. I had to see everything that was said and piece it all together. I was looking for more people to blame and hold responsible."

Although the size and shape of the pain may change, it is omnipresent. A father could not speak his son's name for 18 years. A mother described her realization that her daughter's murder would be a permanent nightmare: "[E]very parent has a nightmare where your child dies but you wake up. This is something you cannot wake up from. This is permanent. This is real."

Challenges. The experiences highlighted by this core construct illustrate the need for safety, a warning system that prepares family members for unexpected events, and the normalization of enduring pain and guilt. Safety is created, in part, by achieving mastery over the elemental horror and fear that registers at a preverbal, psychophysiologic level. Rynearson (2001) maintained that overwhelming fear is so inchoate, however, that the ability to calm oneself is beyond or before words. He argues instead for relaxation strategies such as systematic desensitization, guided imagery, EMDR, art and movement therapy, and the performing of rituals to reduce the flooding caused by intrusive states of horrific awareness, imagery, and affect. These kinds of "pacification" techniques increase the capacity of family members to calm themselves and help reduce trauma to a tolerable level.

Homicide strikes the entire family. The simultaneous effects on and incapacitation of all members leave the family without support from within; magnify each individual's terror, helplessness, and sense of aloneness; and aggravate the worry each has about the well-being of the others. Although they may not be able to change what is happening, their acknowledgment of parallel experiences creates a bond of understanding and point of reference for comparing and universalizing reactions, which decreases isolation. Two sisters described the commonality of their struggle:

> *Sister 1:* Each one of us had an individual hole and none of us could reach over the top to help each other out of the fuckin' hole. And we were just getting deeper and deeper and there was nowhere to go but down.

> *Sister 2:* We would take turns falling apart, of screaming and totally losing it.

> *Sister 1:* My sister moved in here [for] about a year and that's when I started to be able to do more than survive. It was just ok to be nobody, totally unhappy and totally a mess and no words needed to be said at all.

Families can be warned about what lies ahead by talking with them about commonly occurring events in the post-homicide experience. Longer term members of self-help groups often prepare survivors of recent homicides by talking about the unanticipated "surprises" that eroded their own equilibrium. They also validate the reality of ongoing suffering and the endless search for reasons why. Referring family members to support groups, providing reading materials that outline common post-homicide occurrences, and predicting upcoming events give reassurance that the responses of family members are normal and that they best be prepared to be retraumatized regularly. This pessimistic message tends to fortify the family because it furnishes them with knowledge that can help remove them from the sense of personal victimization that is otherwise associated with the experience.

I Feel Betrayed by Those I Thought Cared

Description. Family members expect others to respond sensitively to their needs. Instead, the actions of others leave them bereft of the emotional nourishment they need from friends, relatives, and the community. The impact of the homicide may sever important external family connections because friends or extended family cannot relate to the tragedy. Family members gradually realize that they no long fit as they did before. A wife said, "I went [to my old church] last night for the first time in a long time. It felt cold like I don't belong here anymore. (voice quivering and crying) It's not my home."

Family members also discover that people who should know better act out of their own self-interest rather than with integrity. A father described the rebuff he got from the police when he called to report that his daughter was missing: "[T]he police said, 'Sorry, we do not have time to go looking for every kid that skips school . . . . Go check the mall . . . . She's probably there with her girlfriends.'"

Because they anticipate a sensitive response from people in caregiving positions, they are startled when they receive perfunctory and cursory treatment. Their trust in the benevolence of others gets broken. A son commented on thoughtless condolences. "Anyone who says, 'God never gives us anything that we can't handle' hasn't been through shit. That's all I can tell them. 'You haven't been through it cause you would never say that.'"

As their hopes for support and genuine concern are dashed, family members slowly awaken to the realization that they are, indeed, alone. The world they have known or assumed is no longer there for them. These experiences shatter their faith in a benevolent community and a pre-dictably sensitive response from others to personal tragedy. They also erode a sense of worthiness based on a just-world premise that people who are deserving receive better treatment.

Challenges. The mistrust generated by these situations easily general-izes to anyone who has not experienced a homicide. Consequently, the challenge in this core construct is to counter the emerging mistrust with plausible explanations and the encouragement of acts that either reduce the need for validation or directly address the insensitivity of others.

Although mistrust may build some protection against future on-slaughts, it also contributes to family members' isolation and feelings of helplessness. Because a mistrustful stance is informed by the probability of being in personal jeopardy, it breeds a sense of danger. Giving family members a plausible framework to better understand the attributions or behavior of others helps diffuse that danger. Family members can be told that people who have not experienced homicide have no basis to under-stand the family's experience. Consequently, they are incapable of truly knowing what the family is going through. The making of attributions about the motivations of others helps family members view the behavior as an aspect of human nature rather than a personal betrayal that cannot be forgiven. A clinician who works with homicide survivors tells them that they will be rewriting their address books. Her statement predicts and normalizes the experience of abandonment, but also directs them to look elsewhere for support.

Mistrust is heightened by ongoing disappointment that derives from continuing to look to others for what they cannot give. As family members recognize that their aloneness reflects the uniqueness of their situation, they begin to feel more confident about asserting who they are without waiting for social permission. Although the basic mistrust may still exist, family members find a way around its noxious effects. A family describes how they took matters into their own hands when they met with the fu-neral director to plan their father/husband's service and burial:

Sister: You see, not only are we doers, we are bargain hunters. (laughs) And of course if you can't use a coupon or if you can't get it on clearance or on sale, you just don't do it.

Mother/Wife: This funeral director kept his head down and never looked at us. Never even said, "I am sorry for your loss." He had this long list and kept telling us how much each item would cost. Finally I said, "Do you take coupons?" It just came out.

Son: All of us were laughing. We just busted a gut because this is how our family works.

The paranoia embedded in mistrust is also dissolved when family members realize they must educate the people they most care about. Talking about anniversary reactions with extended family members, for example, provides an avenue for sharing. A daughter salvaged a disappearing friendship after she challenged her friend's response. "When one of my friends gave me a platitude about my father's death, I said, 'What the hell do you say that for. It doesn't mean anything to me.' She said, 'Well I don't know what to say.' So I said, "Well, why don't you tell me you don't know what to say.' And that was a breaking point because that friendship made it while the other ones didn't."

Measures taken to limit the growth of mistrust within the family are particularly important because mistrust can erode the family's cohesiveness. Consequently, family members must address insensitive remarks made by other family members as well.

What Rights Don't I Have Anymore?

Description. Because homicide is a public event that impacts the potential safety of the community, family members quickly discover that their individual rights are subsumed by the public agenda. They feel invisible in the criminal justice system because murder is a crime against the state rather than a crime against them. Yet they are thrust into the limelight by the media, with its claim that the public has a right to information. They also feel marked as an object lesson in the community about what can go wrong in someone's life. Changes in their status happen overnight. Consequently, the rights to privacy and control over their own destinies, which they assumed as private citizens, become rights they no longer have.

Family members, for example, crave information about the suspect, the progress of the police investigation, or the autopsy, but find they are barred, patronized, or discriminated against when they try to get the facts because the priority is given to the criminal investigation. A daughter who hounded the coroner for information about her father was told, "Lady, it is not our job to tell you. We don't have to. We don't want to." A mother declared, "It's been four years and I have seen absolutely nothing from the so-called police investigation."

Besides discovering limits about their rights to information, family members learn that the state's procedures, protocol, and agenda take priority and feel like bit players, who must endure lengthy court delays, courtroom shenanigans, and unjust verdicts. A father explained that because "murderers have a right to a speedy trial, defense attorneys use that right to manipulate time, yet we don't have any of those rights." Family members frequently witness the denigration of their loved one as part of defending of a suspect, but must remain mute in the courtroom so as not to bias the jury. They may be sequestered by the defense as witnesses to limit the jury's potentially empathic response to their presence in the courtroom. Family members feel stripped of their rights to privacy as the media, on behalf of the public, prints or broadcasts all available information and speculation about the murder. How the murder victim is portrayed often distorts who they had been. A mother screamed at a reporter after her son was portrayed as a loser because he lived in a poverty-ridden African-American community: "You didn't even know my son. The only reason you can do this is because he's dead. He can't defend himself." Accordingly, family members may feel they lose control of their truth about the victim. Family members also lose the right to control their standing in the community. They feel marked. "I felt I had a big *M* on my forehead for *Murder*." They feel typed as bad luck families. "It's a stigma to be a parent of a homicide victim. Somehow you failed your kid because she was killed." A sister explained, "There has to be a reason why somebody gets murdered. Either they live in a bad neighborhood, they are involved in a drug deal, they are a different color than me, or they are poor and lazy. There has to be a reason to explain why it [won't] . . . happen to . . . me."

Challenges. The challenge in this core construct is to reduce or mitigate the potential for retraumatization and helplessness by giving control back to the family, skills to manage the ongoing trauma, opportunities to make choices, and support for claiming their own narrative about their loved one and who they are as a family. Although it is not possible to predict all the circumstances that will revictimize family members, some events, such as the criminal trial or discovering information about the murder through the media, are more likely to cause lasting damage because of a person's increased vulnerability. The potential for traumatization can be decreased by forecasting upsetting circumstances, creating safety plans, and building support networks.

Predictable traumatizing events also provide opportunities to fortify the family as a natural support system by capitalizing on the resources they can offer one another. The potential assault on the family, for example, may require family members to put aside differences in order to protect all members against a common enemy. The family's need for the competencies of a marginalized family member may result in a more elevated status for that person after others realize the benefits they gain as a result. Hence, difficult upcoming events can elicit mutual needs for support, careful planning about how to manage and lessen the trauma, and creative ideas about how to respond to one another's difficulties. The preparation and strengthening of the family unit can inoculate family members against the trauma, provide pathways for constructive interdependency in the wake of tragedy, and generate further pride in their accomplishments as an antidote to the shame they may otherwise feel as victims of crime.

The trial for the accomplice of the murderer of Mrs. L's brother was set in a small town three hours away. Mrs. L and her three adult children planned to attend but were concerned about how to avoid reporters, what to do if they ran into relatives of the alleged accomplice or murderer, and how to manage their reactions during the trial if they got upset. The prosecutor had warned them that any emotional display could be used by the defense as the basis for a possible mistrial on the grounds that the display influenced the jury. Mrs. L was a prominent community leader who felt, for the first time ever, that she did not have the stamina to be strong and courageous for her children. She was close to her two daughters, but she worried about her son who played a peripheral role in the family. Mrs. L's brother had been a father figure to Mrs. L's son, whose own father died when he was small.

The therapist suggested a family session to assess each person's needs relative to the upcoming trial. Mrs. L shared her dismay over her lack of strength and asked her children for help. They rose to the occasion by expressing gratitude for the opportunity to give back and reassuring her that they would stick close by. The therapist challenged Mrs. L to let her children be full adults by resisting her usual proclivity to take charge. The family discussed ways to evade the media. Together they plotted to stay at a remote motel owned by a friend. The son offered to make the reservation and to warn the friend about the need to throw off reporters who might be tracking the family's whereabouts. He was also given the job of making contact at the trial with the murder victim's sons, who lived in another state and had maintained minimal contact with their father. The family decided to travel from the motel to the courthouse in one car, to sit together in the courtroom, and to always have one other family member accompany whoever needed to go to the bathroom or attend to personal business. The family felt that this unity would further protect them from reporters who might try to corner them individually for a statement and from the impact of encountering friends and family of the alleged murderer. Concern over reacting to disturbing information presented during the trial was handled by the family's decision to squeeze hands tightly whenever anyone was upset. Being able to share nonverbally would keep the family connected and notified and enhance feelings of safety. Family members also carried notepads so they could write what they wanted to say but could not express verbally. Mrs. L decided she wanted a local priest to meet with the family prior to the first day of the trial and to be available to her and her children throughout the process.

After the trial, Mrs. L and her children returned triumphant about having accomplished their plan. Mrs. L's daughters had increased respect for their younger brother, who himself felt proud and more vital to the family. Mrs. L was able to openly acknowledge her exhaustion and thank her children for their support. Everyone enjoyed outwitting the reporters. Most important, throughout the trial family members had stayed connected, which increased their cohesiveness and laid the groundwork for activating similar plans as the need might arise. They also experienced that acknowledging and making room for each other's needs strengthened rather than depleted them.

In addition to planning how to manage ongoing trauma, control is increased by making family members aware of situations where they can make choices. A mother described how she helped her son manage potential trauma by first alerting him to the fact that there would be new and disturbing information in the newspaper or at the trial and then warning him that he would need to monitor how much he could handle at a time. "He would say, 'Tell me a little bit.' I'd throw little pieces at him and he would process them. Then he would ask questions so he could digest it." The decision to see a loved one's body offers another opportunity to exercise choice. Family members can be told that the decision is theirs. Moreover, they do not have to see their loved one's body alone. If they decide not to view the body but worry they may regret the choice they made, they can be reminded that there will still be pictures of the body taken by the coroner's office and they can get their questions answered at a later date. Giving choice about viewing the loved one's body is an example of delivering concrete services in ways that have therapeutic meaning. The experience of exercising control by making choices both counters family members' feelings of helplessness and serves to restore dignity and self-worth because their needs are shown to matter.

Families lose control in part because extended family members, neighbors, clergy, police, teachers, and others construct their own narratives of the homicide, the victim, and the survivors. Because these narratives are likely to overshadow the family's story, family members can take back some control by forming a narrative that honors the memory of their loved one, embodies loyalty and attachment, and recognizes the enormity of their suffering and fortitude they have needed to just survive. By claiming their own narrative about their loved one and who they are as a family, they counter the diminishment and stigma they may feel from others. Temple (1997), for example, has developed a treatment model based on the work of Boszormenyi-Nagy and his associates (Boszormenyi-Nagy, 1986; Boszormenyi-Nagy & Spark, 1973) to help children create stories with new forms of loyalty and attachment to both the dead and the living following murder. Depending on the circumstances, clinicians can also assist community members such as teachers and clergy to construct narratives that support family members in their attempts to come to grips with the homicide.

Belonging Relieves My Alienation and Loneliness

Description.   In select situations, family members experience a belonging that affirms their common humanity with others. For example, family members may have times when they feel more connected as a family because they mutually bear the trials and tribulations of the homicide. By describing individual variations in guilt, a sister's narrative validated each person in the family while reinforcing the family's unity: "My guilt was 'I want to kill myself because the murder was my fault.' My brother's was 'My dad, my best friend.' My sister's was 'I wasn't close enough to my dad.' My mom's was 'I kicked him out of the house and this is what I get.'"

Family members may feel a union when others truly understand their suffering or they themselves respond to the suffering of others. A mother felt a bond with the judge after the trial: "The judge, this touched me so much, she came over to me. She had tears streaming down her cheeks." A daughter described the "right" questions to open up her pain: "The group leader said, 'Talk about the violence and trauma to your father's body. Tell me about the nightmares. Tell me what you'd like to do to this guy. Do you have revenge fantasies?'"

The pain of remembering ties family members to their loved one. It reminds them that they belong to something larger than their suffering. After visiting his daughter's grave, a father said, "That's my 13-year-old daughter. She'll never get any older. You know she's safe. You know she's good. You know she's in heaven. You don't spend a lot of time at the graveside because it hurts. But you come away smiling." When family members belong, they feel seen. Being cared for affirms their worth. Remembering reminds them of the universality and transcendence of the human condition.

Challenges.   This core construct emphasizes the need for belonging that grows out of the loneliness imposed by death, the alien experience of being a living crime victim, and the shattering of attachments to one's beliefs about the world and how it operates, to friends and family, and to the larger community. Peer-led or -facilitated support groups tend to be the treatment of choice for homicide survivors because they provide family members with a new community that gives them the support they had expected from friends and people in caregiving positions. They also educate group members about how to navigate, among other things, the criminal justice system, the coroner's office, and the media. Moreover, support groups have the potential to counter the stigma and social dislocation that accompany family members' new identity as homicide survivors. Being part of a legitimating social context helps release blockages to grieving and cushion the starkness of the pain (Michalowski, 1976).

The cohesiveness of the family unit can also serve as a buffer against loneliness and alienation. Besides affirming the normalcy of their pain and one another's perspective about events, family members can offer support by banding together against the "outside enemy" (e.g., defense attorneys, gossipy neighbors, taunting children). Consequently, work with the family needs to focus on strengthening unity by reducing the threat posed by individual differences and capitalizing on opportunities for family members to take action on behalf of the family's welfare. Understanding and tolerance for differences in family members' reactions are built first by normalizing the dissimilarities in family members' responses. Families can be told that although everyone grieves for the loss of the same person, each family member grieves for the very unique and individual relationship he or she had with that person. Consequently, the grief of one family member may look very different from the grief of another. Therapists can also educate family members by telling them that they will not do their grieving all together in a neat little package. The potential for shame and a sense of failure can be reduced by reminding families that their reactions may be all over the place, and at times relationships may get nasty. Moreover, therapists who operate on the premise that everyone is going through the aftermath of the murder simultaneously and therefore have little to offer each other can instead begin to shape the family's understanding and acceptance of the uniqueness of each person's process by fostering a climate that encourages nonjudgmental observations of one another as well as comparisons. Besides establishing a frame of reference to address differences, unity is built by adherence to the adage that what happens to any one person in the family, in effect, happens to them all. Isolation, therefore, is countered by the belief that we are all in this together and need one another to get through it. The plan created with the L family was built on and furthered this understanding.

Affirming spiritual connections with a loved one or higher power can also enhance belonging. Family members commonly report transcendental experiences such as being visited in their dreams, having serendipitous events occur, or having an uncanny sense of the ongoing presence of their loved one. When therapists make room for these events, family members feel greater permission to accept the comfort associated with reconnecting with their loved one.

I've Stopped Waiting for Things to Go Back

Description.   The murder of a loved one psychologically stretches family members to the extreme. Instead of landing at a final destination, they find themselves in a state of continuing change and emergence. Besides discovering new aspects of themselves, they become keenly aware of their environments, experience life intensely, and see through to the core of things. A brother, who used to be impervious to shooting scenes in movies, said, "I am completely aware of it now and . . . I will avoid a movie if I think it's going to be violent." A sister explained that the death of her brother caused her to feel "very deeply, which can be both good and bad since I can now tolerate a lot of pain and suffering."

Many of the changes are disabling. After the murder of her brother, a sister recalled that her father began drinking heavily, landed in a nursing home, and eventually died. "He couldn't get up . . . but there was no physical reason . . . he couldn't walk." A son described the permanence of his mother's depression. "I think the day my Mom heals is probably going to be the day she dies." Although family members are aware that they have choices about how they respond to the homicide, their decisions do not feel voluntary. They also feel that their changes further separate them from others who have not experienced murder. A daughter declared, "I feel we know something others do not know."

In addition to personal changes, family members develop a different set of assumptions that provide them with more reliable truths on which to base their living. Their "new normal" consists of the following beliefs: (a) It could happen again. (b) I don't control anything anymore. (c) They [homicide victims] are not coming back. (d) There's no closure. (e) Suffering is natural. (f) I draw my own conclusions. (g) I don't believe past tomorrow. (h) Everyone does it differently. These new beliefs encompass the randomness of events and allow for individual differences. They also normalize suffering and present a more accurate interpretation of time.

Challenges.   Homicide can create fundamental changes in the personality and temperament of surviving family members. Having lost their membership in the society as they had known it, they face learning how to fit in nontraditional ways as a developmental task associated with this core construct. The first step is for family members to realize that besides losing their loved one, they may have lost their sense of safety, trust, spiritual beliefs, anonymity, and who they used to be. Family members, therefore, have to get to know who they are now and how to appreciate who they are as a result of the changes. They also have to adjust to changes in one another. A son commented on changes in his father: "Dad was kind of like a T.V. dad, very one dimensional. After my brother's death, it was like wow! Dad has feelings and emotions. He just became very real."

As family members accept that they are different from other people and from who they were before the homicide, they have less difficulty acting on what they currently believe as a way to make a place for themselves. A father struggled with himself for 2 years before he put a big red bumper sticker on his car that read "Parents of Murdered Children." "It was a hard thing to do at first, but it's been on every car I've ever had since." A mother felt triumphant after she challenged her minister to give homicide sur-vivors as much attention as he was giving to raising the consciousness of the congregation to the needs of prison inmates. The accumulation of acts, over time, builds self-reliance and self-confidence.

Besides helping family members accept and become aware of the op-portunities for personal growth, therapists can help identify and support the emergence of the "new normal." The beliefs that compose the new normal reflect fundamental shifts in family members' assumptions about the world, how it operates, and what to expect. They also provide a foun-dation that cultivates greater intentionality in decision making, living in the here and now, and a reprioritizing of life goals. Although the beliefs arise spontaneously from the impact of the murder and post-homicide experience, listening for and validating their emergence provides credi-bility for the development and expression of personal and novel ideas that are not commonly shared. A family member expressed her differentness in her rendition of the belief that suffering is natural: "We're a culture that doesn't like to suffer. You really have to walk a hard, bumpy, lonely, cold, suffering path to get through . . . . And there isn't going to be any short cuts."

The Intense Pursuit of What Matters Is the Meaning in My Life

Description. Neimeyer (2001) contended that meaning reconstruction in response to loss is the central feature in grieving. Studies of traumati-cally bereaved mourners suggest, however, that meaning making based on traditional definitions of the process may not occur because violent death is irrational and meaningless (Davis et al., 2000; Rynearson, 2001). Specifically, meaning making has been narrowly construed as "making sense" based on a cognitive system of appraisal about the nature of the event or as an existential search for meaning and purpose in life. People blocked from finding meaning in these ways may use other methods both to counter the incoherence inherent in violent acts and rebuild meaning out of the rubble.

In the aftermath of the homicide, family members find that they have intense feelings about what matters now. By following the dictates of these intense feelings, they begin to create meaning in their lives. Family members express what matters in three ways. First, they make pronouncements about the hypocrisy they see around them or verbal assertions about conclusions they have reached for themselves. A mother exposed the dishonest motives of the press as well as her own position: "[W]henever there's media around, no way would you hear a word from me because you're not 'doing it for my good.' You're doing it to sell papers." Second, family members intervene in situations by holding others accountable or claiming what is rightfully theirs. These corrective actions become symbolic statements about the importance of their experience and their right to be seen. A father used the court setting to express his sentiment that justice had been done: "[At the end of the trial] I started clapping and then everybody broke loose and [the murderer] turned around and whipped me the bird. And I thought, 'I did it. I finally got to this guy.'" Third, family members make choices about how to live that become, in effect, testimonies to the fact that their loved one's life mattered as do the lives of others, including theirs. Family members may use their experiences, therefore, either to educate others or as a base of direction for how they want to live out their own lives. A mother, for example, decided to use the police envelopes that held her son's remaining personal effects to educate and shock juvenile delinquents into valuing their own lives. A family chose to do something about their historically destructive communication patterns: "Me and my sisters made a pact that we weren't going to talk about each other behind each other's backs with Mom even if we thought there was good reason to do it. That's when the family really got cohesive."

Challenges.   The challenge in this core construct is for each family member to positively reconstruct the self through performed meanings (Armour, 2003). The behaviors reestablish the coherence and continuity of the self by reducing the dissonance created by the conflict between pre- and post-realities. Moreover, by acting in accordance with their personal beliefs, homicide survivors create an internal resonance that is self-affirming. The internal experience of the family member is that "I/we make sense." Likewise, the formation of causal linkages between meaningful acts generates movement and directionality from event to event. The internal experience of the family member is that "I/we go on." Additionally, pursuits related to what matters help establish a social identity because many of them involve interactions with others who also have a stake in the murder and how it is portrayed (e.g., schoolmates, media representatives).

Because meaning making occurs in response to intrusive stimuli, therapists can further the process by watching for events that furnish the opportunity for action. When family members make declarations that expose hypocritical behavior, therapists can become compassionate witnesses to the truth being expressed. When family members take positions that enhance the potential for self-determination, therapists can bolster their resolve through agreement or support for the conclusions reached. When family members consider interventions that would symbolically express the importance of their experience and their right to be seen, therapists can support a constructive process by encouraging the planning necessary to bring about the desired results. When family members contemplate choices that have a sense of mission, provide purpose, and create meaning out of the senselessness of murder, therapists can again lend credibility to the endeavor by exploring its significance to the person and encouraging instrumental behavior.

The therapist's ability to assist in this process rests on listening for what matters to family members and allowing their striving, however faint, to direct the work. As the significance of the pursuit is recognized, the intensity that accompanies it becomes powerful because of the presence of strong emotions, clarity of purpose, and strength of commitment. The intensity therefore provides an experience of self as enhanced, which helps in self-reconstruction. Therapists can also listen for negative appraisals given to events because these appraisals help elicit meaning-making behaviors connected to naming truth, problem solving, and the revamping of life goals. Indeed, the therapist's capacity to hear vital signals helps family members pay closer attention to their own healing processes and the importance of living more deliberately. The accumulation of their acts over time gives family members the base from which to construct coherent narratives that make their experience central.

WORKING WITH FAMILIES OF HOMICIDE VICTIMS

Although the six core constructs collectively compose the post-homicide experience, there is no order to their emergence. Therapists, therefore, must assess the relative significance of the core constructs for each member based on current events in the family's post-homicide experience. Therapists must also recognize that priorities will continually shift as different events happen. If a father first learns at a long-delayed trial that his daughter was stabbed 75 times, he may experience reactions, for example, from the core construct titled *This Is a Nightmare You Never Wake Up From.*

Therapy with family members is frequently long term because of the emergence of events that continually retraumatize them, the need to reconstruct a self, and the lack of a validating community. Moreover, therapy does not result in "closure," "resolution," or "recovery." Rather, success in therapy is most often measured by the family members' ability to prevail over the murder that threatened to destroy them too. In some cases, family members are able to use the tragedy as a springboard for personal transformation (Parapully, 2002; Tedeschi, Park, & Calhoun, 1998). Posttraumatic growth, however, may be more dependent on dispositional traits than on specific therapy approaches.

Work with families requires the therapist to assume a fundamentally supportive position that works with a family's strengths to build greater cohesiveness. The goal is to promote the solidarity of the family so that individual members feel less alone. Building solidarity also minimizes the chances for personal disintegration because family members can use one another as reference points to normalize their reactions. The family-team concept needs to be activated in challenging situations so that family members feel protected and the family itself is buffered against further onslaughts. Therapists, therefore, need to maintain a family perspective while they make continual adjustments regarding whom they see in the family and for what reasons.

Therapists must be accepting of the slowness of the post-homicide process and respectful of the rights of family members to move only according to their own pace. Therapists must also be aware of how their own reactions to the horrific nature of the death cause them to back off from family members and delay asking the questions that might expose the full intensity of family members' rage, terror, graphic death imagery, and fantasies of revenge. The family's experience may also make therapists more aware of their own losses, the reality of their mortality, and the unpredictability of random violence. Because the potential for vicarious traumatization is high, therapists must build in time between sessions to process and integrate the experience, allow for their own active grieving, and search out activities that nourish life within themselves.

REFERENCES

Amick-McMullan, A., Kilpatrick, D. G., & Resnick, H. S. (1991). Homicide as a risk factor for PTSD among surviving family members. *Behavior Modification, 15,* 545–559.

Archer, L. G., Grant, B. F., & Dawson, D. (1995). What if Americans drank less? The potential effect of the prevalence of alcohol abuse and dependence. *American Journal of Public Health, 85,* 61–66.

Armour, M. (2003). Meaning making in the aftermath of homicide. *Death Studies, 27,* 519–540.

Armour, M. P. (2002a). Experiences of co-victims of homicide: Implications for research and practice. *Trauma, Violence, and Abuse, 3,* 109–124.

Armour, M. P. (2002b). The journey of homicide families: A qualitative study of their post homicide experience. *American Journal of Orthopsychiatry, 72,* 372–382.

Bierhals, A. J., Prigerson, H. G., Fasiczka, A., Frank, E., and Miller, M. (1996). Gender differences in complicated grief among the elderly. *Omega, 32,* 303–317.

Boszormenyi-Nagy, I. (1986). *Between give and take: A clinical guide to contextual therapy.* New York: Brunner/Mazel.

Boszormenyi-Nagy, I., & Spark, G. L. (1973). *Invisible loyalties: Reciprocity in intergenerational family therapy.* Harper & Row: New York.

Davis, C. G., Wortman, C. B., Lehman, D. R., & Silver, R. C. (2000). Searching for meaning in loss: Are clinical assumptions correct? *Death Studies, 24,* 497–540.

Federal Bureau of Investigation. (1999). *Uniform Crime Report, Table 2.6. Available: www.fbi.gov www.fbi.gov/ucr/99cius.htm [2001, May 29].*

Fitzpatrick, K., & Boldizar, J. (1993). The prevalence and consequences of exposure to violence among African-American youth. *Journal of the American Academy of Child and Adolescent Psychiatry, 32,* 424–430.

Freedy, J. R., Resnick, H. S., Kilpatrick, D. G., Dansky, B. S., & Tidwell, R. P. (1994). The psychological adjustment of recent crime victims in the criminal justice system. *Journal of Interpersonal Violence, 9,* 450–468.

Jacobs, S., & Prigerson, H. (1999). Psychotherapy of traumatic grief: A review of evidence for psychotherapeutic treatments. *Death Studies, 24,* 479–495.

Kessler, R. C., Sonnega, A., Bromet, E., Hughes, M., & Nelson, C. B. (1995). Posttraumatic stress disorder in the National Comorbidity Survey. *Archives of General Psychiatry, 52,* 1048–1060.

Larson S. (1994). Witnessing violence damages development. American Academy of Pediatric News.

Levy, A. J., & Wall, J. C. (2000). Children who have witnessed homicide: Incorporating risk and resilience in clinical work. *Families in Society, 81,* 402–411.

Michalowski, R. J. (1976). The social meanings of violent death. *Omega, 7,* 83–93.

Miranda, A. O., Molina, B., & MacVane, S. L. (2003). Coping with the murder of a loved one: Counseling survivors of murder victims in groups. *Journal for Specialists in Group Work, 28,* 48–61.

Moss, E., & Raz, A. (2001). The ones left behind: A siblings' bereavement group. *Group Analysis, 34,* 395–407.

Murphy, S. A., Braun, T., Tillery, L., Cain, K. C., Johnson, L. C., & Beaton, R. D. (1999). PTSD among bereaved parents following the violent deaths of their 12- to 28-year-old children: A longitudinal prospective analysis. *Journal of Traumatic Stress, 12,* 273–291.

Murphy, S. A., Johnson, L. C., & Lohan, J. (2002). The aftermath of the violent death of a child: An integration of the assessments of parents' mental distress and PTSD during the first 5 years of bereavement. *Journal of Loss and Trauma, 7,* 203–222.

Murphy, S. A., Johnson, L. C., & Lohan, J. (2003). Finding meaning in a child's violent death: A five-year prospective analysis of parents' personal narratives and empirical data. *Death Studies, 27,* 381–404.

Murphy, S. A., Johnson, I. C., Lohan, J., & Tapper, V. J. (2002). Bereaved parents' use of individual, family, and community resources 4 to 60 months after a child's violent death. *Family and Community Health, 25,* 71–82.

Neimeyer, R. A. (2001). Reauthoring life narratives: Grief therapy as meaning reconstruction. *Israel Journal of Psychiatry & Related Sciences, 38,* 171–183.

Parapully, J. (2002). Thriving after trauma: The experience of parents of murdered children. *Journal of Humanistic Psychology, 42,* 38–70.

Peach, M. R., & Klass, D. (1987). Special issues in the grief of parents of murdered children. *Death Studies, 11,* 81–88.

Peterson, M. (2000). *The search for meaning in the aftermath of homicide: a hermeneutic phenomenological study of families of homicide victims.* Unpublished doctoral dissertation. University of Minnesota: Minneapolis, MN.

Prigerson, H. G., Bierhals, A. J., Stanislav, V. K., Reynolds III, C. F., Shear, M. K., Day, N., Beery, L. C., Newsom, J. T., & Jacobs, S. (1997). Traumatic grief as a risk factor for mental and physical morbidity. *American Journal of Psychiatry, 154,* 116–123.

Prigerson, H. G., Frank, E., Kasl, S. V., Reynolds III, C. F., Anderson, B., Zubenko, G. S., Houck, P. R., George, C. J., & Kupfer, D. J. (1995). Complicated grief and bereavement-related depression in distinct disorders: Preliminary empirical validation in elderly bereaved spouses. *American Journal of Psychiatry, 152,* 22–30.

Prigerson, H. G., Shear, M. K., Jacobs, S. C., Reynolds III, C. F., Maciejewski, J. R. T., Davidson, R., Rosenheck, R., Pilkonis, P. A., Wortman, C. B., Williams, J. B. W., Widiger, T. A., Frank, E., Kupfer, D. J., & Zisook, S. (1999). Consensus criteria for traumatic grief: A preliminary empirical test. *British Journal of Psychiatry, 174*, 67–73.

Prigerson, H. G., Shear, M. K., Newsom, J. T, Frank, E., Reynolds III, C. F., Maciejewski, P. K., Houck, P. R., Bierhals, A. J., & Kupfer, D. J. (1996). Anxiety among widowed elders: Is it distinct from depression and grief? *Anxiety, 2*, 1–12.

Rando, T. A. (1993). *Treatment of complicated mourning. Champaign, IL: Research Press.*

Reynolds, III, C. F., Miller, M. D., Pasternak, N. E., Frank, E., Perej, J. M., Cornes, C., Huock, P. R., Muzumdar, S., Dew, M. A., & Kupfer, D. J. (1999). Treatment of bereavement-related major depression episodes in later life: A controlled study and acute and continuation treatment with nortriptyline and interpersonal psychotherapy. *American Journal of Psychiatry, 156*, 202–208.

Rynearson, E. K. (1988). The homicide of a child. In F. Ochberg (Ed.), *Posttraumatic therapy and victims of violence. New York: Brunner/Mazel.*

Rynearson, E. K. (1996). Psychotherapy of bereavement: After homicide: Be offensive. *Psychotherapy in Practice, 2*, 47–57.

Rynearson, E. K. (2001). *Retelling violent death. Philadelphia: Brunner-Rutledge.*

Rynearson, E. K., Favell, J., & Saindon, C. (2002). Group intervention for bereavement after violent death. *Psychiatric Services, 53*, 1340.

Rynearson, E. K., & Geoffrey, R. (1999). Bereavement after homicide: Its assessment and treatment. In C. Figley (Ed.), *Traumatology of grieving: Conceptual, theoretical, and treatment foundations (pp. 53–70). Philadelphia: Brunner/Mazel.*

Rynearson, E. K., & McCreery, J. M. (1993). Bereavement after homicide: A synergism of trauma and loss. *American Journal of Psychiatry, 150*, 258–261.

Salloum, A., & Vincent, N. J. (1999). Community-based groups for inner city adolescent survivors of homicide victims. *Journal of Child and Adolescent Group Therapy, 9*, 27–45.

Salloum, A., Avery L., & McClain, R. P. (2001). Group psychotherapy for adolescent survivors of homicide victims: A pilot study. *Journal of the American Academy of Child and Adolescent Psychiatry, 40*, 1261–1267.

Shapiro, E. S. (1996). Family bereavement and cultural diversity: A social developmental perspective. *Family Process, 35*, 313–332.

Smith, C., & Carlson, B. E. (1997). Stress, coping, and resilience in children and youth. *Social Service Review, 71*, 231–256.

Spungen, D. (1998). *Homicide: The hidden victims. Thousand Oaks, CA: Sage.*

Stevens-Guille, M. E. (1999). Intersections of grief and trauma: Family members reactions to homicide. In C. Figley (Ed.), *Traumatology of grieving: Conceptual, theoretical, and treatment foundations (pp. 53–70). Philadelphia: Brunner/Mazel.*

Tedeschi, R. G., Park, C. L., & Calhoun, L. G. (1998). *Posttraumatic growth: Positive change in the aftermath of crisis. Mahwah, NJ: Erlbaum.*

Temple, S. (1997). Treating inner-city families of homicide victims: A contextually oriented approach. *Family Process, 36*, 133–149.

Thompson, M. P., Norris, F. H., & Ruback, R. B. (1998). Comparative distress levels of inner-city family members of homicide victims. *Journal of Traumatic Stress, 11*, 223–242.

Videka-Sherman, L., & Lieberman, M. (1985). The effects of self-help and psychotherapy intervention on child loss: The limits of recovery. *American Journal of Orthopsychiatry, 55*, 70–82.

3

When Children's Parents Are Traumatized: The Din and the Dearth

MARY BETH WILLIAMS

Loretta is a 41-year-old, separated mother of three. She lives in her child-hood home; her parents stay there perhaps one week every two months. As a teenager, she used alcohol to numb out memories of early childhood sexual abuse. While under the influence of alcohol, she was raped by a high school classmate and became pregnant with twins. She did not tell her parents about the rape and, instead, went to her high school counselor to report the rape. The counselor did nothing to help her with her trauma and brushed her off. Her father was a local policeman and she knew she could not turn to him for help; he had recently been accused of showing porn movies at the station (and was later relieved of duty). She then used a knitting needle to cause a miscarriage. Every day she saw her abuser—the rapist—at school; often, she heard his rude comments as she walked down the halls. She never told him of the pregnancy and eventually quit school at age 16 (then the legal age). She has never gotten a GED.

Loretta was diagnosed 2 years ago with dissociative identity disorder (DID). She has at least eight personalities, one of whom is the raped teenager. Another alter is about 4 and was molested by a grandfather and an uncle. She sleeps in the bedroom in which she was raped and is reminded of her trauma on a daily basis. Now her daughter Kathy is 14, is beginning to show some typical teenage behavior, and attends the same school as Loretta. Every time Loretta comes to that school, she flashes back to her own postrape experience. Yet, if Kathy mouths off at her mother, Loretta may regress to a 4-year-old. Kathy uses her newfound verbal power to cause her mother to regress and retreat to her bed, particularly when she wants her freedom to come and go as she pleases. Kathy has anger at her situation and has adopted her mother's intense fear of her mother's husband, her father. She may display inappropriate anger at her two younger brothers, who have a genetically transmitted condition that causes many physical abnormalities as well as low immune system tolerance to illness.

Recently, Kathy had suicidal ideation as she took a bath in the home. She drew a picture of herself and called her mother to report what was going through her head. Her mother was visiting the grandparent's cottage in another state while the grandparents were in the home. Without thought of the consequences, Loretta decided to tell Kathy about her own trauma and her diagnosis of DID. In the meantime, Kathy has had bouts of real—and possibly psychosomatic—illness that have led to extensive absences. Now she does not want to go to school and is on the verge of failing her eighth grade year. She has made a suicide contract with the family therapist, but does not want her father to know of her thoughts because she fears him and refuses to go for visitation. Yet she feels she "should" be there to protect her brothers, particularly if her father gets angry toward them. She is conflicted; she knows she would feel extremely guilty if anything happened to them during their visitation. One of the brothers, age 10, is now "eating himself into obesity" as a source of nurturance. He is depressed—visibly sluggish in his motor movements—and has no friends. The younger boy, age 7, has become less verbal. When he does talk about his feelings, he only describes anxiety.

Loretta is a victim of many traumas; she may more accurately be diagnosed as having a disorder of extreme stress, not otherwise specified (DESNOS) as well as dissociative identity disorder. As the head of the family, she attempts to interact with her children in ways that lead to positive school performance, positive peer relationships, and boundaried intimacy. Yet Loretta's traumatic reenactments and dissociative switches upset that state and the routine of the system. Her history of trauma has led to behaviors that put the family system in danger. When she retreats to her room with migraine headaches, when she becomes the child alters, when she is so filled with fear of her ex-husband that she transmits terror to the children, when she relives the miscarriage and/or rape—when these and other traumatic reenactments occur, she may cause her children also to become traumatized by association and chiasmal transmission of the trauma (Blevins, 1993; Catherall, 1992; Figley, 1989).

Loretta's attachment to the world and, ultimately, to her children is disorganized. Her home is filled with *din:* the din of nightmares, outbursts of temper and rage, and chaos when things don't get done. Yet there is also *dearth*—a dearth of joy, humor, peace—and a silence marked by Loretta's retreats to her bed. Her self-organization is dissociative, disturbed, and lacks emotional stability. Her response to stress is poor, to say the least. It is very difficult for her to ground and incorporate reflective thought and behavior into her normal pattern of impulsive reactivity. In spite of all of these characteristics, she is a survivor (Higgins, 1994).

THE TRAUMATIZED FAMILY

When a parent in a family has been the victim of trauma and suffers from some form of traumatic stress reaction, that parent often is not the only family member who suffers the consequences of the past. Trauma has ramifications throughout the family and may exhibit itself in the form of secondary posttraumatic stress in other family members, especially the victim's spouse and/or children. Sometimes children become silent in their watchfulness, waiting for the next reenactment, the next regression, the next dissociative split in the parent. Their hypervigilance may heighten their reactivity in the form of either intrusive or avoidant symptoms of posttraumatic stress.

Loretta is often overinvolved in her children's lives. She keeps them home from school at the least sniffle or sign of an illness. She sees herself as a mother lion when one of them is challenged or attacked. Some aspects of her children's traumatic reactions may be the result of her caring too much—her constant presence increases their exposure to her triggers and fears. As time passes, the family may become less open to intervention, and dysfunctional rules of relationships and behaviors (e.g., "Do not go to court to get support money" and "Avoid conflict at all costs") may become the norm.

When a family member is traumatized or has been traumatized in the past, the behaviors of the family may lead to shattered or challenged family bonds. In this family, the children have not yet begun to pull away; they still seek to be connected as a family. However, as they age and individuate, this closeness may wane and they may seek to dissociate themselves from each other. Loretta's family even now has certain rigid rules for behavior. Rules like "Don't tell Daddy what is going on" and "Don't let outsiders into the family" convey Loretta's underlying belief that people must prove their trustworthiness beyond any doubt (McCubbin & McCubbin, 1989).

Only recently has Loretta begun to speak of her trauma history to her children. Yet she did not do so in a logical, age-appropriate manner. On one occasion, she cried openly during a school staffing and related her rape history while her daughter was present. She has not obtained appropriate treatment, primarily because her health care provider does not have qualified mental health professionals available. If Loretta does not get help and work through her trauma, she may never be able to develop an intimate relationship with another; her children may leave the family—either by choice or through outside intervention; and she may decompensate even further. Currently, her children's schools are pressuring her to get help.

Loretta's story illustrates how the impact of trauma, both short and long term, is not confined only to those who experience traumatic events directly. Secondary exposure to trauma in parents may undermine basic safety and trust in children and lead them to question their own personal beliefs and connections (Williams, 1996). These children may become unable to modulate their impulses, emotions, and behaviors. This can lead to aggression and self-harm, disturbances in their sense of self, and relationship disturbances involving lack of trust and negative perceptions of self and other. Their core beliefs, formed within a context of impaired self-regulation, are often disturbed and counterproductive—they have not learned that it is safe to have a self that can relate in a continuous manner.

Trauma and Attachment

Attachment is a deep and enduring connection, a bond between parent and child ideally established in the first days, weeks, and months of life. Attachment—or lack of attachment—influences every aspect of the self. An attachment bond is ongoing and reciprocal as parents and children fulfill basic needs for connection. The basic function of attachment is to provide safety and protection for children by parents. Children who have failed to attach to parents or whose parents have failed to attach to them may exhibit some or all of the following:

- Superficially charming behavior
- Lack of eye contact
- Indiscriminate affection
- Lack of true cuddle behavior
- Self-destructive acts
- Destruction of others' property
- Cruelty to animals
- Lack of impulse control
- Lack of conscience and cause-and-effect thinking
- Poor peer relationships
- Lack of ability to give and receive true affection
- Failure to accept obligations or rules

- Inability to empathize
- Chronic inability to modulate (emotions, behaviors, impulses)
- Disturbed core beliefs of safety, trust, power, esteem, and intimacy
- Dissociative and anesthetizing abilities
- Preocccupation with blood and gore
- Impulsivity
- Resistance to authority
- Failure to accept obligations
- Lying tendencies
- Minimizing behavior
- Blaming of others
- Lack of respect for others
- Inability to initiate positive affection

On the other hand, the securely attached child

- Smiles
- Shows and accepts appropriate affection
- Makes eye contact
- Asks questions
- Explores his or her environment through interaction
- Takes care of others appropriately
- Has a sense of right and wrong and acts on that sense of conscience
- Wants to please caretakers
- Wants to keep caretakers close
- Tries to solve problems proactively
- Responds to direction in a positive fashion
- Feels safe in his or her world
- Initiates affection
- Reacts appropriately to pain and pleasure
- Is able to self-soothe (if the pain is not too great)
- Has age-appropriate social skills
- Knows and names personal needs
- Gives and receives love (reciprocal interaction and caring)
- Has self-mastery and individuates

   Typical reactions of traumatized families include problems in developing attached relationships, as exhibited in areas such as the lack of intimacy and emotional numbing, withdrawal from social contact, outbursts of anger, substance abuse, verbal abuse of others in authority, lack of competency in everyday life, and problems with the five basic psychological needs of safety, trust, power/control, esteem, and intimacy (Rosenbloom & Williams, 1999; Niles, 1990). According to Rosenthal, Sadler, and Edwards (1987), families of trauma survivors may develop the following symptom patterns:

- Secondary posttraumatic stress disorder (PTSD) symptoms
- Boundary distortions and violations
- Somatization of rage and grief
- Mistrust of others
- Parentification of children
- Normative family avoidance
- Ambivalent feelings of children/spouse toward the victim/survivor
- Extreme need for social support
- Substance abuse and other means to encourage numbing
- Survivor guilt
- Self-destructive behavior
- Extreme need to be in control for each member
- Attempts to meet others' needs at personal expense
- Attempts to control the behavior of other family members when self cannot be controlled.

According to Schore (1999) and others, those families also develop patterns of disorganized attachment, the most dysfunctional attachment style to be transmitted from parent to child (Williams-Keeler, 2002). Bartholomew and Horowitz (1991) noted that the child with disorganized attachment always calculates the degree of 1safety when close to the caregiving parent. In other words, is it safe to relate and interact or must the child keep distance and fear for retaliation or outbursts?

At times, Loretta's children sit near and talk with her; they go with her to extracurricular activities or to shop. Other times, they remain distant and stay away, hiding in other parts of the house or immersing themselves in activities such as video games. The younger children, both boys, have no friends and either play with each other or alone. Only the daughter has made friends with other girls, all from dysfunctional homes. The children are ambivalent about direct contact with their mother because she demonstrates disorganized attachment. As Williams-Keeler (2002) noted, someone like Loretta has sustained "an irreparable trauma that forever shattered her ability to trust, to love, and to cherish without being intermittently immobilized by the fear that attended her original involvement in (a) traumatic events" (p. 8).

Loretta has never resolved her early childhood abuse, later rape, abandonment, and spousal abuse. She relates to her children in an unpredictable fashion, at times warm and caring, even attacking of those who threaten the children (the Lioness alter) and at other times punitive and rageful. Recently, one of the boys was angry at her; she lay in front of his door until he threw a tissue box at her head to get her to move so that he could use the bathroom. Loretta expects much from her children, but she is more likely to blame external systems for her children's failure to succeed than to look at her own role in the children's behaviors, emotional reactions, and beliefs.

The Partner

As other chapters in this volume attest, partners of survivors are affected both directly and indirectly by family trauma. Loretta's husband, Joe, opted to leave the marriage; he sees his sons every other weekend. He has had angry outbursts during the visitations—smashing dishes and causing his children great distress because of his behavior. Joe still is not fully aware of Loretta's trauma history because she has never shared it with him. He became frustrated with his wife's unwillingness to be sexually active with him and then found it impossible to provide emotional support to her.

Gilbert (1995) stated that there are two primary reasons for the development of secondary traumatic stress in spouses. The first centers on the need of a family to have a stable relationship that does not change. The second centers on emotional connection and the desire to help a spouse resolve or escape from the impact of trauma. These two needs are often thwarted, possibly leading to a secondary trauma disorder. In addition, the spouse may use the trauma survivor/victim as a reason to exist and as a means to avoid personal issues or traumas. The partner of a trauma survivor may be called upon to be almost superhuman—to be incredibly hypervigilant and aware of the survivor's needs and limits, as well as their own (Davis, 1991). The partner is often required to deal with crises in the spouse, including self-mutilation and suicide threats, gestures, or attempts.

For many partners of trauma survivors, the burden of care becomes too great. When the partner has his or her own psychopathology, the mix can be disastrous for marital and family stability. When conflict within the family is high, the survivor's recovery is even more compromised (Lyons and Root, 2001). The disorganized attachment patterns that drive a lot of anger and contribute to the din in the family of a trauma survivor tax coping abilities and keep the survivor from connecting with both partner and children (Williams-Keeler, 2001). This level of noise/din contaminates relationships; as the disconnected periods of avoidance, dissociation, depression, and dysfunction can be contagious and lead to even more avoidant behavior, emotional blunting in partner and children, and a dearth of warmth and caring.

Traumatic Reactions in Children Whose Parents Are Victims

Much of the literature describing children's reactions to parental victimization comes from Holocaust research (Danieli, 1981). Klein-Parker (1988) found that children of Holocaust survivors had intense, somewhat superficial relationships with parents, yet those relationships became more personal over the years because parent and child were deeply attached and interdependent. Children of trauma survivors often express horror when hearing stories of their parents' victimizations. They may have nightmares of the events their parents experienced or become mournful and tearful when they think about what their parents had to do to survive; or they may distance themselves, run away, or threaten suicide (Williams, 1996).

Many children of trauma survivors feel a sense of alienation within their families and may choose to escape into personal isolation, emotional distance, and/or geographic distance—often the result of their own disorganized attachment patterns of relating. However, parental nonavailability may have resulted in an actual lack of nurturance and subsequent fear of abandonment. The children often are confused about the generalities and specifics of their parents' trauma history. They learn that asking questions about what happened may lead to reenactments, suicide attempts, outbursts, or avoidant behaviors such as retreating to the bed. Matsakis (1996) found that children of Vietnam veterans often internalized the attachment style of their parent and had emotional difficulties ranging from fear and anxiety to stifled anger or repression of anger to overt eruption of anger. These children also often distanced themselves from the parent and tended to relive parental experiences and exhibit parental symptoms.

Age-Specific Reactions. According to a list of responses found in the City of Falls Church, Virginia's Crisis Response Plan (Williams & Becker, 2000) for its schools, the following responses are age/stage specific:

Reactions of Toddlers and Preschoolers

- Reactions reflecting those of parents
- Regressing behavior
- Decreased appetite
- Sleep disorders, nightmares, night terrors
- Stuttering, muteness, or speech delays
- Excessive clinging
- Reenactment of their parent's trauma through play
- Exaggerated startle response
- Experiences of many trauma-related fears
- Increased sensitivities and poor sensorimotor integration
- Immobility or confusion

Reactions of Elementary School Students

- Anxiety and worry about their own safety and the safety of other family members
- Worrying that "bad things" in the family with recur
- Increase or decrease in activity level
- Decreased concentration and attention
- Eruptions of outbursts of anger

- Decreased school attendance
- Increased incidents of headaches, stomachaches, and other pain
- Profuse talk about what has happened
- Oversensitivity to sounds, smells, and other triggers
- Changes in appetite and sleep patterns
- Irritability and whininess
- Withdrawal from friends

Possible Reactions of Middle School Students

- Anxiety or worry about their own safety and the safety of other members of their family
- Changes in behavior similar to that of younger children
- Changes in academic performance and decreased school attendance
- Increased incidents of bodily complaints and pains
- Increased sensitivity to sounds, smells, and other triggers
- Loss of trust in family members or systems that fail the family
- Lessened interest in normal routine activities
- Expressions of defiance or deeper emotions (fear, anger, sadness)
- Sleep and appetite disturbances
- Increased rebelliousness more at home and refuse to do chores

Possible Reactions of High School Students

- Any of the reactions of middle school students
- Feelings of vulnerability (which they may not like)
- Denial of the impact
- Exhibit a more adult manner (Gurwitch, Silovsky, Schultz, Kees, & Burlingame, 2001)
- Become hypochondriacal
- Become more irresponsible and even delinquent
- Exhibit a lessening or increase in their emancipatory struggles
- Become tense and exhibit appetite and sleep disturbances (Marin and San Mateo County School Staffs, 1982)

Symptoms and patterns exist beyond the individual child and affect the family as a whole. Albeck (1994) calls these patterns generational consequences of trauma. They include, according to Rosenthal, Sadler, and Edwards (1987):

- Boundary distortions related to the disorganized attachment patterns that impact intimacy, individuation, and separation
- Somatization of trauma experiences into physical symptoms in partners and/or children, often mimicking parental trauma survivor's symptoms

- Role reversals in which children are forced or manipulated into taking on parental roles
- Alienation toward the survivor parent by the other parent, who is tired and no longer wants to/chooses to/is able to cope
- Ambivalence toward the survivor parent as that parent switches attachment style and/or interaction pattern ranging from love and tolerance to disgust and hate
- Extreme need for unhealthy social support, often from inappropriate individuals (peers or adults)
- Feelings of guilt and shame
- Self-destructive behaviors
- Inappropriate attempts to control the parent survivor and/or the family through acting out or acting in
- Abusive language and/or behavior toward the survivor parent by even the youngest family member, often modeled by the nonsurvivor parent (or the parent who is seen as less damaged)
- Interruption of the normal developmental life cycle leading to regression, stagnation, or even pseudoadulthood
- Overreaction to normal stresses of daily life

When both parents are trauma survivors, the ability to provide support to children can be severely compromised (Williams, 1998). Ironically, this is particularly true if the parents are focused primarily on self-healing and introspection. Having rage episodes, disorganized attachment reactions, nightmares, and/or hypervigilant scanning is often the norm for these parents, who are not able to provide stability or function as positive role models to their children.

Assessment of the Child

It is important to assess the child thoroughly before determining the type(s) and extent of treatment to provide. Part of that assessment is to look at the child's attachment style and the quality of the child's patterns of interaction with others (Carroll, Foy, Cannon, & Zweir, 1991). It is also important to assess the child's role or position in the family structure—as perceived by the child, parent(s), and siblings, if possible. To what degree is the child responsible for caring for a parent or for other siblings? What contributions does the child make toward family continuity and connection (Okun, 1984)? This assessment also looks at the existence of clear boundaries regarding personal space, privacy, ventilation of anger/aggression, and expression of other emotions. A variety of instruments are available for this purpose.

It is important to assess the child's coping abilities. How much secondary stress can the child tolerate should the survivor parent begin to work through traumatic experiences in an intense fashion? How well can the child tolerate exposure to the trauma(s) that happened as well as flashbacks, nightmares, or abreactions?

When Loretta's daughter sees her mother take to the bed and hide, is her reaction to hide herself, to think of suicide, or to try to push her mother's buttons? In the last instance, her daughter has become the transference figure of an earlier abuser; Loretta may then treat her with avoidance and dissociation or with verbal and physical outbursts.

Treatment of Secondary Trauma

To address the secondary effects of parental trauma on children, therapists must consider the nature of the trauma, the extent of the parent's resolution of his or her trauma, and the impact on the children's sense of safety. The following section describes a logical therapeutic framework that allows these factors to be addressed.

THERAPEUTIC FRAMEWORK

Trauma Assessment

Ideally, treatment must be family based, beginning with an in-depth assessment of family dynamics, strengths, and weaknesses. Figley (1989) noted that such an assessment needs to examine patterns of distancing/ cohesion, rigidity/adaptability, social skills, and conflict resolution abilities. It is important to examine the family's readiness and motivation to cope with a variety of traumatic experiences and sequelae in both parent and children. The major goal of this initial assessment is to determine whether or not the family is a safe enough place to begin the trauma work that needs to be done. It must take cultural factors and the role of culture in the particular family into consideration. Assessment also needs to include an investigation of the personal meaning of the trauma to each family member and how any change in meaning will affect daily life.

Parental Resolution of Personal Trauma

Before a traumatized family can heal, the trauma survivor must come to some resolution of his or her own history, work on personal issues, and focus on personal healing. The most therapeutic approach to treatment is probably a combination of individual, couple, and family sessions. Resolving personal issues usually precedes issues in relationships (Graber, 1991); however, when an entire family is directly and secondarily traumatized, the definition of who constitutes the client varies. For example, Loretta needs individual therapy to address her sexual abuse history and multiplicity; her ex-husband needs anger management work; each of the children would benefit from a personal therapist; and the children together and the marital couple, though separated, would be other foci for therapy.

Initial Treatment

The initial role of the therapist is to help family members deal with the primary survivor and their own posttraumatic stress reactions to that survivor. The competent trauma therapist has the knowledge, skills, and techniques to help the family through provision of educational information about PTSD, skills acquisition, behavior modification, and identification of personal reactions. It is essential to educate all family members about primary and secondary trauma reactions within developmental levels. Sharing appropriate information about the parent's traumatic past (without unduly upsetting) is part of this education as an awareness builds of what is happening and has happened within the lives of family members and within the family as a whole. The therapist also helps the family set appropriate rules and limits concerning duties, relationships, and behaviors. These rules need to be appropriate, flexible, healthy, easily communicated, easily remembered, and acceptable to all family members (Williams, 1991).

Safety and Beliefs

The fundamental goal of therapy is to make the family a safe place for all. Once safety is established, then members may build or rebuild trusting relationships, establish appropriate sources of personal power, and build self-esteem. An effective way to identify personal beliefs about needs is to have each member state a belief and then make a series of statements that reflect on the implications of his or her belief. The first statement reflects on the belief itself, the second statement reflects on the implication of the first, and the third statement reflects on the implication of the second. The final answer to the third statement reveals a more accurate core belief than did the first initial statement (Rosenbloom and Williams, 1999). The three statements are as follows:

What this says about me is _____.
What that says about me is _____.
What that says about me is _____.

Role of the Therapist

The role of the therapist in such treatment is complicated and demanding. The therapist must create a healing partnership between him- or herself and all family members so that some minimal degree of trust can begin to be built. Williams-Keeler (2001) describes this as the development of a trustful alliance with a steady stream of psychoeducation and a steady dose of realistic hope. The therapist provides a consistent level of positive regard and creates opportunities for all family members to try to reconnect and reattach. Initially, the therapist serves as the secure base for the family. Over time, that security is transferred to the family itself as members change and the therapist teaches family members self-soothing and self-calming techniques to regulate the din and the dearth within themselves and within the family as a whole.

Treatment and Support Suggestions by Developmental Stage

It is crucial that children who have experienced primary or secondary trauma be able to feel personally safe. Often, they can establish a sense of control through taking some form of action. That action might be as small as talking to a teacher about feelings or drawing a picture of what happened at home the night before. As the National Association of School Psychologists (2001) wrote after September 11, 2001, "the closer a child is to the location of a threatening and/or frightening event and the longer the exposure, the greater the likelihood of severe distress" (p. 1).

Infancy to Three Years of Age. What might caregivers and others do to help the very young child who is living in a traumatized family setting? It is important to remember that children at this age are highly susceptible to the impact of traumatized individuals (Perry, 2002) and are prone to dissociation and splitting should the traumatic events become unbearable around them. Thus it is important to

- Maintain the child's routines of sleeping, eating, and napping
- Encourage attachment with primary caregivers that is warm and accepting
- Help traumatized caregivers to maintain a calm atmosphere
- Help traumatized caregivers to soothe children when children need soothing (including developing an awareness of the children's needs)
- Help children with language to give names to what they are experiencing—teaching children to name feelings and reactions, to recognize reactions and feelings in others, to identify feelings on faces and charts

- Give children props for play that can help them to work out traumatic reactions

Three to Six Years of Age.   Children in this age group are making their
first encounters with the world outside the family—they usually have
begun preschool or are in kindergarten or first grade. Developmentally,
they are beginning to individuate. What might help the secondarily traumatized child in this age/stage to heal? The caretaker, whether parent or
teacher, might choose to

- Listen and tolerate retellings of exposure to parental trauma
- Limit reexposure to traumatic reenactments (e.g., if Daddy gets
drunk on Friday nights and then explodes, spend Friday nights
away at Grandmother's house)
- Help children name strong feelings during short conversations and
identify those feelings in themselves and others
- Set firm limits on harmful play
- Encourage and model attachment to the child
- Help maintain predictable routines to give comfort and safety
- Discuss nightmares—name them, identify that they come from in-
ternal fears and that nightmares are not real
- Help children identify triggers that might lead to acting out, acting
in, or other traumatic manifestations
- Listen for misunderstandings about parental behavior and help to
correct those faulty beliefs
- Provide safety
- Help develop a realistic understanding of "why things got this way"
as well as the family's trauma history
- Build opportunities into children's lives for them to have control and
make choices

Six to Eleven Years of Age.   The school-aged child grows immensely in
a few short years in physical, emotional, cognitive, spiritual, and relational realms. Developmentally, they are becoming increasingly focused
on their ability to function competently in the outside world. Yet school-
aged children still can be "stuck" in traumatic reenactments and misunderstandings, feeling lost and alone, alienated and unattached from their
primary caretakers. What are some ways to help these children?

- Listen to and tolerate their retellings of what occurs at home, in appropriate settings (not in the open classroom).
- Respect children's fears and help them cope.
- Monitor play for trauma themes and set limits on scary, hurtful play.
- Introduce new, more mature ways to cope with fears and try other
ways to help children (e.g., sleep with a radio on, listening to a relaxation tape).

- Encourage children to talk about events, feelings, and concerns.
- Teach children the language of trauma; they are not too young to learn about traumatic events, the family's traumatic history, and the impacts of the traumas.
- Maintain rules and safety to give children a container for accomplishment.
- Help children develop realistic understandings of traumatic events and histories.
- Help children make appropriate choices.

Eleven to Eighteen Years of Age. Preadolescent children still can be greatly affected by parental traumatic reenactments. Many of these children have been thrust into early adulthood and have not had a carefree period in which to experiment with identity choices and gradually develop a sense of who they are. Others seek to maintain their own childhoods into their 20s or 30s—their way to cope is to not leave home, to not become independent, and to not individuate or separate. How can caregivers help preteens and teens who have grown up in a world of family trauma?

- Encourage them to talk about their experiences in safe, appropriate settings.
- Provide children with socially supportive groups and activities.
- Help children discuss strong feelings.
- Build attachments of children between peers and appropriate adults.
- Help construct activities that will allow mastery, control, and development of self-esteem.
- Refer children to outside counseling if serious depression, self-harm, acting out, accident proneness, recklessness, personality change, or substance abuse occurs.
- Help children develop realistic perspectives on trauma and recovery.

A final reminder: Children of all ages express traumatic reactions individually. There is no single one-plan-fits-all pattern of response. Thus it is important for anyone involved in a traumatized child's life to get to know the child personally so that changes in behavior can be monitored and guidance can be individualized. Grieving, traumatized children often mimic children with attention deficit disorder and attention deficit hyperactivity disorder. Educators and caretakers must be cautious in trying to fit a child who has lived in a world of trauma into the box of learning disabilities, other health impairments, or disability. The most important thing is to provide opportunities for connection and attachment to these children, no matter what age they are.

Guidelines for Adjustment of Children

After the disaster of September 11, 2001, many organizations offered suggestions regarding ways to help traumatized children of all ages and stages (American Counseling Association, 2001; American Red Cross, 2001; Gurwitch et al., 2001). The following suggestions apply to children who have been traumatized secondarily through family events and histories as well as for children who have experienced primary exposure to trauma:

- Talk to children about what happened.
- Support their reactions.
- Listen to them.
- Tell them appropriate facts.
- Share your feelings (appropriately).
- Reassure them and help them attach.
- Reaffirm the life direction of the family.
- Reunite as a family with whomever is in the home or whomever has connections.
- Establish or reaffirm the family's belief systems, whether religious or philosophical or spiritual.
- Share only what you yourself know (no one has all the answers).

Whatever model of trauma treatment is utilized, the first focus must be on the necessity for family safety and stabilization. There must be a measure of stability in the family's current life before beginning the more disruptive aspects of trauma work—dealing with traumatic memories and emotional processing. Assigning meaning to family events and history comes next, followed by the development of social skills, such as problem solving and conflict management. The therapist functions in a variety of roles, including case manager, as he or she leads the family to appropriate resources.

Coping and Children

Not all children are seriously affected by family trauma; in fact many are resilient and cope effectively. Those who cope better are children who have positive, stable emotional relationships with others, positive self-esteem, a supportive, safe educational environment, at least average cognitive abilities, and active coping methods (doing, acting, choosing).

The Role of the School System

When children have been traumatized within the family, the role of the school system is less direct than if there were a school crisis or a national crisis. Garbarino, Dubrow, Kostelny, and Pardo (1992) contended that it is essential that the school take the role of a caregiving environment for secondarily traumatized children. Teachers often know students the best—when a teacher observes changes in a student, that teacher may ask for information: "What's going on, I notice that you have been looking out the window a lot. Where are you?" If there is a concern that the student is having emotional difficulties, referring the student to the guidance counselor, crisis counselor, school social worker, or school psychologist is often a good choice of action, even to rule out the possibility of problems or possible traumatic sequelae.

Most schools are not, and do not see themselves as, therapeutic institutions. They prefer to restrict interventions to group and individual counseling. A smaller number of school systems actually employ licensed therapists to provide counseling to their most disturbed or needy students, often under the blanket of special education services through an individualized educational plan.

The classroom teacher can serve as a bastion of safety and security for the child simply through being consistent and maintaining a predictable schedule and rules. Doing classroom activities that reinforce safety and the power of choice can help students express themselves and make decisions. Allowing for a temporary decline in performance or productivity is also a way to help the child cope in the case of a family crisis or if the child is displaying a posttraumatic stress reaction. Teachers can use worksheets, writing assignments, music and art, and other interventions to address aspects of trauma and loss (Pynoos & Nader, 1988). School staff can design games, structured or unstructured, to help children express feelings, or they can use journal assignments for catharsis. Groups also may be designed around specific topics (divorce, absent fathers, parental death) to provide support. When group members are children of trauma survivors, there may be a tendency for them to share inappropriate family history, particularly if students have had varying levels of exposure to traumatic details. However, when handled correctly, groups of this nature can teach children to separate themselves from their parents' traumas and not envision themselves in the parent's place. Children can be freed from the role of witness of the effects of their parents' traumas.

The teacher also may want to schedule a parent conference or ask for a staffing with parent, counselor, principal, and all of the student's teachers. In schools in Virginia, because of the Comprehensive Services Act, students and families can participate in the child specific team (CST) process. This process brings together a team of educators, representatives of community agencies, and the family to discuss the family's strengths and needs and make a plan for intervention. The school social worker serves as school representative.

At the request of the principal and eighth grade team, the school social worker brought together a large group of individuals to form a CST after

Loretta's daughter, Kathy, revealed suicidal ideation. In attendance were the therapist for the family and the therapist's supervisor; the principal, assistant principal, and guidance counselor; the court services representative, family services representative, school social worker, and mental health representative; and Loretta. Kathy's father was invited but did not attend, and Kathy herself was ill at home. Loretta shared her daughter's journals. CST members decided that the need for intensive services in the family was great; they requested that the Department of Family Services representative approve referral to the Family Assessment and Planning Team (FAPT), a team of upper level management officials who make financial decisions, and approve home-based family services for up to 25 hours of family intervention per month. That request was approved to go to the FAPT, but it has been difficult to find a provider.

Individual Treatment for the Child

In some instances, schools and other nontherapeutic interventions cannot meet children's needs, and the children must be included in family therapy and/or have individual therapy. Children must be included in the therapeutic process in order to lessen denial, change behaviors, and work on attachment issues. In some instances, a parent's therapist may have a few sessions with the children. In others, it is important that children have their own therapists. This course of treatment has four stages: (a) encounter/education, (b) exploration of the trauma and its impact, (c) skill building and empowerment, and (d) integration and termination (Williams, 1998).

The goal of individual treatment for children, as well as for parents, is to build resilience while challenging and rebuilding core beliefs about safety, trust, power/control, esteem, and intimacy of self, others, and the world (Rosenbloom & Williams, 1999). The resilient family uses strengths to function independently in give-and-take situations, providing support when needed. Through treatment, parents learn to attach to children and children attach to parents. Parents allow children to make independent decisions based on personal empowerment and to take responsibility for themselves.

CONCLUSION

What does the future hold for Loretta and her family? Without appropriate treatment for her, their situation looks grim. A series of meetings at the school involving the child specific team has led to the recommendation that the family be funded for at least 25 hours of home-based services monthly for up to one year. These services would provide counseling and mentoring to supplement the weekly one-hour therapy the family is receiving in a local therapist-training program of a major university. Loretta cannot get appropriate treatment for DID from her mental health HMO provider. The children continue to suffer with attentional issues, self-destructive behaviors, intrusive thoughts and images, and incredibly low self-esteem. The goal of work by the home-based service providers, should services be approved, is to establish some sense of basic safety in the family. However, finding a home-based services provider who is willing to treat DID (or who has any familiarity with the diagnosis) is a difficult task.

The consequences of inheriting a disorganized attachment style (as a secondary victim of parental traumas) can "forever doom the affected child to have a series of unrequited and unrewarding attachment experiences for the rest of his/her life" (Williams-Keeler, 2002, p. 20). With intervention in the family, a more secure attachment between parent/child and family/outsiders could develop. Therapy can become the secure base from which to explore the world (Johnson, 2002) and help the traumatized parent become more secure and develop a more functional sense of emotional connectedness, insight into children's problems, communication skills, nonreactive responding, and a safe style of comfortable relating that does not retraumatize. Through this process, the parent will share appropriate information about his or her developmental legacy and join the children in engaging in interaction and exploration (Sroufe, 1996).

One of the most important healing factors in overcoming the impact of exposure to trauma in the self or others is the ability to derive comfort from another. Therapy must be flexible, creative, and focus on family-wide healing, including normalization of the traumatic response (Williams, 1991). After all, knowledge is power and education is one of the major goals of treatment. Treatment can help family members attach to one another, maintain an atmosphere of safety and stability, connect with a larger community (e.g., through home-based services), and overcome traumatic sequelae (Catherall, 1997).

EPILOGUE: LORETTA'S LIFE SINCE

Loretta was at a treatment impasse when this chapter was first written. However, since that time, as the book came into fruition, changes in the world around her have allowed her to participate in the type of flexible, creative, connective therapy described herein. The school social worker who was instrumental in designing the CST intervention that was never utilized no longer works for the school system. Instead, she became an authorized provider for Loretta's HMO and has been working with Loretta for over a year. During that time, Loretta has worked through the first few chapters of *The PTSD Workbook* (Williams & Poijula, 2002), looking in depth at some of the traumatic experiences that led to the creation of her alters. She has developed a close, trusting relationship with the social worker/therapist, and has developed excellent parenting skills that no longer are as protective and restrictive, allowing her children to venture out from her on their own. Her daughter Christine now has a boyfriend, as well as a diagnosis of chronic fatigue, which is limiting her ability to attend school. However, Loretta now is not encouraging her daughter's illness and instead is insisting that her daughter attend one class a day, and she is ready to challenge the school system to provide home-based services. Her daughter now wants to be in school and is upset that her illness is preventing full-time daily attendance. Loretta is committed to her healing and is pleased at the progress she has made.

REFERENCES

Albeck, J. H. (1994). Intergenerational consequences of trauma: Reframing traps in treatment theory—a second generation perspective. In M. B. Williams & J. F. Sommer, Jr. (Eds.), *Handbook of posttraumatic therapy* (pp. 106–125). Westport, CT: Greenwood Press.

American Counseling Association (2001). *Responding to tragedy: How much should you tell your children?* (Available from the American Counseling Association, 5999 Stevenson Ave., Alexandria, VA, 22304).

American Red Cross (2001). *Disaster services.* Falls Church, VA: Author.

Bartholomew, K., & Horowitz., L. M. (1991). Attachment styles among young adults: A test of a four-category model. *Journal of Personality and Social Psychology, 61,* 226–244.

Blevins, W. (1993). *Your family, your self: How to analyze your family system to understand yourself and achieve more satisfying relationships with your loved ones.* Oakland, CA: New Harbinger.

Carlson, E. B. (Ed.). (1997). *Trauma assessments.* New York: Guilford Press.

Carroll, E. M., Foy, D. W., Cannon, B. J., & Zweir, G. (1991). Assessment issues involving the families of trauma victims. *Journal of Traumatic Stress, 4,* 25–40.

Catherall, D. R. (1992). *Back from the brink: A family guide to overcoming posttraumatic stress.* New York: Bantam

Catherall, D. R. (1997) Family treatment when a member has PTSD. *Clinical Quarterly, 17,* 19–21.

Danieli, Y. (1981). Families of survivors of the Nazi Holocaust. Some short and long term effects. In C. D. Spielberger, J. G. Arason, & N. Milgram (Eds.), *Stress and anxiety* (Vol. 8, pp. 405–421). New York: McGraw-Hill Hemisphere.

Davis, L. (1991). *Allies in healing: When the person you love was sexually abused as a child.* New York: Harper/Collins.

Figley, C. R. (1989). *Helping traumatized families.* San Francisco: Jossey-Bass.

Garbarino, J., Dubrow, N., Kostelny, K., & Pardo, C. (1992). *Children in danger: Coping with the consequences of community violence.* San Francisco: Jossey-Bass.

Gilbert, K. R. (1995). Spouses and secondary traumatic stress. In C. R. Figley (Ed.), *Trauma and its wake III: Secondary traumatic stress syndromes.* New York: Brunner/Mazel.

Graber, K. (1991). *Ghosts in the bedroom: A guide for partners of incest survivors.* Deerfield Beach, FL: Health Communications.

Gurwitch, R. H., Silovsky, J. F., Schultz, S., Kees, M., Burlingame, B. A. (2001). *Reactions and guidelines for children following trauma/disaster.* Washington, DC: American Psychological Association.

Higgins, G. O. (1994). *Resilient adults: Overcoming a cruel past.* San Francisco: Jossey-Bass.

International Critical Incident Stress Foundation, Inc. (2001). *Children's reactions and needs after disaster.* Ellicott City, MD: Author.

Johnson, S. M. (2002). *Emotionally focused couple therapy with trauma survivors: Strengthening attachment bonds.* New York: Guilford Press.

Klein-Parker, F. (1988). Dominant attitudes of adult children of Holocaust survivors toward their parents. In J. P. Wilson, Z. Harel, & B. Kahana (Eds.), *Human adaptation to extreme stress: From the Holocaust to Vietnam* (pp. 193–218). New York: Brunner/Mazel.

Lyons, J. A., & Root, L. P. (2001). Family members of the PTSD veteran: Treatment needs and barriers. Vet Center Voice, *10*(3), 48–52.

Marin and San Mateo Counties school staffs (1982). *Outreach materials for teachers: Tips for teachers in times of disasters.* Marin County and Santa Cruz County, CA: Community Mental Health Services.

Matsakis, A. (1996). *Vietnam wives: Facing the challenges of life with veterans suffering posttraumatic stress* (2nd ed.). Lutherville, MD: Sidran Press.

McCubbin, M. A., & McCubbin, H. I. (1989). Theoretical orientations to family stress and coping. In C. R. Figley (Ed.), *Traumatic stress in families* (pp. 1–43). New York: Brunner/Mazel.

National Association of School Psychologists. (2001). *Identifying seriously traumatized children: Tips for parents and educators.* Retrieved September 20, 2001, from www.nasponline.org

Niles, D. (1990). PTSD: Family implications. *International Association of Marriage and Family Counselors Newsletter, 1,* 2.

Okun, B. (1984). Family therapy and the schools. In B. Okun (Ed.), *Family therapy with school related problems* (pp. 1–12). Rockville, MD: Aspen Publications.

Perry, B. D. (2002). *Maltreated children: Experience, brain development and the next generation.* New York: W. W. Norton.

Pynoos, R., & Nader, K. (1988). Psychological first aid and treatment approach for children exposed to community violence: research implications. *Journal of Traumatic Stress, 1,* 445–473.

Rosenbloom, D., & Williams, M. B. (1999). *Life after trauma: A workbook for healing.* New York: Guilford Press.

Rosenthal, D., Sadler, A., & Edwards, W. (1987). Families and posttraumatic stress disorder. In D. Rosenthal (Ed.), *Family stress* (pp. 81–96). Rockville, MD: Aspen Publications.

Schore, A. N. (1999). Early trauma and the development of the right brain. Presentation at course and institute entitled: Psychological trauma: Maturational processes and therapeutic interventions. Boston: Boston University School of Medicine.

Sroufe, L. A. (1996). *Emotional development: The organization of emotional life in the early years.* Cambridge, UK: Cambridge University Press.

Stamm, B. H. (1996). *Measurement of stress, trauma, and adaptation.* Lutherville, MD: Sidran Press.

Williams, M. B. (1991). Clinical work with families of MPD patients: Assessment and issues for practice. *Dissociation, 4*(2), 92–98.

Williams, M. B. (1996). Trauma and the family. In M. Harway (Ed.), *Treating the changing family: Handling normative and unusual events* (pp. 144–162). New York: John Wiley & Sons.

Williams, M. B. (1998). Treating STSD in children. In C. R. Figley (Ed.), *Burnout in families: The systemic costs of caring* (pp. 91–138). Boca Raton, FL: CRC Press.

Williams, M. B., & Becker, J. (2000). *Crisis plan for Falls Church City Public Schools.* Falls Church, VA: Falls Church City Schools.

Williams, M. B., & Poijula, S. (2002). *The PTSD workbook.* Oakland, CA: New Harbinger Press.

Williams-Keeler, L. (2001, December). How to do couples therapy with trauma survivors: Paper presented at Pre-meeting Institute of the 17th Annual Meeting of the International Society for Traumatic Stress Studies, New Orleans, LA.

Williams-Keeler, L (2002). What attachment theory suggests about the prospects of forgiveness for mother. Unpublished manuscript.

4

When a Child Is Traumatized or Physically Injured: The Secondary Trauma of Parents

MICHAEL F. BARNES

The task of ensuring that our children will safely navigate the physical, emotional, and developmental stages from infancy to adulthood has become increasingly difficult in the twenty-first century. The number of incidences of traumatic injury, life-threatening illness, abuse, violence, and other sources of unexpected death to children and adolescents in our society are staggering. Even in the most conscientious families, unexpected and unthinkable traumatic events occur, with consequences for the child and parents that can be catastrophic. The National Center for Injury Prevention and Control (www.cdc.gov/ncipc/default.htm) has reported that each year 700,000 children are identified as victims of abuse and neglect, 140,000 children are treated in emergency rooms for injuries sustained in bicycle accidents, 200,000 are treated for falls from playground equipment, and 320,000 for injuries sustained in automobile accidents (2001). Over 100,000 children are treated in emergency rooms for traumatic brain injuries resulting from falls, accidents, and athletic injuries (Rivara et al., 1992), and thousands of children will be diagnosed with some form of cancer (Varni, Katz, Colegrove, & Dolgin, 1996). If these statistics are hard to believe, visit a hospital emergency waiting room or pay close attention to the articles that fill our newspapers concerning the accidents, illnesses, and abuses that befall our children.

It is clear from the traumatology literature (Jones & Peterson, 1993; Lipovsky, 1991) that physically abused, severely injured, and critically ill children will show signs of psychological trauma. But what about the parents and other family members? For the vast majority of these traumatized children, family members are at risk for experiencing their own psychological trauma. Often parents or siblings of the traumatized child are present at the time of the event and have to deal with their own terror, uncertainty, and urgent need to ensure that lifesaving interventions are administered appropriately. Others have to deal with the sudden and unexpected telephone call informing them that their child has been injured and is presently being treated in a local emergency room. For many, long periods of medical or psychological treatment must be endured, while possible death or long-term physical, intellectual, and emotional disabilities remain in question.

Many families will be burdened with months or years of medical and emotional therapy to assist their child in dealing with the scars resulting from the traumatic event. In many cases, parents will be forced to deal with their own shattered dreams for their child's future, as well as ongoing questions and concerns about what they could have done to prevent this horrible situation. Although medical and emotional services are often available to assist the primary trauma victim, the family members are all too often overlooked as victims of their own secondary traumatic stress reaction (Figley, 1995).

Figley (1998) defined secondary traumatic stress as tension experienced as a result of the demands of living with and caring for someone with posttraumatic stress disorder (PTSD). A secondary traumatic stress disorder is therefore the resulting emotional exhaustion and burnout that comes from this caregiving relationship. Parents who must deal with the sudden traumatization of someone they love, cope with the physical, emotional, and behavioral changes that follow the trauma and who must face their own uncertainty and personal vulnerability are clearly candidates for this secondary traumatization (Barnes, 1998a).

The majority of the seminal works in the study of secondary traumatization have focused on the systemic interactional patterns of adult trauma survivors and their family members, but a growing body of research investigates the impact that injured, abused, or critically ill children have on the cognitive, emotional, and behavioral functioning of their parents, siblings, and the family system as a whole (Barnes, 1998a). This chapter discusses such primary and secondary trauma symptoms and reviews the literature associated with the secondary trauma of parents and families, and concludes with a review of six axioms that have been identified from the literature review and upon which future research questions can be developed.

PRIMARY AND SECONDARY RESPONSES TO TRAUMA

The traumatic stress response is generally considered to be primary when the victim of the traumatizing event is the one either who is personally threatened or who has witnessed others who have been threatened or injured. Secondary trauma occurs when the victim is traumatized through the process of learning about the primary trauma that has been experienced by a loved one or by the secondary victim's frequent interactions with a primary trauma victim.[1]

Figley (1995) noted that although secondary traumatic stress disorder (STSD) would be experienced by the victim as a syndrome of symptoms that are nearly identical to PTSD, there is a fundamental difference between the response patterns of the primary and secondary trauma victim. The difference is that the "primary trauma victim experiences symptoms that are directly associated with some aspect of the traumatic event, whereas the secondary trauma victim experiences symptoms that are associated with the primary trauma victim" (Barnes, 1998a, p. 77). For the family members of the ill or injured child, this is a significant distinction.

PTSD Symptoms in Children

The diagnosis of PTSD is based upon the patient's exhibition of symptoms from three primary symptom categories: (a) persistent experiencing of the stressor, (b) persistent avoidance of reminders of the event and numbing of general responsiveness, and (c) persistent symptoms of arousal (American Psychiatric Association, 2000). Symptoms that are commonly associated with children who suffer from persistent reexperience of traumatic stressors include nightmares, flashbacks, repetitive trauma-focused play, intense distress associated with reminders, and intrusive repetitive thoughts about the event. Symptoms associated with avoidance may include avoidance of reminders of the traumatic event, decreased interest in significant activities, regressive behaviors, numbing and restrictions in range of emotions, amnesia related to the traumatic event, and feelings of detachment from others. Finally, symptoms associated with persistent arousal may include sleep difficulties, irritability, difficulty concentrating, hyperalertness, and hypervigilance (Cohen, Berliner, & March, 2000; Lipovsky, 1991; Shah & Mudholkar, 2000).

---

[1]Editor's note: Strictly speaking, individuals learning of a trauma to a loved one are classified with PTSD; however, their symptomatic focus is associated with the primary victim rather than their own direct experience of the trauma and thus most traumatologists conceptualize them as secondary victims.

Risk Factors in Children

The extent to which children are at risk for experiencing posttraumatic symptoms appears to be related to several factors. Cohen et al. (2000) identified three primary factors that have been found to predict the development of PTSD symptoms: (a) the severity of the trauma exposure, (b) parental trauma-related distress, and (c) temporal proximity to the traumatic event. Pfefferbaum (1997) concurred, stating that the trauma response is highly correlated with the child's exposure to the traumatic event, which is influenced by both physical and emotional proximity. The impact of the exposure is mediated by (a) the child's perceptions associated with their risk of being killed or seriously injured, (b) the child's perceptions associated with the degree of danger experienced by significant others, and (c) the actual responses of significant others following the traumatic event (Lipovsky, 1991). The child's affective experience of fear associated with his or her perceived risk of death or injury has been found to increase symptoms of PTSD, as does the child's tendency to suppress thoughts and feelings related to their injuries. Aaron, Zaglul, and Emery (1999) reported that suppression was not only predictive of PTSD avoidance symptoms, but was also "highly correlated with PTSD re-experiencing and overall PTSD symptomatology" (p. 341).

Developmental Factors

The age and developmental level of the victimized child plays a significant role in influencing these predictive factors. Pfefferbaum (1997) contended that the child's "exposure to risk, perception and understanding of trauma, susceptibility to parental distress, quality of response, coping style and skills, and memory of the event" (p. 1505) are all influenced by the child's developmental ability and awareness. As children grow and become more emotionally mature and socially aware, the PTSD symptoms that they experience begin to resemble the symptoms that are experienced by adults in our society. Younger children tend to exhibit symptoms that do not fit well into the diagnostic categories for PTSD as outlined in the DSM-IV. Cohen et al. (2000) contended that this is primarily due to the child's lack of advanced cognitive and expressive language skills, which are required to carry out many of the symptoms listed in the diagnostic criteria for PTSD.

Younger children will exhibit a significantly different set of posttrauma symptoms than their adolescent counterparts. Younger children appear to experience symptoms that enable them to avoid painful feelings associated with the traumatic memories, whereas older victims experience more symptoms associated with reexperiencing the traumatic memories and associated hyperarousal (Schwarz & Kowalski, 1991). Younger children may exhibit symptoms that are more consistent with a generalized anxiety disorder that indicates significantly greater fear and anxiety, whereas older victims demonstrate greater anger, aggression, and acting out behaviors. Younger children may experience regressive symptoms such as difficulty sleeping alone, a reversal of toilet training, and infantile speech, whereas older victims may exhibit greater dissociative symptoms such as derealization, depersonalization or self-injurious behaviors. Finally, younger children may be able to express their issues associated with traumatic memories only through a process of expressive play or drawing, whereas older victims will be able to talk about their memories and emotions (Cohen et al., 2000).

Freud defined trauma as a "sudden overwhelming stimulation that immobilizes the ego functions and results in a state of helplessness" (quoted in Mishne, 2001, p. 65). James (1997) hypothesized that a child's development of posttraumatic symptoms is related to the degree to which he or she is able to deal with the fear/terror associated with the traumatic event, without overwhelming the ego defenses that serve as protective structures. The quality of the attachment relationships that the child has with his or her parents and the parental posttraumatic response significantly influences the child's defensive abilities. Overwhelmed ego defenses can result in significant memory disorders, dysregulation of affect, and avoidance of intimacy (James) for both primary and secondary trauma victims.

PARENTAL/FAMILY SECONDARY TRAUMA

A growing body of literature addresses the issues associated with the secondary traumatization of parents and other family members of medically or physically traumatized children. Recent publications have addressed such issues as acute physical injury (Aaron et al., 1999), severe traumatic brain injury (Levi, Drotor, Yeates, & Taylor, 1999), life-threatening illness (Madan-Swain et al., 2000; Smith, Redd, Peyser, & Vogl, 1999; Stuber, 1996), and painful or frightening treatment for severe medical conditions (Stuber, Nader, Yasuda, Pynoos, & Cohen, 1991). What has emerged is support for the contention that sudden and unexpected medical emergencies are often followed by a form of systemic trauma characterized by family system disturbance, primary and secondary traumatization, and psychological and marital distress (Barnes, Todahl, & Barnes, 2002). Family members appear to engage in a circular process through which parents and children respond to one another's stress responses, with the parents ultimately serving as the model for how to cope with the traumatic event (Pfefferbaum, 1997).

Reports from Emergency Medical and ICU Personnel

Barnes, Todahl, and Barnes (2002) polled experts (intensive care unit nurses, physicians, social workers, psychologists, and family therapists) who work with physically traumatized children on pediatric intensive care units (PICUs) to determine their views concerning family response patterns that occur immediately following the traumatic event and throughout the ICU hospital experience. These experts identified family response patterns that are consistent with symptoms of a secondary traumatic stress reaction that are evident immediately post trauma and throughout the family's ICU experience.

The family response patterns were consistent with each of the diagnostic criteria for PTSD, as set forth in the DSM-IV-TR (APA, 2000). The family response patterns that meet the criteria for persistent reexperiencing of the traumatizing event include the following: The parents spend a significant amount of time and attention on the overall health and welfare of the child; they focus on the possibility that the child may die; they have anxiety about a prognosis of permanent disability; they have many fears about the child's unknown future; and they are preoccupied with the child's specific injuries and associated pain. The experts observed that the families would be preoccupied with these concerns and would ask the same questions over and over again, soliciting answers from physicians, nurses and other support staff. Examples of avoidance of the stimuli associated with the trauma included the use of intellectualization, memory deficits, standing around mutely, depression of affective responses, and denial of the reality and potential consequences associated with the traumatizing event. The experts hypothesized that family members used these avoidance behaviors to distance themselves from experiencing the painful emotions associated with the child's injuries. Symptoms of increased arousal included sleep difficulties, difficulty concentrating, and hypervigilance. Family members were said be reluctant to leave their child at any time, resulting in increased fatigue, hunger, and agitation. The experts also noticed a manner in which many families become hypervigilant about the standard of care their child receives—they identify a specific staff member(s) with whom they feel comfortable and then hold that individual's caregiving behaviors as the standard for all caregivers who work with the child. This often results in conflict between the parents and PICU administration and direct-care staff.

These examples indicate that the majority of family response patterns focus on some aspect of (a) the child's experience of the traumatic event, (b) the medical care being provided, and/or (c) the victim's future functioning. These findings support Figley's (1995) contention that the symptoms exhibited in a secondary traumatic stress response would be similar to the primary victim's, but with a focus on the primary victim rather than the specific traumatic event.

Barnes et al. (2002) also indicated that the experts identified multiple family response patterns that demonstrate family members' need for trust, safety, and control while the child is a patient in the PICU. Family members are concerned about personal and family vulnerability, exerting significant energy to convince other family members that everything is going to be all right. They become easily frustrated if they do not believe that questions are being answered in a timely and honest fashion, and they express great difficulty when alarms activate in the child's room for no apparent reason. This need for safety and control is also demonstrated by the family members constant focus on all possible consequences of the child's injuries and their need to insure that the right staff members are present to care for their child.

Barnes et al. (2002) proposed that family members' attempts to deal with multiple stressors associated with the traumatic event, the constant anxiety about life-and-death issues, and the constant stress associated with the PICU environment result in a cumulative experience of a systemic traumatic stress reaction within the family system. The experts in this study clearly supported the belief that family members demonstrate affective, cognitive, and behavioral changes following the traumatic event. They also suggested that stable relationship patterns between family members must, by necessity, change in response to the individual changes listed and the demands associated with the care of the injured child:

> This reallocation of time and attention to the injured child, as well as long periods of time away from the home at the hospital, is believed to result in diminished contact with the spouse and siblings and limited attention to the emotional needs of the other children (Barnes et al., 2002, p. 21.)

Barnes (1998a) proposed the term *systemic traumatic stress* as the most appropriate for the sudden demands imposed on each member of the family system and the resultant changes in relationship patterns. The collaborators agreed that if family members do not attend to the stressors of the PICU environment, then familial interactional patterns could escalate into arguments, resentments, triangulation, attention-seeking sibling behaviors, and fault finding/blame (Barnes et al., 2002).

Peebles-Kleiger (2000) stated that a pediatric/neonatal ICU hospitalization is a traumatic stressor according to criteria set forth in the DSM-IV (APA, 1994) due to the fact that the individual and family is dealing with "actual or threatened death or serious injury, or a threat to the physical integrity of self or others" (p. 259). She noted that family members will experience involuntary and intrusive thoughts that can be experienced for months following the PICU admission. She also asserted that family members "alternate between intrusion and avoidance as a way of processing what would otherwise be too overwhelming to comprehend" (p. 261). The significance of this process is that family members will differ in their ability to talk openly about feelings and in their choice of coping strategies throughout their child's hospital stay. This is to some degree based on their ability to tolerate anxiety resulting from conscious contact with traumatic material. Peebles-Kleiger contended that avoidance of feelings is normal and is more often a sign that the individual is overwhelmed, rather than an indication of an absence of feelings. Therefore, it is important for family members to have space for quiet reflection and attentive listeners who allow them to speak when they are ready.

Peebles-Kleiger (2000) also noted that family members demonstrate symptoms of increased arousal. She identified several examples, including sleep disturbances, edginess, fatigue, and physical complaints. She warned that sleep deprivation is a significant issue in the PICU environment, stating that it can "create irritability and lability, decrease reaction time, impede judgment, and hamper efficient cognitive processing" (p. 266). Care should be taken to identify any increase in alcohol or other substance intake as a means of self-medicating to alleviate symptoms of increased arousal.

Finally, Peebles-Kleiger (2000) supported the contention of Barnes et al. (2002) that family members will show evidence of attempts to maintain some semblance of control in their lives. She views these control behaviors as a response to the overwhelming sense of helplessness that is experienced while in the PICU environment. She proposed that unchanneled aggression (anger that has no simple target) is a normal response when an individual is assaulted and feeling helpless. It is this anger that results in family members' angry outbursts, blaming behavior, and wishes for revenge. Angry outbursts are often focused on hospital staff for failure to provide timely information, lack of privacy, or a perceived oversight or slight. Outbursts can also be focused on other family members, which may result in increased distance and damage to familial relationships at a time when support is needed most. Finding a reason for this catastrophic event (or a source of blame) is an intellectual process that allows family members to avoid feelings of fear and helplessness and enables them to feel more in control of the situation. Unfortunately, these control behaviors "rarely succeed in restoring equilibrium; instead they typically create additional harm, maladaptation, and energy-depleting crises" (Peebles-Kleiger, p. 267).

Pediatric Cancer

The study of pediatric cancer and its relationship to primary and secondary trauma of both victims and their family members has increased in the past 20 years. Strong evidence indicates both groups are at significant risk for posttraumatic stress symptoms.

Impact on Parents.   Barakat et al. (1997) suggested that the "diagnosis and treatment for childhood cancer may have significant long-term effects, which are manifest in symptoms of posttraumatic stress, for parents of childhood cancer survivors" (p. 854). Manne, Duhamel, and Redd (2000) supported this proposition and stated that 10 to 40% of these parents experience high levels of posttraumatic stress symptoms that include intrusive thoughts, increased arousal, hypervigilance, and avoidance of reminders associated with the child's medical treatment. In fact, parents reported greater frequency and intensity of cancer-related posttraumatic stress symptoms than their children did (Barakat et al., 1997). Because proximity to the stressor is associated with greater risk for PTSD, the child who is facing his or her own life-and-death situation presumably would experience greater posttrauma symptoms than their parents. Barakat et al. hypothesized that this difference may be due, in part, to the fact that children receive "support from family, friends, and hospital staff with an aim to enhance mastery over their treatment experience" (p. 856), which serves to buffer their perception of how life-threatening the illness is. The parents, on the other hand, are faced with the painful and frightening reality of life and death each day!

The Mother's Experience.   Pelcovitz et al. (1996) found that mothers of children who have survived pediatric cancer demonstrated significantly higher rates of PTSD than community comparison groups, and appear to have symptom patterns that are more common with this population than among other trauma survivors. Avoidance symptoms such as diminished interest in activities, feelings of detachment, and a sense of a foreshortened future are common, whereas evidence of psychogenic amnesia is extremely uncommon. Also, symptoms associated with increased arousal, such as hypervigilance, sleep disturbances, and concentration difficulties are commonly reported, whereas physiologic reactivity and startle response are rarely reported.

Manne et al. (2000) found several factors that appear to influence these maternal experiences of posttraumatic stress symptoms. One factor that appears to play a significant role in the mother's symptom development is maternal perceptions about treatment and social support. Manne et al. contended that the severity of maternal posttraumatic symptoms is influenced by the mother's perceptions of (a) the cancer treatment as a threat to the child's life, (b) the treatment and its level of intensity, and (c) the amount of threat she experiences as a result of social constraints. A clear finding was that mothers experienced greater PTSD symptoms when they felt inhibited about expressing cancer-related thoughts and feelings. Such constraints can lead to increased posttrauma symptoms because (a) parents have more difficulty finding meaning or obtaining advice and coping assistance from others; (b) negative reactions by others can themselves be experienced as traumatic; and (c) increased verbal inhibition may contribute to increased use of other avoidant coping strategies. Sloper's (2000) study supported the significance of maternal perception as a guiding force in the mother's ability to deal effectively with the daily traumatic stresses of cancer recovery. She found that the mother's appraisal of the amount of strain experienced as a result of the child's illness was more closely associated with reported subjective distress than with actual changes in the child's medical condition.

Impact on the Family. The influence of family functioning and cohesiveness following the diagnosis of pediatric cancer has also been investigated. Hoekstra-Weebers, Jaspers, Kamps, and Klip (1998) proposed that throughout the course of cancer treatment, the mother-child relationship becomes closer than the father-child relationship. This relationship places the mother in the role of guardian; she is compelled to manage the child's medical care and ensure that the child is protected. The impact of these additional responsibilities on her ability to cope with day-to-day stressors is believed to influence the quality of all family relationships. Thus, Noojin, Causey, Gros, Bertolone, and Carter (1999) stated that although family interactions are bidirectional and circular in nature, "family functioning is directly influenced by the success of the mother in coping with this challenge" (p. 91).

Cohesion is defined as the degree to which family members are emotionally bonded to one another. Varni et al. (1996) found that with newly diagnosed families, high family cohesiveness was predictive of lower psychological distress and higher social competence as well as "most consistently predictive of child adaptation across both concurrent and prospective associations" (p 325). However, a different finding is that families who report significant family system cohesion are more likely to have a survivor who exhibits poorer adjustment (Newby, Brown, Pawletko, Gold, & Whitt, 2000). The researchers hypothesized that over time in a traumatized family, alterations in family organization and parental needs for safety and control may result in the establishment of an intense level of emotional bonding that represents a movement from emotional closeness and supportiveness to a more emotionally enmeshed parent-child relationship. Newby et al. proposed that "children who have survived cancer may have greater needs for autonomy than their healthy peers. Thus, any perceptions of intrusion from the family system may be associated with symptoms of adjustment difficulties" (p. 122).

Impact on Siblings. The impact of family system reorganization, especially changes associated with family roles, has been identified as a significant source of distress for the siblings of pediatric cancer survivors. Koch (1985) discovered that after the diagnosis parenting responsibilities tended to shift, from a focus on daily family needs to the care and protection of the cancer patient. This shift resulted in the siblings spending less time with the parents and receiving less parental attention. Other role changes included the utilization of older siblings in adult caretaker roles. These adaptive roles included taking care of the physical needs of the ill sibling and the emotional needs of the parents, who continue to struggle with stressors associated with the child's illness. Koch found that siblings reacted to these systemic changes by acting out in an attempt to regain parental attention or by the rapid development of thoughts, feelings, and actions that exceed an age-appropriate level of maturity.

Madan-Swain, Sexson, Brown, and Ragab (1993) investigated the coping and adaptation skills of siblings of childhood cancer survivors; their findings support Koch's findings associated with role changes. They found that older siblings assumed parental roles and caretaker responsibilities, which seemed to blur the parent-child boundaries and result in the siblings' perception of being less involved in family activities. In the Madan-Swain et al. study, the bond that was established between the cancer patient and the parents through the period of medical treatment served to further isolate siblings from the parents and from the cancer patient. Sargent et al. (1995) found the lack of attention paid to the siblings and the family focus on the ill child were reported as a source of distress for the siblings. The findings of Koch, Madan-Swain et al., and Sargent et al. support those of Barnes et al. (2002) regarding systemic traumatic stress reaction among families supporting a member with life-threatening medical problems.

Traumatic Brain Injury

The literature associated with head trauma has provided several resources that address family coping strategies following a pediatric brain injury.

Use of Denial.   Zarski, DePompei, and Zook (1988) studied the spouses and parents of head-injured adults and children, respectively, and found that families who utilized denial as their primary coping strategy to deal with the traumatic injury reported lower family satisfaction and a major focus on the limitations of the head-injured individual. This negative emphasis resulted in the family organizing around the dysfunction of the child, which contributed to even lower levels of functioning for the traumatized child. Families who were able to honestly face the reality of the traumatic event were better able to make appropriate adjustments in power structure, role relationships, and relationship rules in response to the posttraumatic stress.

Wade et al. (2001) also found that parental "denial was associated with greater caregiver psychological distress" (p. 411). This distress appears to be the result of the family members' efforts to suppress or deny painful affect, which paradoxically results in increased experience of anxiety and a more significant self-report of psychological distress. Wade et al. warned that parental denial and disengagement may reflect the emergence of an acute stress disorder in response to the trauma of the injury. Parents commonly experienced symptoms such as numbing, detachment, absence of emotional responsiveness, and marked avoidance of stimuli that might provoke recollections of the trauma (Wade et al.).

Impact on Functioning. Bragg, Klockars, and Berninger (1992) studied the impact on individual and family functioning in families with a pediatric brain injury survivor. The family members scored significantly lower scores on problem solving, communication, role dimensions, affective responsiveness, affective involvement, and general functioning than did the control group families. A second finding was that the head trauma families reported significantly lower perceptions of member autonomy than did the control group families.

Wade et al. (2001) proposed that families experience significant organizational alterations. Marital conflicts may arise due to triangulation, in which one partner assumes a disproportionate burden of caregiving and discipline (most frequently the mother) and the other shuts down to avoid confronting their own feelings about the injury. This triangular relationship prevents the partners from receiving much needed social support. As with pediatric cancer, parental relationships with siblings of the brain-injured child may also be significantly strained due to (a) changes in the quantity and quality of time spent with them and (b) role changes that require the siblings to accept more responsibility for caring for the injured child.

Nursing and Family Medicine

Miles (1985) studied family response patterns following the death of a child. A significant finding was that the parents' perceived stress was more influential on symptom development than actual, observable stressors. Shaw and Halliday (1992) also supported the proposition that family perceptions are a major influencing factor in how a family responds to a crisis. They proposed that in the case of a chronic illness, the crisis is not the central problem, rather it is the family's "constraining beliefs that restrict alternative views about the crisis that becomes the problem" (p. 541). These findings were supported by the Manne et al. (2000) study regarding the mothers of pediatric cancer survivors. Figley (1988) also argued that perception plays a major role in the family response to a traumatic event; he proposed that families that maintain or construct a more positive worldview associated with the crisis or traumatic event will deal with it in a more positive manner.

As in the nursing literature, the family medicine literature emphasizes the role of family perception in family members' response to chronic illness. Gallo (1991) and Thompson, Gustafson, Hamlett, and Spock (1992) each studied family response patterns associated with chronic, life-threatening pediatric illness and found that family perceptions played a large role in the family choice of coping mechanisms. Thompson et al. (1992) proposed that parental psychological distress is explained more by their perceptions than by the actual medical condition of the child.

AXIOMS ASSOCIATED WITH SECONDARY TRAUMA OF FAMILY MEMBERS

A primary goal of this chapter is to identify testable axioms associated with the secondary traumatization of parents. Popper (1965) defined *axioms* as either conventions or scientific hypotheses. Six axioms can be derived from the literature on family response patterns following the traumatization or illness of a child family member. These six axioms provide a foundation for understanding the process of secondary traumatization in these families and for generating future research questions.

Axiom 1—Individual PTSD-Like Reactions

Following the traumatization of a child, the parents and siblings will report having experienced emotional, cognitive, and behavioral symptoms similar to those reported by primary victims of PTSD. The symptoms associated with a secondary traumatization that have been reported in this literature include intrusive thoughts, nightmares, flashbacks, feelings of detachment or estrangement from others, restricted affect, emotional and physiological distress associated with the traumatic event, avoidance of activities that remind the family member of the child's traumatization, sleep disturbance, hypervigilance, and fatigue.

Axiom 2—Parental Focus on the Child

The focus of the parents' secondary trauma symptoms will be on the physical and emotional condition of the primary trauma victim. Barnes et al. (2002) addressed this issue at length, supporting Figley's (1995) contention that secondary traumatic stress reactions will be focused on issues associated with the primary trauma victim's physical and emotional condition. Koch (1985) also supported this issue when he proposed that increased negative affect is associated with parental concerns about the child's critical condition and its effects on the siblings of the cancer patient. Both Koch and Madan-Swain et al. (1993) discussed the preoccupation that parents maintain with the ill child, at the expense of their relationship with the other siblings.

Axiom 3—Altered Parental Worldview

Parental worldview associated with personal vulnerability, safety, and control will be altered as a result of the traumatizing event. Catherall (1998) proposed that all human systems develop their own unique and idiosyncratic interpretations of reality within their world. It is through this reality filter that families develop unique attitudes, beliefs, values, rituals, and ways of operating and behaving that become reinforced through intrafamily and extrafamily interactions. Following a traumatic event, families commonly experience a shift in attitudes and beliefs that represents a need to focus on safety issues, as they relate to the self and others. Catherall contended that safety issues are "expressed in the family's worldview in the form of suspicious, distrustful attributions concerning the motivations of others, but it can also be seen in various symptoms of family members (i.e., fearfulness, phobias, and other anxiety reactions)" (p. 203).

Janoff-Bulman (1992) contended that alterations in the worldview of the traumatized individual can directly influence the victim's experience of depression, intrusive thoughts, breakdowns in interpersonal trust, anger, rage, feelings of vulnerability, disillusionment, lost sense of safety, and loss of self-worth and self-confidence. Family members consequently develop issues associated with vulnerability and control. Barnes et al. (2002) and Peebles-Kleiger (2000) each identified this axiom as being significant for understanding family hypervigilance and conflict with staff in the PICU. Barnes et al. proposed that family members often assume a more controlling stance in order to avoid experiencing the symptoms associated with an altered worldview. The risk of experiencing these symptoms would seem to be equally likely for both primary and secondary victims.

Axiom 4—Centrality of Parental Perceptions

Parental perceptions of the amount of stress resulting from the traumatizing event will influence interactional patterns, selection of coping mechanisms, and the degree of emotional sequelae experienced by the parents. This point is strongly supported by Gallo (1991), Manne et al. (2000), Miles (1985), and Thompson et al. (1992). Parental perceptions appear to play a major role in the recovery process for families as well. Koch (1985) proposed that many families believed that the challenge of the crisis resulted in a more cohesive and emotionally closer family, and Figley

(1988) suggested that families that are able to recognize the strengths they have developed through their struggles following the traumatic event are better able to recover from their experience of secondary trauma.

Axiom 5—Structural Changes

The traumatization of a child family member will cause significant alterations in family organization, including major changes in communication patterns and role behaviors. Studies by Koch (1985), Madan-Swain et al. (1993), and Wade et al. (1995) agree that parents and siblings of the traumatized child experience role changes that serve to protect the parents, while alienating the siblings from the parents and the primary victim.

Axiom 6—Systemic Reactions

Multiple stressors resulting from the immediate needs of the parents, siblings, and traumatized child will result in a systemic traumatic stress reaction among family members. Barnes et al. (2002) reported that a traumatizing event may result in immediate stressors that can affect the lives of all family members for days, weeks, months, or years. This wound to the family system can affect much more than the family's life routines and may be observable through disruptions in family members' stable patterns associated with behavior, communication, discipline, and emotional support. The expert collaborators in the Barnes et al. study agreed that failure on the part of the family to deal with these disruptions in family interactional patterns would ultimately result in arguments, resentments, and attention-seeking behaviors between family members. If systemic stressors continue to go unattended, noticeable patterns of triangulation and blaming become common family dynamics.

CONCLUSION

Family members of traumatized or critically ill children experience significant disturbances in individual and systemic functioning, beginning almost immediately following the traumatizing event. Health care workers from all disciplines need to be aware of the nature of both primary and secondary responses to trauma, so that interventions for each member of the family can be initiated as quickly as possible. In hospital settings, nurses and social workers must be trained to recognize symptoms of secondary and systemic trauma. Medical staff members must be alert to signs that family members are becoming overwhelmed so that they can intervene before the family's need for safety and control results in conflict between the family members and the medical staff.

It is important for mental health professionals to realize that the psychological/emotional problems exhibited by primary trauma victims are greatly influenced by the emotional, behavioral, and interactional struggles of their parents outside the medical environment. Most families will not receive clinical assistance while in the hospital setting, so many families will ultimately seek assistance for the emerging primary and secondary traumatic stress reactions in outpatient settings. It is especially important for marriage and family therapists to recognize that these families will often present with traditionally systemic difficulties such as marital problems, boundary issues, disrupted parenting styles, and difficulties associated with their children's behaviors (Barnes et al., 2002). Often, families will not make the connection between their current problems and the past traumatic experience(s). Therefore, therapists need to be alert to historical factors when assessing the family system functioning. Barnes (1998b) proposed that once the family trauma has been identified, an initial focus on structural family therapy (Minuchin, 1974) with a transition to Figley's empowerment model (Figley, 1989) is a useful integration that provides the family with the safety needed to begin to face the traumatic material and the opportunity to move beyond personal experiences to a unified family healing theory.

REFERENCES

Aaron, J., Zaglul, H., & Emery, R. I. (1999). Posttraumatic stress in children following acute physical injury. *Journal of Pediatric Psychology, 24*, 335–343.
American Psychiatric Association. (1994). *Diagnostic and Statistical Manual of Mental Disorders* (4th ed.). Washington, DC: American Psychiatric Association.
American Psychiatric Association. (2000). *Diagnostic and Statistical Manual of Mental Disorders* (4th ed., Text Revision). Washington, DC: American Psychiatric Association.
Barakat, L. P., Kazak, A. E., Meadows, A. T., Casey, R., Meeske, K., & Stuber, M. L. (1997). Families surviving childhood cancer: A comparison of posttraumatic stress symptoms with families of healthy children. *Journal of Pediatric Psychology, 22*, 843–859.
Barnes, M. F. (1998a). Understanding the secondary traumatic stress of parents. In C. R. Figley (Ed.), *Burnout in families: Secondary traumatic stress in everyday life* (pp. 75–89). Boca Raton, FL: CRC Press.
Barnes, M. F. (1998b). Treating burnout in families following childhood trauma. In C. R. Figley (Ed.), *Burnout in families: Secondary traumatic stress in everyday life* (pp. 177–185). Boca Raton: CRC Press.
Barnes, M. F., Todahl, J. L., & Barnes, A. (2002). Family secondary trauma on the pediatric critical care unit. *Journal of Trauma Practice, 1*(2), 5–29.
Bragg, R. M., Klockars, A. J., & Berninger, V. W. (1992). Comparison of families with and without adolescents with traumatic brain injury. *Journal of Head Trauma Rehabilitation, 7*(3), 94–108.
Catherall, D. R. (1998). Treating traumatized families. In C. R. Figley (Ed.), *Burnout in families: Secondary traumatic stress in everyday life* (pp. 187–215). Boca Raton, FL: CRC Press.

Cohen, J. A., Berliner, L., & March, J. S. (2000). Treatment of children and adolescents. In E. B. Foa, T. M. Keane, & M. J. Friedman (Eds.), *Effective treatments for PTSD: Practice guidelines from the International Society for Traumatic Stress Studies* (pp. 106–138). New York: The Guilford Press.

Figley, C. R. (1988). Treating traumatic stress in family therapy. *Journal of Traumatic Stress, 1*, 1.

Figley, C. R. (1989). *Helping traumatized families.* San Francisco: Jossey-Bass.

Figley, C. R. (1995). Compassion fatigue as secondary traumatic stress disorder: An overview. In C.R. Figley (Ed.), *Compassion fatigue: Secondary traumatic stress disorder in treating the traumatized* (pp. 1–20). New York: Brunner/Mazel.

Figley, C. R. (1998). Burnout as systemic traumatic stress: A model for helping traumatized family members. In C. R. Figley (Ed.), *Burnout in families: The systemic costs of caring* (pp. 15–28). Boca Raton, FL: CRC Press.

Gallo, A. M. (1991). Family adaptation in childhood chronic illness: A case report. *Journal of Pediatric Health Care, 5*(2), 78–85.

Hoekstra-Weebers, J. E., Jaspers, J. P. C., Kamps, W. A., & Klip, E. C. (1998). Marital dissatisfaction, psychological distress, and the coping of parents of pediatric cancer patients. *Journal of Marriage and the family, 60*, 1012–1021.

James, B. (1997). Family treatment of attachment trauma problems in children. In U. P. Gielen & A. L. Comunian (Eds.), *The family and family therapy in international perspective* (pp. 418–437). College Park: International Association For Cross Cultural Psychology.

Janoff-Bulman, R. (1992). *Shattered assumptions: Towards a new psychology of trauma.* New York: The Free Press.

Jones, R. W., & Peterson, L. W. (1993). Posttraumatic stress disorder in a child following an automobile accident. *The Journal of Family Practice, 36*, 223–225.

Koch, A. (1985). "If only it could be me": The families of pediatric cancer patients. *Family Relations, 34*, 63–70.

Levi, R. B., Drotar, D., Yeates, K. O., & Taylor, H. G. (1999). Posttraumatic stress symptoms in children following orthopedic or traumatic brain injury. *Journal of Clinical Child Psychology, 28*, 232–243.

Lipovsky, J. A. (1991). Posttraumatic stress disorder in children. *Family Community Health, 14*(3), 42–51.

Madan-Swain, A., Brown, R. T., Foster, M. A., Vega, R., Byars, K., Rodenberger, W., Bell, B., & Lambert, R. (2000). Identity in adolescent survivors of childhood cancer. *Journal of Pediatric Psychology, 25*, 105–115.

Madan-Swain, A., Sexson, S. B., Brown, R. T., & Ragab, A. (1993). Family adaptation and coping among siblings of cancer patients, their brothers and sisters, and nonclinical controls. *The American Journal of Family Therapy, 21*, 60–70.

Manne, S., Duhamel, K., & Redd, W. (2000). Association of psychological vulnerability factors to posttraumatic stress symptomatology in mothers of pediatric cancer survivors. *Psycho-Oncology, 9*, 372–384.

Miles, M. S. (1985). Emotional symptoms and physical health in bereaved parents. *Nursing Research, 34*, 76–81.

Minuchin, S. (1974). *Families and family therapy.* Cambridge, MA: Harvard University Press.

Mishne, J. M. (2001). Psychological trauma in adolescence: Familial disillusionment and loss of personal identity. *The American Journal of Psychoanalysis, 61*, 63–83.

Newby, W. L., Brown, R. T., Pawletko, T. M., Gold, S. H., & Whitt, J. K. (2000). Social skills and psychological adjustment of child and adolescent cancer survivors. *Psycho-Oncology, 9*, 113–126.

Noojin, A. B., Causey, D. L., Gros, B. J., Bertolone, S., & Carter, B. D. (1999). The influence of maternal stress resistance and family relationships on depression in children with cancer. *Journal of Psychosocial Oncology, 17*, 79–97.

Peebles-Kleiger, M. J. (2000). Pediatric and neonatal intensive care hospitalization as traumatic stressor: Implications for intervention. *Bulletin of the Menninger Clinic, 64*, 257–280.

Pelcovitz, D., Goldenberg, B., Kaplan, S., Weinblatt, M., Mandel, F., Meyers, B., & Vinciguerra, V. (1996). Posttraumatic stress disorder in mothers of pediatric cancer survivors. *Psychosomatics, 37*, 116–126.

Pfefferbaum, B. (1997). Posttraumatic stress disorder in children: A review of the past 10 years. *Journal of the American Academy of Child and Adolescent Psychiatry, 36*, 1503–1511.

Popper, K. R. (1965). *The logic of scientific discovery*. New York: Harper & Row.

Rivara, J. B., Fay, G. C., Jaffe, K. M., Polissar, N. L., Shurtleff, H. A., & Martin, K. M. (1992). Predictors of family functioning one year following traumatic brain injury in children. *Archives of Physical Medicine and Rehabilitation, 73*, 899–910.

Sargent, J. R., Sahler, O. J. Z., Roghmann, K. J., Mulhern, R. K., Barbarian, O. A., Carpenter, P. J. et al. (1995). Sibling adaptation to childhood cancer collaborative study: Siblings' perceptions of the cancer experience. *Journal of Pediatric Psychology, 20*, 151–164.

Schwarz, E. D., & Kowalski, J. M. (1991). Malignant memories: PTSD in children and adults after a school shooting. *Journal of the American Academy of Child and Adolescent Psychiatry, 20*, 936–944.

Shah, N., & Mudholkar, S. (2000). Clinical aspects of posttraumatic stress disorder in children and adolescents. In K. N. Dwivedi (Ed.), *PostTraumatic stress disorder in children and adolescents* (pp. 97–111). London: Whurr Publishers.

Shaw, M. C., & Halliday, P. H. (1992). The family, crisis and chronic illness: An evolutionary model. *Journal of Advanced Nursing, 17*, 537–543.

Sloper, P. (2000). Predictors of distress in parents of children with cancer: A prospective study. *Journal of Pediatric Psychology, 25*, 79–91.

Smith, M. Y., Redd, W. H., Peyser, C., & Vogl, D. (1999). Posttraumatic stress disorder in cancer: A review. *Psycho-Oncology, 8*, 521–537.

Stuber, M. L., Nader, K., Yasuda, P., Pynoos, R. S., & Cohen, S. (1991). Stress responses after pediatric bone marrow transplantation: Preliminary results of a prospective longitudinal study. *Journal of the American Academy of Child and Adolescent Psychiatry, 30*, 952–957.

Thompson, R. J., Gustafson, K. E., Hamlett, K. W., & Spock, A. (1992). Stress, coping and family functioning in the psychological adjustment of mothers of children and adolescents with cystic fibrosis. *Journal of Pediatric Psychology, 17*, 573–585.

Varni, J. W., Katz, E. R., Colegrove, R., & Dolgin, M. (1996). Family functioning predictors of adjustment in children with newly diagnosed cancer: A prospective analysis. *Journal of Child Psychology and Psychiatry, 37*, 321–328.

Wade, S. L., Borawski, E. A., Taylor, H. G., Drotar, D., Yeates, K. O., & Stancin, T. (2001). The relationship of caregiver coping to family outcomes during the initial year following pediatric traumatic injury. *Journal of Consulting and Clinical Psychology, 69*, 406–415.

Zarski, J. J., DePompei, R., & Zook, A. (1988). Traumatic head injury: Dimensions of family responsivity. *Journal of Head Trauma Rehabilitation, 3*(4), 31–41.

5

When One Partner Has Been Sexually Abused as a Child

CHRISTINE A. COURTOIS

Incest and child sexual abuse are particularly virulent forms of interpersonal trauma that hold high potential to harm a child's development, especially when they occur repetitively and cumulatively during childhood and particularly within the context of important attachment relationships. Although not all sexual abuse occurs in ways that are traumatic, such abuse must always be considered as potentially traumatic for the involved child by virtue of the various dynamics that come into play. Sexual abuse involves premeditation and the use of the child for the gratification of some need of the perpetrator (not always a sexual need but achieved through a sexual activity), betrayal of relational bonds and responsibility for the child's safety and protection, and premature and often traumatic sexual initiation and sexualization, all accompanied with shaming and forced silence. When sexual abuse is perpetrated by a family member these dynamics become more complex, and relationships become very conflicted; a child abused within the family is less likely to be believed and protected and more likely to be blamed than a child abused by an acquaintance or a stranger. Abuse by a stranger does not generate the divided loyalty and resultant denial or dismissal of abuse disclosure that is the case when abuse is intrafamilial, especially when it occurs in the nuclear family (involving parent and/or siblings).

Contemporary study of the effects of incest/child sexual abuse has now been ongoing for approximately 25 years and has resulted in a broad accrual of knowledge. The methodology of these studies has improved during this time, and a number of summaries (Briere, 1996; Chu, 1998; Courtois, 1988; Beitchman, Zucker, Hood, daCosta, & Ackman, 1991; Beitchman et al., 1992; Herman, 1992b; Russell, 1986, 1999) and meta-analyses (Kendall-Tackett, Williams, & Finkelhor, 1993; Neumann, Houskamp, Pollock, & Briere, 1996; Polusny & Follette, 1995) are now available. Experts agree that child sexual abuse often meets criteria as a traumatic stressor and can result in posttraumatic reactions and disorders at the time of the abuse or later. Reactions might be ongoing and chronic from the time of the abuse or they can lie dormant for periods of time, even years, to emerge in delayed fashion in adulthood. Although not all children are seriously or negatively affected by sexual abuse (especially abuse that was nonincestuous, mild or noncontact, short term, not particularly upsetting to the child, elicited intervention and protection; and did not involve blaming the child), a substantial percentage of abused children suffer serious to severe consequences including posttraumatic stress disorder (PTSD). Abused subjects in general, and the incestuously abused in particular, report more depression, irrational guilt, shame and self-blame, atypical yet pervasive anxiety reactions, dissociation, somatization, urges to self-harm, revictimization, relational disturbances, sexual dysfunction, substance abuse and other addictive-compulsive behaviors, major cognitive distortions, and polarities of behavior along with other posttraumatic symptoms when compared with nonabused subjects (Briere, 1996; Briere & Runtz, 1993; Chu, 1998; Courtois, 1988; Herman, 1992b).

Besides the effects that are straightforwardly posttraumatic in nature, these other effects can be dichotomized into those that are *intrapsychic* and those that are *interpersonal*, although these categories are not mutually exclusive because feelings about the self certainly affect the quality of relationships and vice versa.

INTRAPSYCHIC EFFECTS

Intrapsychic effects involve damage to the sense of self and identity, including personal disconnections and alterations.

Damage to the Sense of Self

The damage to the sense of self includes (a) an unstable self-image based on shame and a core belief that one is permanently damaged, unlovable, and undeserving of love and protection but deserving of maltreatment and abuse and (b) damage to the ability to identify and regulate emotions. Difficulty with emotional regulation often involves a high degree of reactivity and hypervigilance and difficulty controlling emotions, especially anger, which in turn can lead to the use of maladaptive coping mechanisms to deal with the ongoing distress associated with posttraumatic depressive, anxiety, and somatic symptoms. These coping methods include but are not limited to use of drugs and alcohol, self-mutilation, suicidality, and revictimization.

Personal Disconnections and Alterations

Alterations can occur in consciousness, autobiographical memory, physical sensations and perceptions, personal awareness, and identity, the last sometimes resulting in the development of ego states and, in the case of dissociative identity disorder, alternate personalities.

Alterations in Perception of the Perpetrator

These alterations can range from accepting and adopting the perpetrator's mindset to murderous rage toward the perpetrator. Ambivalent attachment to the perpetrator is often the norm, especially is he or she offered the child attention and caring as an offset to the abuse.

Alterations in Existential Meanings and Worldviews

These alterations usually involve massive disillusionment with life and with other people, alienation from others, and a pervasive despair that no one could possibly understand their experience or their anguish.

INTERPERSONAL EFFECTS

Interpersonal effects involve a generalized mistrust of others and their motives and a variety of relational styles. Relational stress and strain has been found to extend to relationships of all types. Sexual abuse survivors report difficulty in family relations, friendships, intimate relationships, intimacy and sexuality, parenting, work relationships, and social functioning in general (Courtois, 1979, 1988; Maltz & Holman, 1987; Westerlund, 1992). They typically have difficulty managing boundaries and understanding the relational motivations of others as well as their own.

Attachment Patterns

In recent years, the work of John Bowlby on attachment styles and the corresponding inner working models of attachment (Bowlby, 1969, 1988) has been productively applied to the study of abused children and adults. Individuals who have been abused and mistreated in their primary relationships often develop insecure patterns of attachment that cause them at one extreme to be overly dependent on others and hypervigilant in pleasing and meeting others' needs, and at the other to be wary of attachment, alienated, highly guarded, and self-sufficient to the extreme. Some individuals have been found to shift between these styles and relational patterns and to behave in ways that are inconsistent and seemingly random and disorganized. These are typically those individuals who experienced the most unpredictability, neglect, and abuse in their histories, and their inconsistent strategy, although seemingly disorganized, has been found to be an organized strategy for dealing with the inconsistency in their past environment (Alexander, 1992). These individuals are also the most likely to be dissociative, with their primary defense in childhood extending into adulthood and affecting their functioning and relationships with others (Liotti, 1992, 1999).

Interpersonal Patterns

Typically, those individuals who experienced the most unpredictability, neglect, and abuse are constantly on alert for real or imagined relational slights and abandonment, and use anticipatory coping strategies that may cause them to alienate others and distance from them, thus paradoxically recreating the feared abandonment in present relationships. They are difficult to relate to and have difficulty sustaining ongoing relationships, a pattern that certainly extends to intimate relationships as well.

Historically, individuals with this type of personal and relational distress have met the criteria for the diagnosis of borderline personality disorder (American Psychiatric Association, 1994) and have been maligned quite routinely by others (including mental health professionals) for their personality characteristics and relational difficulties. Recently, attempts have been made to reconceptualize this distress in more neutral and less pejorative ways that attend to its developmental and traumatic antecedents (Linehan, 1993). Two newly developed diagnostic conceptualizations identify complex posttraumatic stress disorder (or complex trauma) (Herman, 1992a, b) and disorder of extreme stress, not otherwise specified (DESNOS) (Pelcovitz et al., 1997). Additionally, these individuals often meet criteria for a dissociative disorder, especially dissociative amnesia, depersonalization, or dissociative disorder, not otherwise specified, and some are appropriately diagnosed with dissociative identity disorder (Chu, 1998; Courtois, 1999).

Impact in Adulthood

Despite the fact that these effects of child sexual abuse have been acknowledged for some time, it has only been recently that the impact of abuse on survivors' adult intimate relationships (including sexual functioning) has been adequately recognized and addressed. This chapter focuses on the effects of abuse as they result in distress in intimate and marital relationships and presents an overview of a therapeutic model and techniques that may be applied to treat the abuse survivor and his or her partner. Johnson (2002) provided the following succinct summary: ". . . if a person's connection with significant others is not part of the coping and healing process, then, inevitably, it becomes part of the problem and *even a source of retraumatization*" (p. 7, emphasis added). She took this even further, observing that "there is a potentially more powerful corrective relationship than the relationship with a therapist. This is the relationship with the person's life partner. This relationship is often overlooked or discounted by health professionals as an active source of healing" (pp. 6–7). The present chapter espouses this perspective in discussing the significance of including the partners of sexual abuse survivors in treatment and providing couple therapy where feasible. It also takes the position that the therapist should not assume that the progress in individual therapy necessarily extends to or positively affects the couple relationship (Follette, 1991). In fact, therapeutic progress can unbalance the couple's normal mode of functioning and worsen their distress. Thus, it behooves the individual therapist to assess the status of the couple relationship periodically and remain alert to reports of changes (whether positive or negative). These can certainly affect the survivor's status even to the point of derailing the individual treatment, the intimate relationship, or both.

THE EFFECTS OF ABUSE ON INTIMATE RELATIONSHIPS

Although the intrapsychic and interpersonal issues described would be expected to affect all types of relationships, their impact is likely to be felt most directly in those involving an intimate partner. Abuse survivors routinely report longing for emotional connection with others, as they simultaneously fear the potential for revictimization and vulnerability that such connection creates. Thus, they enter relationships searching and hoping for better than they had, all the while fearing a repeat of the same. They bring their relational template and predominant attachment style to bear, finding partners with complementary relational styles and issues. Abuse survivors may have such major difficulties with trust and the ability to relate that true intimacy is seriously compromised and/or unattainable. Survivors may seek out those whose style is compatible with or similar to their own and unwittingly recreate the past.

It is important to note that not every survivor of child sexual abuse is relationally compromised. Some survivors emerge relatively unscathed relationally and/or sexually, and many are able to enter into relationships with partners who are healthy enough. These survivors are often able to develop relationships that are healthy enough to change the relational template from the past, their "inner working model," per Bowlby (Bowlby, 1969; Johnson, 2002). And some succeed in their determination to learn good relational skills and to not do to others what was done to them. However, the focus of this chapter is on those who suffer from significant relational impairment and some of the issues that arise in couple therapy with that subset of survivors. Therapists still should be aware that even in the most relationally compromised individuals they may come across pockets of functionality or relating that, on the surface, appear functional and healthy. These may be real or may be the result of defensive compensation and involve pseudomature relational responses developed early on as a means of coping with the abuse and, when intrafamilial, with the family dysfunction in which the abuse is embedded.

Relational Effects

Research findings and clinical observations consistently establish that sexual abuse survivors experience a variety of problems with intimate and marital relationships. Their abuse legacy of interpersonal betrayal and exploitation, its impact on intrapsychic and interpersonal development, and its long-term symptoms (including but not limited to depression, dissociation, anxiety, posttraumatic disorders, medical concerns) can all have corrosive effects on the ability to relate to others in ways that are healthy and sustaining. Any combination of these symptoms can have a major life impact; however, a number of authorities on the effects of PTSD remind clinicians of the high potential of this diagnosis alone to create instability in intimate and family relationships (Catherall, 1992; Figley, 1985, 1986; Johnson, 2002; Wilson & Kurtz, 2000). And the impact may be reciprocal and paradoxical, that is, the relationship itself may function as a trigger to the abuse of the past and/or the relationship might be haunted by the past. This point was made by both Graber (1991) in the title of his book, *Ghosts in the Bedroom: A Guide for Partners of Incest Survivors*, and by Nadelson and Polonsky (1991) in the title of their article on couple therapy, "Childhood Sexual Abuse: The Invisible Ghost in Couple Therapy."

As these titles imply, the abuse is not always known to the couple, the survivor's partner, or the therapist, even though its influence on the relationship and on therapy might be profound. Issues of awareness and disclosure are discussed subsequently.

Starting with the earliest of the contemporary research on incest/child sexual abuse, relationship and sexual difficulties have been among the most consistently reported problems (Courtois, 1979, 1988; Finkelhor, 1984; Finkelhor, Hotaling, Lewis, & Smith, 1989; Herman, 1981; Meiselman, 1978; Russell, 1986). As compared to groups of nonabused individuals, the most common findings involve issues of (a) mistrust and fear; (b) alienation from others; (c) inability to form intimate relationships and resultant social and interpersonal isolation; (d) problems with communication; (e) relational discord, instability, and chaos (in some cases involving intimate violence and the abuse of children); (f) lack of relational satisfaction in general and sexual satisfaction in particular; and (g) high rates of relational dissolution or divorce. Additionally, Wilson and Kurtz (2000) identified the following as the most common symptoms and behavioral problems in couples with PTSD in one or both partners: (a) loss of intimacy; (b) breakdown in communications; (c) decreased sexual activity; (d) diminished, impaired, or ineffective decision making; (e) detachment from significant others; (f) increased anger and irritability; (g) displaced, overt, or passive hostility; (h) decreased levels of normal social activities; (i) marital or partner dissatisfaction; (j) generalized anxiety and fears (e.g., fear of abandonment); (k) instability in core areas of relationship (responsibilities, decision making, role expectations, etc.); (l) low self-disclosure of personal concerns; (m) confusion, shame, doubt, and guilt; (n) changes in hygiene, self-care, and sleep patterns; (o) isolation, withdrawal, and social and self-alienation; (p) discernible changes in normal coping patterns; (q) loss of interests in shared activities, hobbies, holidays, and vacations; and (r) depression, dysphoria, and anhedonia.

Sexual Effects

Sexual aftereffects have also been extensively researched (Carnes, 1991; Jehu, 1989; Maltz, 1991; Westerlund, 1992). Sprei and Courtois (1988), in their review article on sexual dysfunction arising from sexual abuse, reported the following as categories of sexual distress and dysfunction that can occur alone or in combination: (a) desire disorder—low desire due to fear, aversion to sex, and phobias; (b) arousal disorder; (c) orgasmic disorder; (d) coital pain, including vaginismus, dyspareunia, and genital pain; (e) general sexual dissatisfaction and/or frequency dissatisfaction; and (f) other problems, such as paraphilias, promiscuity and indiscriminate sexual activity, compulsive sex, ritualized sex, sexual abstinence, (sado)masochistic practices, flashbacks, and chemical and/or relationship dependencies. Although this review pertained to women survivors only, male survivors have been found to suffer from the same range of effects but in gender-specific ways (e.g., erectile/arousal difficulties).

Gartner (1999) has described how sexual abuse has a profound impact on a boy's masculinity (an impact that can vary by gender of the perpetrator and how the abuse was perpetrated) that, in turn, affects his view of sexuality and his ability to function sexually. For example, males experience much more same-sex sexual abuse, which they usually mistake as homosexual behavior, often causing them conflict regarding their gender orientation and preference. Additionally, males might experience gender shame and develop a negative identification with other males and abusive male behavior. Many such men then compensate by disavowing any feelings of anger and becoming excessively good. This might play out in their sexual functioning and in their ability to be intimate with a partner. Finally, several investigators have suggested that sexual abuse may contribute to confusion regarding sexual orientation in both men and women and that the same types of relational and sexual disturbances described here occur in same-sex as well as heterosexual couples.

Emergence of Effects

Courtois (1979, 1988) found a sleeper effect in which the relational and sexual effects of abuse, although not present and/or disruptive at the time of the abuse, may emerge as the victim/survivor enters adolescence and adulthood and attempts sexual activity, a normal developmental task of these life stages. Difficulty with sexual activity plagues some survivors right from the start. For others (especially those who experienced incest), maintaining sexual functioning within an intimate relationship becomes the problem. In a common scenario, the survivor is able to function sexually relatively well until a relationship becomes serious and/or committed, at which time sexual feelings and functioning markedly deteriorate. This pattern makes sense within the context of sexual abuse. Many abuse survivors describe how their fear and vulnerability increases rather than decreases when a relationship becomes more intimate. The lessons of the past—namely, love equals abuse, and commitment connotes entrapment, powerlessness, and loss of control—contribute to the inhibition of sexual feelings and functioning.

Other Sequelae

One last finding deserves mention, namely, the overlap that has been observed between sexual abuse and chemical, relational, and sexual addictions and/or coaddictions (some of which involve sadomasochism and other perversions) in both men and women (Carnes, 1991; Klausner & Hasselbring, 1990; Ogden, 1990). Sexual abuse can result in many dependent and addictive-type patterns of relating and being sexual. Survivors often learn that emotions and conflict are best managed sexually and relationally in ways that avoid true intimacy or satisfaction. Many behaviors described as addictive, coaddictive, or codependent originated as mechanisms used to survive or accommodate abuse, and can be identified as once useful (and even essential and life-saving) coping mechanisms that have outlived their usefulness and become problematic.

Integrating these findings with the attachment styles described by Bowlby (1969), one can conclude that most survivors of sexual abuse have insecure patterns of attachment that undergird their intimate and familial relationships. Those survivors whose abuse was incestuous are likely to have a disorganized/dissociative attachment pattern. Understanding these attachment patterns and using them as a theoretical foundation of the treatment process can greatly assist the recovery process.

Characteristics of Partners

Partners of abuse survivors, by virtue of being those in closest connection to the survivor, are in the position of dealing with the personal and relational legacy of the abuse, whether such abuse is known to them or not. It is not unusual for abuse history to be kept secret and not be disclosed for a number of reasons to be discussed later. As a result, partners of survivors are those most likely to experience the effects of abuse within their relationship but to be in the dark about their origins. And because they are not blood related, partners are those in relation to the survivor who are the most vulnerable to the severance of the relationship. Wilson and Kurtz (2000) summarized the situation in this way: "The reciprocal effects of PTSD in a relationship result in a dyadic dance with trauma's wake" (p. 35).

Data are beginning to accumulate about partners of survivors and how they react (although they have received less research attention than the primary abuse victims). Partners have described a variety of primary feelings toward their survivor-partners, including confusion, sadness, desperation, worry, depression, anxiety, pain, uncertainty, helplessness, resignation, resentment, and anger (Bacon & Lein, 1996; Davis, 1991; Johnson, 2002; Maltz, 1991; Matsakis, 1998). Once they learn of the sexual abuse, they may be deeply concerned and even enraged by the knowledge that their partner was violated. They may feel as though they were secondarily victimized by the perpetrator of the original abuse. If the perpetrator is known and the relationship is such that they are required to interact, they may seek a confrontation and in some cases actively seek revenge. Partners may also feel victimized by seeing their partner in ongoing emotional turmoil and, as is often the case, may feel victimized by being repeatedly sexually and emotionally rejected themselves. Additionally, they may feel victimized by ongoing relational insecurity and inconsistency and may fear that their relationship will not survive the stresses and strains of the recovery process (if the survivor partner is in active treatment and/or if they are in couple therapy). Parents may worry about the emotional and relational repercussions on their children's well-being and worry for their safety if they have contact with the perpetrator.

Partners may themselves have relational deficits and problems, as well as those that are directly linked to those of the primary victim. Specifically, they may have their own history of abuse/trauma and suffer effects that, in parallel fashion to those of their partner, may be chronic or may emerge in delayed fashion after periods of being dormant. Partners enter into relationships with those whose style is familiar to them. In the case of abuse survivors, this might mean they end up with someone who is abusive like others in his or her past, or, alternatively, they may seek out someone who is emotionally distant and hence safe, in control, and unthreatening. Unfortunately, reenactments in the primary relationship, seen principally in patterns of revictimization and couple violence as well as extreme emotional disengagement and shutdown, are not uncommon, as couples may come together almost exclusively on the basis of known behavioral patterns as victim and victimizer. Relationships involving abuse and violence are obviously the most destructive, but may have enormous staying power due to ambivalent and/or sadomasochistic attachments and perhaps the "addiction to chaos" noted in the literature on domestic violence (Walker, 1984).

TREATMENT APPROACHES AND ISSUES

Treatment of a couple in which one partner has been abused largely parallels the treatment of the individual trauma survivor and is best conducted in stages, following a period of assessment.

Stages of Treatment

The sequenced, or stage-oriented, model appears to be linear, but is more like a recursive spiral: The survivor client might move from one stage to the next and then back again as issues are revisited and reworked. This progressive model comprises three stages: (a) the early stage of treatment is devoted primarily to safety, stabilization, skills building, affect management and emotional regulation, and education/debriefing; (b) the middle stage concerns processing and resolution of the trauma; and (c) the final stage advances intrapsychic and interpersonal development (Chu, 1998; Courtois, 1999; Gold, 2000; Herman, 1992b; Kepner, 1995). In the couple work, the stages are focused on the relationship: (a) The early stage is devoted to developing safety and stabilization within the relationship (creating a safe haven) and educating the couple about the effects of trauma, (b) the second to restructuring bonds and developing new modes of relating to others (altering attachment schema and styles), and (c) the third to the continued application of the learning from the first two stages to the relationship.

Sexual healing occurs in parallel; although most healing in the sexual domain is done after the majority of the emotional/trauma processing work (Maltz, 2001; Sprei & Courtois, 1988), some does occur earlier in the treatment. Remer (2004) has helpfully pointed out the complexities and variabilities that are likely to be encountered in the therapy process; likewise I have cautioned that a one-size-fits-all or cookie-cutter approach is much too simplistic, but that a meta model, such as a stage-oriented model, is essential to direct the treatment and to organize the interventions (Courtois, 1999).

Combining Couple and Individual Therapies

Some authors have advocated beginning couple therapy as soon in the individual treatment process as feasible (Johnson, 2002; Kirschner, Kirschner, & Rappaport, 1993; Wilson & Kurtz, 2000) yet noting that it is optimal for individual healing of the primary survivor to be well under way. In an early article, Johnson (1989) espoused simultaneous and alternating individual and couple work by the same therapist. Others have recommended that the same therapist not conduct both individual and couple work unless absolutely necessary due to the potential for triangulation and the need to keep clear boundaries and avoid any semblance of dual relationships (Courtois, 1988; Follette, 1991). In her more recent comprehensive work, Johnson (2002) strongly advocated the emotionally focused couple therapy for trauma survivors and their partners be undertaken as soon as is feasible for the survivor. She believes in educating survivors and partners about the importance of the sanctuary offered by a secure attachment in a relationship, especially one in which a partner(s) has been traumatized. Insecurity in the primary attachment bond will inevitably retraumatize the survivor and damage the relationship, whereas the security that comes from working together rather than at odds with one another holds much greater promise for strengthening the attachment bond and thus reversing the interpersonal damage of the trauma.

Skills Building

Because some survivors have enormous difficulty establishing relationships in general, much less relationships that involve intimacy, some
clinicians who specialize in the treatment of abuse survivors advocate attention to general relationship skills early in the treatment process (Chu,
1998; Courtois, 1999; Gold, 2000; Harris, 1998).[1] The treatment plan for socially isolated/alienated survivors and those with very poor social skills
is the development of such skills and the establishment of relationships at
a pace that is tolerable. The goal is to provide a context of support for the
survivor apart from the therapist in order to discourage overdependence
and unrealistic expectations about what the therapist can provide and/or
to encourage connection to others as a means of much-needed support to
counter the mistrust and alienation generated by the abuse (Chu, 1998;
Gold, 2000; Linehan, Armstrong, Suarez, Almon, & Heard, 1991). Group
formats for the development of specific skills and for learning to give and
to take in a group context have been described in the literature (Courtois,
1988; Donaldson & Cordes-Green, 1995; Harris, 1998; Linehan, 1993;
Vannicelli, 1989; Webb & Leehan, 1996). This approach can be adjunctive
to either individual or couple therapy.

Assessment

Early in the treatment process of either the survivor alone or the couple, the therapist should conduct a thorough assessment of the intimate
relationship in order to ascertain its strengths and weaknesses. In the case
of individual work, it is important to assess the likelihood that the relationship will either assist or undermine the individual recovery process
and whether couple work is warranted. As noted by both Follette (1991)
and Johnson (2002), clinicians should be aware that dyadic problems
could exacerbate individual survivor issues, just as survivor issues impact
the dyadic relationship.

Disclosure to Partner As part of the individual assessment, the therapist must inquire about whether the survivor has disclosed the abuse to
the partner and the partner's response and its quality. The therapist
should not assume that a history of abuse/trauma has been disclosed,
even by a survivor-client who is highly symptomatic and whose partner
knows that she or he is in mental health treatment. If the abuse has not
been disclosed, the therapist should attempt to determine the survivor's

---

[1]See chapter 15 of Gold (2000) for a discussion of the importance of attending to the skills that
were not provided in the family. He argued that developing these missing skills often can be
more important to the person's eventual recovery than processing the traumatic memories.

reasoning but must not mandate or pressure for a disclosure, especially early in treatment. At some point, it will be necessary for the therapist to assist the survivor to assess the cost/benefit of nondisclosure and possibly to plan how and when to reveal the history. In the author's experience, sometimes the history has been divulged and then the disclosure forgotten or repressed. Some partners are therefore not surprised to hear of the abuse, only surprised that prior disclosure was forgotten. Such a situation is more likely with a survivor who uses dissociative defenses or whose style is highly dissociative.

Reasons for Nondisclosure. Some of the customary reasons given by survivors for keeping their abuse history hidden from others, including their partners, involve the following (Courtois, 1988):

1. They may not have made the connection between remote events and their current distress and symptoms. Survivors may be uneducated about the possibility of delayed effects.
2. The information might be withheld due to fear of personal acknowledgment. Some survivors fear that they will suffer an emotional breakdown if they admit what happened to them—in themselves or in others.
3. The abuse memory may have been unavailable and/or discontinuous, making it easier to deny or doubt when it reemerges. Survivors often feel that they are crazy when abuse memories emerge and/or they become symptomatic "out of the blue." They may fear they will be labeled as crazy by others, accused of having false memories or of trying to hurt or create trouble for the perpetrator (and the rest of the family in the case of incest).
4. Survivors are often extremely shamed and fear rejection and abandonment. They expect that others will judge them as harshly as they judge themselves and will ultimately desert them. Unfortunately, some survivors may have already had the experience of a hostile, pejorative, blaming, or rejecting response to their disclosure and so fear a repeat.
5. They also fear being disbelieved, blamed and further shamed, made to feel responsible for what happened to them and for not finding a way to prevent or stop the abuse.
6. They may fear the anger of their partner and specifically fear retaliation against a perpetrator known to their partner.
7. They may have strong loyalty/ambivalence to the perpetrator (and the entire family in the case of incest) and protect them by following the usual incest injunctions, secrecy and nondisclosure (Courtois, 1988), even at their own expense.

Disclosure and Response. On the other hand, if abuse has been disclosed to the partner, the therapist must inquire about the response. A number of common response patterns to the disclosure of abuse have been identified that roughly correspond to relationship issues and can be generally conceptualized as being on a continuum, from good/healthy to poor/abusive.

Healthy Response.   Starting from the healthy pole, some partners are genuinely empathic and supportive and do all they can to assist the survivor, but with appropriate concern and boundaries. A less healthy scenario occurs with a generally supportive partner who does too much and is actually compensating for or enabling the survivor in his or her life and in their relationship (the partner might also be attempting to prove that she or he is unlike the perpetrator(s) and work far too hard to prove trustworthiness and reliability). Davis (1991) called attention to this pattern in her classic book *Allies in Healing* and underscored that although survivors must expend enormous energy and need a great deal of support in their healing and recovery efforts, these should not be undertaken to the exclusion of all else; the couple's relationship and family and work life must also have priority (except, of course, during times of acuity and emergency).

Partners should not be expected to put their lives (and the lives of their children) on hold for years as the survivor's recovery takes precedence. Ultimately, such a scenario, although well intentioned, can parallel the rescuer transference response identified by therapists who work with trauma survivors. In therapy, such a response can result in exhaustion, resentment, burnout, and, not uncommonly, termination/abandonment (Courtois, 1988; Davies & Frawley, 1994; Pearlman & Saakvitne, 1995). In the case of the couple, this might result in a slow erosion and ultimate dissolution of the relationship.

Benevolent Blaming.   Moving across the continuum, it is not unusual for partners to merely appear to be supportive. Follette (1991) warned the therapist to be aware of the problem of "benevolent blame." In this scenario, the partner is supportive while simultaneously blaming all relationship/marital issues on the survivor and the abuse history, thereby abdicating any responsibility for the condition and quality of the relationship. The partner may paint him- or herself as the normal one, from a normal family, who is now saddled with the survivor's past and family. A variation on this theme is the partner who refuses to discuss the abuse after the initial disclosure or seek to understand its impact. Such a partner may push the survivor to "just get over it" and "put it all behind" so they can get on with being a normal couple. In another variation, the survivor has partnered with someone who is emotionally detached and unavailable (sometimes this individual is dissociative and may have his or her own trauma history) because this person is safe and noninquisitive or nonintrusive. This pattern works until such time that the survivor requires emotional support.

Nonbenevolent Shaming.   A more deleterious scenario occurs when partner uses the information to shame and control the survivor partner and, in the process, may violate privacy and force decisions or courses of action. For example, this partner may insist on disclosure to family members or others and/or confrontation of the perpetrator and may undertake them personally, even against the wishes of the survivor. This partner may also respond insensitively in ways that reinforce the survivor's sense of guilt, responsibility, and shame. The partner may subtly or not so subtly blame or criticize the survivor or imply that the survivor did something to provoke the abuse and/or secretly enjoyed it or even wants it to resume. Such criticisms and implications patently meet criteria for emotional abuse and strengthen the survivor's sense of badness and negative self-worth.

Abusive Response.   At the far negative pole of the continuum are responses and relational patterns that constitute direct abuse, whether physical, sexual, or emotional, as well as neglect, and often involve all four factors. As discussed previously, the process of revictimization is all too common for abuse survivors who may end up in destructive relationships that mimic those of the past and that result in reenactments of the original abuse. Researchers have routinely reported patterns of revictimization in adult survivors of sexual abuse and have detailed how vulnerable these men and women are to repeat abuses over their life span, both at the hands of strangers and those of their intimate partners (Courtois, 1988; Herman, 1992b; Russell, 1999; Walker, 1984).

Obviously, couples who seek treatment for difficulties that are on the negative end of the continuum have a lot to do to make a relationship healthy. In the case of outright abuse, the question is whether to treat the relationship or not, a difficult decision for a therapist to make. Follette (1991) recommended that in those cases where it is clear that the survivor is determined to stay in the relationship, therapists who choose to treat the couple consider setting very specific guidelines for therapy and only agree to work with the couple under those conditions. Therapists should not undertake treatment of this sort without specific training in how to work with abusive couples nor should they proceed without adequate supervision, consultation, and support.

To summarize, the abuse history might be known and the consequences dealt with on virtually a daily basis by the couple as an overt part of their relationship, or it may have been kept hidden and dealt with covertly, its effects interwoven into the relationship at unconscious levels. Reasons for nondisclosure should be explored, and where feasible the survivor should be encouraged to divulge the abuse history because having a secret about such a major life experience hinders true intimacy. Therapist and survivor can explore options, with the survivor electing to exercise them when she or he feels ready. Although delayed disclosure often constitutes a crisis, it may also be a relief to both partners to have it out in the open. The therapist must be prepared to support both partners during the disclosure period and may be called upon to help the nonsurvivor-partner communicate her or his reaction and provide appropriate emotional support.

This review of types of relationship difficulties is abbreviated and addresses only the most obvious and common, those that have been identified by a number of researchers and clinicians. A continuum of the sort presented here only begins to touch on the myriad ways that survivors and their partners respond to one another and the complicated issues that might arise in trying to treat the individual and the couple. Remer (2004) rightfully points out the variability of responses in both primary victims and their partners (whom she identified as secondary victims) and the nonlinearity and nonindependence of their responses and their healing processes.

Other Therapy Issues

The scope, intensity, and duration of the couple therapy varies according to the ego strength of each partner, the severity and chronicity of their problems (individual and dyadic), their commitment to one another, and the strengths they bring to bear in the relationship. The multidimensional nature of the effects of trauma and their severity across the continuum call for different interventions for different problems and for the therapist to be flexible in application and able to tolerate change and chaos that are the legacy of trauma (Johnson, 2002).

Throughout the process of either individual or couple therapy, the therapist must be sensitive to issues of transference/countertransference and, as pertains to the couple, issues of triangulation. Transference and countertransference issues that arise in treatment of the traumatized have been found to put unusually high demands on the emotional resources of the therapist (Pearlman & Saakvitne, 1995; Wilson & Lindy, 1996) and warrant careful monitoring. Furthermore, therapists must scrupulously avoid fostering an alliance with (or colluding with) one partner against the other, even though the temptation to do so may be very compelling. Historically, as partners were routinely left out of the treatment process, many complained that their survivor-partner seemed to have more emotional intimacy with the therapist than with them, a trap that the therapist must avoid.

CONCLUSION

The trauma associated with incest/child sexual abuse has profound interpersonal, intrapsychic, and posttraumatic effects, all of which can seriously affect intimate relationships. Until fairly recently, therapists have tended to treat the survivor alone using individual or group modalities and have failed to assess the impact of the trauma on couple functioning or to include the partner in treatment. Couple therapy for trauma survivors and their partners has grown as the importance of primary relationships to the survivor's well-being has been increasingly recognized. The goal of treatment is to strengthen attachment bonds and to create increased levels of security within the relationship to reverse the negative interpersonal/relational effects of trauma.

REFERENCES

Alexander, P. (1992). Application of attachment theory to the study of sexual abuse. *Journal of Consulting and Clinical Psychology, 60*, 185–195.

American Psychiatric Association. (1994). *DSM-IV: Diagnostic and statistical manual of mental disorders, 4th ed.* Washington, DC: American Psychiatric Association.

Bacon, B., & Lein, L. (1996). Living with a female sexual abuse survivor: Male partners' perspectives. *Journal of Child Sexual Abuse, 5*(2), 1–16.

Beitchman, J., Zucker, K., Hood, J., daCosta, G., & Ackman, D. (1991). A review of the short-term effects of childhood sexual abuse. *Child Abuse and Neglect, 15*, 537–556.

Beitchman, J. H., Zucker, K. J., Hood, J. E., daCosta, G. A., Akman, D., & Cassavia, E. (1992). A review of the long-term effects of childhood sexual abuse. *Child Abuse and Neglect, 16*, 101–118.

Bowlby, J. (1969). *Attachment and loss: Vol. 1. Attachment.* New York: Basic Books.

Bowlby, J. (1988). *Parent-child attachment and healthy human development.* New York: Basic Books.

Briere, J. (1996). *Therapy for adults molested as children: Beyond survival.* New York: Springer Publishing.

Briere, J., & Runtz, M. (1993). Childhood sexual abuse: Long-term sequelae and implications for psychological assessment. *Journal of Interpersonal Violence, 8*, 312–330.

Carnes, P. (1991). *Don't call it love: Recovery from sexual addiction.* New York: Bantam.

Catherall, D. (1992). *Back from the brink: A family guide to overcoming traumatic stress.* New York: Bantam.

Chu, J. A. (1998). *Rebuilding shattered lives: The responsible treatment of complex posttraumatic and dissociative disorders.* New York: Wiley.

Courtois, C.A. (1979). Characteristics of a volunteer sample of adult women who experienced incest in childhood and adolescence. *Dissertation Abstracts International, 40A*, Nov.-Dec. 1979, 3194-A.

Courtois, C.A. (1988). *Healing the incest wound: Adult survivors in therapy.* New York: W.W. Norton & Company.

Courtois, C.A. (1999). *Recollections of sexual abuse: Treatment principles and guidelines.* New York: W. W. Norton & Company.

Davies, J., & Frawley, M. G. (1994). *Treating the adult survivor of childhood sexual abuse: A psychoanalytic perspective.* New York: Basic Books.

Davis, L. (1991). *Allies in healing: When the person you love was sexually abused as a child.* New York: Harper Perennial.

Donaldson, M. A., & Cordes-Green, S. (1995). *Group treatment of adult incest survivors.* Thousand Oaks, CA: Sage.

Figley, C. R. (Ed.). (1985). *Trauma and its wake. Vol. 1: The study and treatment of posttraumatic stress disorder.* New York: Brunner/Mazel.

Figley, C. R. (Ed.). (1986). *Trauma and its wake. Vol. 2; Traumatic stress theory, research, and intervention*. New York: Brunner/Mazel.

Finkelhor, D. (1984). *Child sexual abuse: New theory and research*. New York: The Free Press.

Finkelhor, D., Hotaling, G., Lewis, I., & Smith, C. (1989). Sexual abuse and its relationship to later sexual satisfaction, marital status, religion, and attitudes. *Journal of Interpersonal Violence, 4*, 379–399.

Follette, V. M. (1991). Marital therapy for sexual abuse survivors. In J. Briere (Ed.), *New Directions for Mental Health Services, Vol. 51: Treating victims of child sexual abuse* (pp. 61–71). San Francisco: Jossey-Bass

Gartner, R. B. (1999). *Betrayed as boys: Psychodynamic treatment of sexually abused men*. New York: The Guilford Press.

Gold, S. N. (2000). *Not trauma alone: Therapy for child abuse survivors in family and social context*. Philadelphia: Taylor & Francis.

Graber, K. (1991). *Ghosts in the bedroom: A guide for partners of incest survivors*. Health Communications.

Harris, M. (1998). *Trauma recovery and empowerment: A clinician's guide for working with women in groups*. New York: The Free Press.

Herman, J. L. (1981). *Father–daughter incest*. Cambridge, MA: Harvard University Press.

Herman, J. L. (1992a). Complex PTSD: A syndrome in survivors of prolonged and repeated trauma. *Journal of Traumatic Stress, 5*, 377–391.

Herman, J. L. (1992b). *Trauma and recovery: The aftermath of violence-from domestic to political terror*. New York: Basic Books.

Jehu, D. (1989). Sexual dysfunctions among women clients who were sexually abused in childhood. *Behavioral Psychotherapy, 17*, 53–70.

Johnson, S. (2002). *Emotionally focused couple therapy with trauma survivors: Strengthening attachment bonds*. New York: Guilford.

Johnson, S. M. (1989). Integrating marital and individual therapy for incest survivors: A case study. *Psychotherapy: Theory, Research, and Practice, 26*, 96–102.

Kendall-Tackett, K. A., Williams, L. M., & Finkelhor, D. (1993). Impact of sexual abuse on children: A review and synthesis of recent empirical studies. *Psychological Bulletin, 113*, 164–180.

Kepner, J. I. (1995). *Healing tasks: Psychotherapy with adult survivors of childhood abuse*. San Francisco: Jossey-Bass.

Kirschner, S., Kirschner, D. A., & Rappaport, R. L. (1993). *Working with adult incest survivors: The healing journey*. New York: Brunner/Mazel.

Klausner, M., & Hasselbring, B. (1990). *Aching for love: The sexual drama of the adult child*. New York: Harper and Row.

Linehan, M. (1993). *Cognitive-behavioral treatment of borderline personality disorder*. New York: The Guilford Press.

Linehan, M. M., Armstrong, H. E., Suarez, A., Almon, D., & Heard, H. L. (1991). Cognitive-behavioral treatment of chronically parasuicidal borderline patients. *Archives of General Psychiatry, 48*, 1060–1064.

Liotti, G. (1992). Disorganized/disoriented attachment in the etiology of the dissociative disorders. *Dissociation, 5*(4), 196–204.

Liotti, G. (1999). Understanding the dissociative processes: The contribution of attachment theory. *Psychoanalytic Inquiry, 19*, 757–783.

Maltz, W. (1991). *The sexual healing journey: A guide for survivors of sexual abuse*. New York: Harper Collins.

Maltz, W. (2001). *The sexual healing journey: A guide for survivors of sexual abuse*. New York: Quill.

Maltz, W., & Holman, B. (1987). *Incest and sexuality: A guide to understanding and healing*. Lexington, MA: Lexington Books.

Matsakis, A. (1998). *Trust after trauma: A guide to relationships for survivors and those who love them*. Oakland, CA: New Harbinger Publications.

Meiselman, K. C. (1978). *Incest: A psychological study of causes and effects with treatment recommendations*. San Francisco: Jossey-Bass.

Nadelson, C., & Polonsky, D. (1991). Childhood sexual abuse: The invisible ghost in couple therapy. *Psychiatric Annals, 21,* 479–484.

Neumann, D. S., Houskamp, B. M., Pollock, V. E., & Briere, J. (1996). The long-term sequelae of childhood sexual abuse in women: A meta-analytic review. *Child Maltreatment, 1,* 6–17.

Ogden, G. (1990). *Sexual recovery: Every woman's guide through sexual co-dependency*. New York: Health Communications, Inc.

Pearlman, L. A., & Saakvitne, K. W. (1995). *Trauma and the therapist: Countertransference and vicarious traumatization in psychotherapy with incest survivors*. New York: W. W. Norton & Company.

Pelcovitz, D., van der Kolk, B. A., Roth, S., Mandel, F. S., Kaplan, S., & Resick, P. A. (1997). Development of a criteria set and a structured interview for disorders of extreme stress (SIDES). *Journal of Traumatic Stress, 10,* 3–17.

Polusny, M., & Follette, V. (1995). Long term correlates of child sexual abuse: Theory and review of the empirical literature. *Applied and Preventive Psychology: Current Scientific Perspectives, 4,* 143–166.

Remer, R. (2004). The partner's experience: Learning to cope with chaos. In D. R. Catheral (Ed.), *Handbook of stress, trauma, and the family* (pp. 51–68). New York: Brunner-Routledge.

Russell, D. (1986). *The secret trauma: Incest in the lives of girls and women*. New York: Basic Books.

Russell, D. (1999). *The secret trauma: Incest in the lives of girls and women* (Rev. ed.). New York: Basic Books.

Sprei, J. E., & Courtois, C. A. (1988). The treatment of women's sexual dysfunctions arising from sexual assault. In R. A. Brown & J. R. Field (Eds.), *Treatment of sexual problems in individuals and couples therapy* (pp. 267–299). New York: Aperture.

Vannicelli, M. (1989). *Group psychotherapy with adult children of alcoholics. Treatment techniques and countertransference considerations*. New York: Guilford.

Walker, L. E. (1984). *The battered woman syndrome*. New York: Springer.

Webb, L. P., & Leehan, J. (1996). *Group treatment for adult survivors of abuse: A manual for practitioners*. Thousand Oaks, CA: Sage.

Westerlund, E. (1992). *Women's sexuality after childhood incest*. New York: W. W. Norton & Company.

Wilson, J., & Lindy, J. (Eds.). (1996). *Countertransference in the treatment of PTSD*. New York: Guilford.

Wilson, J. P., & Kurtz, R. R. (2000). Assessing PTSD in couples and partners: The dyadic dance of trauma. *NC-PTSD Clinical Quarterly, 9*(3), 33–38.

6

When a Couple Cannot Conceive: Traumatic Consequences of Infertility

BRYN W. JESSUP

"THIS CAN'T BE HAPPENING TO US!"

My first impression of the young couple in the waiting room is that they seem tired. "We never thought we would need to see a therapist for this," begins Julie as she and her husband, Rob, seat themselves in my office. "But we just don't seem to be having much luck—" At this her voice catches and her eyes well up with tears. Rob stares at his shoes while Julie swallows hard and then continues: "We've been trying to have a baby, but we haven't been able to. We've been through three cycles of IVF so far. Our doctor thinks we should do another cycle, that the last one almost worked, but I'm worn out. I don't think I can take another miscarriage—I've had two already"— the tears return, but this time Julie keeps on without pausing for her grief—"and I just hate this whole stupid process. My life seems like it just came to a halt 2 years ago when we realized that something wasn't working right for us to have a baby. I feel like I should just forget about becoming a parent and donate my body to science instead." She reaches for a tissue and allows herself a rueful smile. "It already belongs to the doctors as it is."

115

I turn to look again at Rob, who glances up at me. "It's true. Since we started this whole baby pursuit, our life together has gone down the tubes. I feel like I hardly know Julie anymore. The drugs she has to take make her incredibly moody, she cries all the time now, and nothing I do or say is right. I'm beginning to question whether this whole thing is worth it. Maybe we just aren't meant to have children." At this, Julie's head snaps up and she stares at Rob fiercely. He meets her eyes for a moment, as though determined to make a stand. But then his determination sags and he looks away, his face a mask of sadness and resignation. Julie lets out an anguished sigh. Neither speaks, and I realize it's my turn to say something. I decide to invite them to say more about the pain that brings them here before gathering details about their medical workups and treatments, marital history, and family backgrounds—information I know from past experience will be crucial to our work together.

"What you're both going through together now must be so different from what you expected," I offer. Both nod and then look at each other, less grimly this time, before Julie speaks. "It's *nothing* like what I expected. Sometimes I don't even remember what things used to be like or how we got here. I can't even believe it sometimes." Rob nods. Then Julie adds something that I've heard other clients struggling with a traumatic event say, something that speaks to the trauma survivor's astonishment at the enormity of their impending loss: "I keep thinking, *this can't be happening to us.*"

Twenty years ago, I had scarcely heard of infertility. I knew that some people, for whatever reason, could not make a baby—their bodies simply didn't cooperate when it came time to start a family. Sometimes those people went on to build families through adoption, or they became foster parents of older children who needed shelter from the child welfare system, or maybe they simply became more involved with other people's children—nieces and nephews, for instance. There was something endearing yet also a little bit sad about the couple everyone knew who "couldn't have children."

But all of that changed sometime during the past 20 years. Baby Louise Brown's birth from an in vitro conception made news across the world, and a new medical specialty, reproductive endocrinology, took root not only in the medical community but in the hearts and minds of a growing number of couples whose biological destiny to become parents had somehow stalled. A dizzying array of medical terms and acronyms entered the lexicon, becoming the working vocabulary of therapists and their clients struggling with infertility treatment. People talked about gametes and zygotes for the first time since high school biology. IUI, IVF, GIFT, and ZIFT belonged to a new medical language that made it seem as though people were speaking in code about biological warfare. Not far behind these developments came trend watchers and statisticians, who documented that infertility and its treatment are not confined to a particular social cultural stratum. At least 10 to 15% of couples in the United States who want to conceive find they cannot (Meyers, Diamond et al., 1995). Of those who seek treatment, approximately two thirds receive a specific diagnosis of infertility—male-factor, female-factor, or some combination of the two. About half of the remaining group is eventually diagnosed; the other half falls into the medical purgatory of the undiagnosed.

Trends and statistics only hint at the clinical phenomena that therapists encounter whenever infertility pops up in their consulting rooms. The psychosocial issues facing those couples for whom biological parenthood doesn't come easily are profound and unusually daunting. The reasons for this are found in the intimate association of infertility with loss and grief, disruptive and invasive medical treatments, and repetitive cycles of hope and failure. Infertility is neither a disease nor a cause of disease. But it can properly be considered a chronic medical condition, one with life-altering consequences for couples who encounter it. It is, moreover, less an *individual's* medical condition than a condition that belongs to a *couple*, a condition with the power to disrupt, contravene, and reshape the attitudes, feelings, and behaviors that constitute the shared life of a couple, their time and energy spent together, their sexual intimacy, and their life plans and dreams.

This chapter focuses on the psychological impact of infertility in the lives of couples. Infertility is understood to be a major stressor in the life cycle of a couple, one that entails both real and anticipatory losses for those affected and their families. Gender differences are discussed, and key therapeutic issues are highlighted to enable the clinician who treats couples to navigate through the difficult terrain of ambiguous loss and attenuated grief.

IMPACT ON SELF-REGULATION

Physical Effects

Infertility can have long-lasting and devastating effects upon the lives of those it touches. Yet it does not kill; it does not shorten anyone's life, as other kinds of trauma may. It is not, strictly speaking, life threatening and does not meet the definitional criteria of the *DSM-IV* for designation as a "qualifying event" in discussions of posttraumatic stress disorder (PTSD). Yet its consequences are no less traumatic for many of those afflicted, who can feel just as wrenched physically, psychologically, and spiritually as those who have experienced life-threatening traumas.

One thing that infertility shares with trauma of all kinds is a distinctly physical imprint. As one client put it, "Infertility is an unwanted event taking place in your own body without your consent." The inability to conceive (or carry to term) a baby is experienced as a personal failure, a betrayal of the body. It is not unusual for persons undergoing infertility treatment to feel alienated from their own bodies, to feel physically damaged, dysfunctional, or incapacitated.

Couples in treatment must also contend with the intrusion of the medical establishment into the most private and intimate sphere of their lives. Such treatments can extend over a fairly lengthy period of time, from months to years, and tend to leave couples feeling chronically depleted by the steady drain of complex medical procedures, protocols and medications on one or both partner's physical energy, time, and resources.

Affect Dysregulation

These pressures place considerable strain on self-regulation. Couples routinely report significant and often bewildering effects on their emotional adjustment. Taxing medical procedures and unfamiliar medications can have broad systemic effects on the individual who undergoes them, disrupting normal rhythm, mood, energy level, etc. These alterations can be as abrupt as they are intense, likening some clients to refer to themselves or their partners (humorously) as having been "possessed." The language that clients use to describe such states points to their ego-alien quality, as well as to the couple's underlying sense of helplessness. As one woman put it: "Since we have been doing this treatment, my emotions have been a total roller coaster. I go from being ridiculously cheerful to incredibly bitchy. No wonder my husband isn't sure who he's living with from one moment to the next. I don't even recognize myself half the time, and yet I can't seem to help it."

These complaints are not unique to infertile couples in therapy, but the therapist who is unacquainted with the effects of traumatic stress may gloss over the physical and thereby overlook an important dimension of her or his clients' psychological adjustment.

One couple in therapy complained that they were fighting repeatedly over whether to continue their medical treatment. Referred by their reproductive endocrinologist (a man known for his sensitivity to the disruptive effects of fertility treatment on a couple's mental health), the couple reported that they could not agree about whether they should merely suspend ("take a break") a course of treatment that both described as "grueling" or abandon further medical treatment altogether in favor of pursuing adoption. Rather than delve immediately into the process of their recurring arguments, the therapist instead asked both partners what each one liked least about the medical regimen they were presently enduring together. It became clear that both found especially distressing the phase of treatment in which the woman was required to take a particular medication known to have powerful systemic effects on the patient's affect regulation. The therapist's inquiry opened a whole new dialog between the couple about the physical toll that treatment had been taking on them both. The words poured out from each of them about their shared ordeal. And for the first time in months, they were able to regard themselves and each other with sympathy and compassion. Both agreed that their prior focus on results and outcome had allowed them to become emotionally disconnected from one another. At one point in this discussion, the husband realized that he had been caught up in trying to deny the likely cause of his wife's increasing moodiness even as he had been growing more resentful about how miserable *her* moods were making him.

TRAUMA AND THE BRAIN

The ever-growing literature on the effects of trauma attests to the essential *physical* basis of traumatic experience. Titles such as *The Body Remembers* (Rothschild, 2000) and "The Body Keeps the Score" (van der Kolk, 1994) point to this fact. In his studies of children exposed at an early age to traumatic conditions, Perry (1994) has found that children's brains develop differently as a result of their exposure to trauma. Experience produces morphological change that becomes encoded in the brain's structural development. This is not a case of nature writing upon the blank tablet of the developing brain, Perry argues, but of trauma changing the way that the brain will be shaped or affected by experience yet to come. Further, a wealth of evidence now suggests that the morphogenic effects of trauma occur not just with children, who we readily conceive to have more pliable, malleable brains, but with adults as well. Indeed any extreme somatosensory experience can precipitate a cascade of physiological events that, if the original experience is sufficiently powerful (e.g., an automobile accident) and/or sustained (e.g., a battlefield siege), can alter the individual's future capacity to perceive and respond to sensory events of a much less extreme nature (e.g., the sound of a car door closing or the rumble of a passing truck).

MULTIPLE SOURCES OF DYSREGULATION

The trauma literature offers a useful paradigm for understanding the intense and comprehensive impact of infertility on self-regulation. Researchers such as Perry (1994) and van der Kolk (2002) have drawn attention to the vital relationship between the body and the psyche, advising therapists that distressing events that persist over time can alter people's experience of themselves, their significant others, and future events. This means that many of the psychological complaints heard from couples undergoing medical treatment for infertility may stem, at least in part, from physical traumatic effects—effects, the trauma researchers remind us, that produce states of heightened arousal, decreased problem-solving capacity, diminished flexibility of responsiveness, flattened or restricted range of affect, distractibility, and a general tendency of the individual toward guardedness and conservation. Trauma researchers liken this condition to the activation of the organism's basic fight or flight response, only in this case the affected individual suffers the repeated reactivation of this state of heightened arousal. According to van der Kolk, trauma of all kinds results in the preferential activation of the brain's right hemisphere, which includes the limbic system. In the middle of this right brain orchestration, the so-called left brain—the seat of rational deliberation and problem solving—goes off-line (van der Kolk, personal communication, October 3, 2003).

In the case of infertility, particularly in cases where medical treatment is invasive, systemic (i.e., where medication and/or surgery is involved), and sustained over a period of weeks or months (or, in many cases, years), extreme somatosensory events can be par for the course. While they are usually not life threatening to the individual in treatment, they may be far reaching in their traumatic effects on the body and hence the psyche. Infertile couples in medical treatment thus contend with two sources of dysregulation: (a) the fertility medications themselves and (b) the traumatic imprint of invasive medical regimens that tax the body and produce long-lasting alterations in mood, energy level, and self-esteem regulation.

IMPACT ON MARITAL INTIMACY

We have seen that infertility can have disruptive effects on individual self-regulation. Its impact on couples is no less profound and reaches into every sphere of married life. The effects here are less physical than psychological; they pertain to the couple's shared systems of meaning, communication, and agency, as we shall see.

Loss

For couples undergoing treatment for infertility, a dark shadow hangs over their determined efforts to make a baby. The shadow is loss, and in the case of infertility it is a layered, often ambiguous loss that darkens the hopes, plans, and dreams of the men and women affected. The inability to conceive or carry to term a successful pregnancy lies at the center of a complex web of other losses. Infertile couples face the prospect of losing the opportunity to become biological parents—to give birth to, breast-feed, and care for babies genetically related to them. For some, this loss of genetic continuity strikes at the heart of what it means to be a family, what it means to be a husband or wife, and what it means to be a man or woman. There is corresponding damage to other important psychological dimensions of selfhood, including personal adequacy, desirability, self-worth, potency, and related conceptions of masculinity or femininity.

In an influential article describing how families contend with future losses, Rolland (1990) argued that *anticipatory* losses can be "as challenging and painful for families as the death of a family member" (p. 229). His framework for understanding the effects of anticipatory loss on a family gives particular significance to the timing of the loss in the family's life cycle. Some losses are especially hard on families when they occur out of phase with the normal developmental tasks and expectations of the life cycle (Walsh & McGoldrick, 1991). Further, an off-phase loss that occurs during a life-cycle transition—for example, the transition from new marriage to incipient parenthood—can be the most disruptive of all. Infertility represents a case in point.

Infertility is likely the first prolonged marital crisis for the majority of couples who experience it, the first serious test for a young marriage. Faced with the prospect of being unable to realize their dreams and expectations of parenthood, infertile couples tend to feel cheated out of their rightful place in the normal sequence of events in the life course. Infertility makes couples especially vulnerable to "the emotional upheaval generated by anticipatory loss" (Rolland, 1990, p. 237) because it occurs at a time when couples are already beginning to organize their thoughts, feelings, and plans around becoming parents.

Another important aspect of loss associated with infertility is its *unbounded* nature. Because infertility can irrevocably alter a couple's life plans and outcomes, its effects extend throughout the life cycle. Unbounded losses are generally much more difficult for individuals to bear, more extensive in terms of their duration and scope, and more difficult to delineate, contain, and repair (Rolland, 1990). Many of the losses associated with infertility are similarly interminable and hence impossible to identify precisely or entirely resolve. Several writers have also commented about the *ambiguous* nature of infertility loss (Gilbert, chapter 1 of this volume; McDaniel, Hepworth, & Doherty, 1992). Many of the losses associated with infertility are intangible, such as the loss of a child not yet conceived or the loss of genetic continuity. Others, given the difficulty of fixing a specific cause and prognosis to a couple's inability to conceive, may remain shrouded in mystery—Is it male-factor or female-factor infertility? With whom does the basic fault/deficiency/dysfunction reside? Can it be corrected? If not now, then later? Ever? Infertile men and women routinely pose these questions to themselves, to each other, and to their doctors, but the absence of definitive answers, as may often be the case, can be an ongoing burden to them in their effort to come to grips with their infertility.

Social Disconnections and Shame

This effort to highlight some of the losses associated with infertility points to another important dimension of infertility's traumatic impact: the effects of grief and shame upon a couple's social support. Generally, individuals and families with supportive ties to extended families, friends, and other sources of social support cope better with trauma and loss (Catherall, 1992; Herman, 1992). The same may be true for infertility. Some couples readily seek support from understanding friends and informed family members. However, many couples find it extremely difficult to discuss their situation with their families and friends (Johnston, 1994). The reasons for this difficulty may be complex but likely involve shame associated with the painful sense of failing at something so basic and integral to married life. The effect of this kind of shame is readily seen in the reluctance of many couples even to admit to others that there might be a problem (RESOLVE, 2002). Social awareness of infertility may be increasing steadily, as publicity surrounding advanced medical procedures grows alongside greater public scrutiny of the laws and policies governing insurance reimbursement of those procedures. But the decision to inform one's relatives and friends about one's own infertility remains a highly personal one, usually made reluctantly and often after considerable time has passed since the initial diagnostic workup. This means that many couples struggle with their infertility-related grief, at least in the early stages, without the benefit of emotional support from their friends and family. They keep their losses to themselves, especially in the early stages, when it still seems possible to rejoin the fertile community.

Infertile couples who cope by keeping their infertility losses to themselves also report an unexpected loss of the sense of belonging to the community of their peers who are becoming parents without apparent difficulty or dysfunction (Johnston, 1994; RESOLVE, 2002). Social relationships with friends, coworkers, and the fertile world at large often lose their ease and familiarity. Like the bereaved parents described by Gilbert and Smart (1992), these infertile couples feel out of sync with normal life much of the time.

For those couples who cannot find their way back to the community of their peers and loved ones, whose shame and grief leave them further isolated from previous sources of social support, recovery and reconnection will require the assistance of a therapist.

The shadow of loss darkens every sphere of an infertile couple's life together, from the personal to the social, the private to the public. As seen, infertility can wreak havoc with the physical and psychological underpinnings of selfhood. It can undermine the couple's sense of belonging among family, friends, and peers; and it can drive couples off the path of their own life histories. The protracted difficulty to conceive or carry a successful pregnancy can engender intense feelings of failure, deficiency, and inadequacy. Intense and unpredictable feelings of shame begin to congeal in the marriage, stifling the flow of empathy, disrupting the normal ease of marital communication, and unbalancing the delicate emotional system that sustains the couple's most intimate moments together.

Sexual Disconnections

Virtually all couples struggling with infertility find their sexual pleasure and activity curtailed or disrupted for an extended time (Johnston, 1994). Complaints about a partner's lack of interest in sex or difficulties with sustaining or achieving arousal are common. Part of the problem can be related to side effects of fertility-enhancing medications, which can alter autonomic nervous system pathways that govern, among other things, sexual arousal and orgasm. This results in diminished capacity for arousal and orgasm in women and episodic erectile dysfunction in men. Another source of interference relates to the steady drain on physical energy and time due to frequent, intrusive, and often debilitating medical procedures that can leave one or both members of a couple feeling chronically depleted.

For those couples in treatment, the intrusion of the medical establishment into the most private, intimate sphere of their lives together usually robs sex of much of its pleasure and virtually all of its spontaneity. Treatment protocols often prescribe exactly when and how often a couple should engage in procreative sex. Wives in therapy speak ruefully of having as much physical intimacy with their medical team as with their husbands, and husbands report feeling that their role has been reduced to that of sperm donor. Both parties are subject to feeling that sex together has become mechanized, medicalized, and closely scrutinized by a clinical third party (the medical team). Add to these conditions the ever-present specter of failure and disappointment, and it is no wonder that infertility wreaks havoc with sexual intimacy.

It is important to bear in mind that most people do not spend a lot of time thinking about the conditions necessary for healthy sexual functioning. Even people in treatment for infertility may understand little about the psychological underpinnings of sexual intimacy (Stammer, Wischmann, & Verres, 2002), or they may hold unrealistic expectations for themselves about maintaining an exuberant, spontaneous sex life while submitting to a medical regimen of sex by prescription (Galst, 1986). Sex therapists remind us that sexual functioning requires a reasonably cohesive sense of self; the ability to surrender control and abandon oneself to internal and external sources of sexual stimulation; and the ability to assert one's needs and desires effectively with a partner while also being able to hold or soothe oneself in the face of small disjunctions or disconnections (Schnarch, 1997, 2002; Zoldbrod, 1997). Infertility treatment can interfere with each of these, but the resulting disruption of sexual functioning often comes as a painful surprise to many couples, yet another unexpected loss. By assisting couples in therapy to step back and take stock of the varied sources of strain on their sexual relationship (both physical and psychological), therapists can help them avoid becoming mired in reactive patterns of blame and withdrawal (Stammer et al.).

Marital Conservation and Sexual Withdrawal

What happens under the siege of infertility treatment is that both members of the couple begin to adopt countermeasures to preserve their energy, their privacy, their personal control, and their sense of self-worth. Instead of letting go with each other, they hold on. They conserve. They might even shut down. The manifold losses associated with infertility, both real and threatened, activate powerful needs for self-protection, conservation, and withdrawal. In addition, repeated failures to conceive often reawaken feelings of guilt associated with past sexual behavior, contraceptive methods, pregnancy losses, and so on, which further interferes with sexual desire.

CASE EXAMPLE: LIKE A DAM BURSTING

Elly and Bruce, both in their late 30s, had been married 8 years when they presented for therapy at the recommendation of a social worker affiliated with their reproductive endocrinologist. The presenting complaint was that they had become increasingly distant from one another emotionally. They seemed to be able to handle the routine tasks of their busy lives together without much difficulty or conflict, but they no longer felt emotionally connected to one another. And both thought a big part of the problem was that they had stopped having sex together. Following the long-awaited birth of their only child, a tow-headed 6-year-old boy, who Elly referred to as "our miracle baby," their dream of having a second child was thwarted by a series of three miscarriages that occurred in the year following their son's second birthday. They eventually consulted a specialist, who was now in the process of starting them on a new protocol of regular coitus with careful monitoring of any subsequent conception. However, at this point neither Bruce nor Elly had much interest in engaging in any sort of sexual activity together, procreative or otherwise.

The therapist wondered about the cumulative effects on the couple of Elly's three miscarriages. What unfolded was a story of attenuated grief and extreme solicitousness on the part of each toward the other. In the 3 years since the last miscarriage, as they struggled to get over their losses and forge ahead, they gradually stowed away their pain, and in the process began to avoid the kinds of intimate encounters that might threaten their emotional containment strategy. Sexual encounters grew rare and were characterized by extreme diffidence on both sides. Each had reason for being tentative, given the specter of pregnancy loss that hung over them both, and this led to a heightened sensitivity to any indication in the other of uncertainty, hesitation, or ambivalence. Each became preoccupied with obtaining a clear signal of the other's willingness to be sexually intimate. The net result was a dampening of erotic interest and a heightened investment in control and restraint.

The therapist elected to support the couple's expressed interest in restoring their intimate connection by helping them plan a series of intimate encounters. Both recognized at once that they had been arranging their busy lives in such a way as to allow virtually no intimate time together aside from sleep and trips to their doctor's office. In their first planned encounter, they arranged for a babysitter and spent the evening lingering over a candlelight dinner at one of the city's nicer restaurants. Several more nonsexual encounters were planned and carried out before the couple felt ready to bring their newly revived intimacy into the bedroom. Once they did so, it felt, according to Elly, "like a dam bursting." What poured out from both were the long-suppressed feelings of anxiety and loss associated with their previous failed attempts at carrying a healthy baby. Many tears and long discussions ensued. When they finally took up again the question of whether and how to pursue having a second child, they did so with a stronger sense of themselves as a couple bound together through shared losses as well as shared parenting.

GENDER DIFFERENCES

A number of authors on the subject of coping with infertility have noted that spouses rarely experience the stresses of infertility in the same way and at the same time (Becker, 1990; Carter & Carter, 1989; Johnston, 1994; Meyers, Weinshel et al., 1995). The effects appear to divide along gender lines, tracing pathways remarkably congruent with traditional gender stereotypes. Studies suggest, for example, that men are likely to face the challenges of infertility in a task-instrumental way; women, on the other hand, are more likely to focus on the socioemotional costs of infertility's encroaching losses (Meyers, Weinshel et al., 1995).

Stress and Coping

Although both men and women endorse the idea that their infertility poses a grave threat to their well-being, women report much greater levels of distress throughout the course of their infertility than do men. For example, 50% of women but only 15% of men view infertility as the most upsetting experience of their lives (Freeman, Boxer, Rickels, Tureck, & Mastrioanni, 1985). Even when comparisons are made between men with male-factor infertility and women with female-factor infertility, differences between the sexes continue to stand out: Infertile women are more likely to describe themselves as "feeling incomplete," whereas infertile men are more likely to feel a diminished sense of virility (Kraft et al., 1980); women are more likely to be pessimistic about the outcome of treatment, whereas men are more likely to endorse optimistic statements about the efficacy of their medical regimen *du jour* (Abbey, Halman, & Andrews, 1992); and women are more likely to seek out others in the infertile community for emotional support, whereas men are more likely to avoid identifying with the infertile community (RESOLVE, 2002).

These differences reflect more than the effect of social stigma. They indicate the extent to which infertility shakes each person's core sense of efficacy, worth, and selfhood. Men approach their infertility more as a problem to be solved than as a loss to be mourned; in the process, they tend to keep their feelings to themselves and avoid emotionally charged conversations about anticipatory losses. Women seek out social support and actively pursue new lines of communication with their spouses in order to voice their distress, rather than suppress or deflect their feelings. Each pursues a course of action designed to cope with and repair his or her own, gender-specific psychological damages.

In the wake of infertility, couples experience relational and performance losses differently. Some recent studies suggest that women are more likely than men to voice greater distress, report higher levels of marital and sexual dissatisfaction, and blame themselves and their behavior for their infertility. Men, on the other hand, are more likely to temporize their self-reported distress with accounts of instrumental attempts to overcome their infertility. They are also more likely than their wives to rely on avoidant coping strategies, such as denial and withdrawal into work, and to attribute cause for their infertility to chance factors rather than to themselves.

Sex and Infertility

In the bedroom, both sexes experience relational disruptions (e.g., heightened feelings of vulnerability, irritability, and discomfort in relation to one's partner) as well as performance pressures. Men often feel they are expected to produce or perform on demand, leading to a diminished sense of their worth or value to their partner. (As more than one husband in treatment has remarked, "I feel like I'm just a means to an end for her.") Women too can experience a kind of performance pressure associated with treatment protocols that dictate when and how often sexual intercourse should occur. Under such conditions, couples experience a growing disconnection between their own, internally generated sexual rhythms and their physical participation in sexual activity (i.e., intercourse). Infertility treatment can upset each partner's internal balance between surrender and control, as well as the delicate interplays between partners that create and sustain sexual interest. Both desire and arousal pathways can be affected.

Not surprisingly we find gender differences here, too, among couples in treatment for infertility. Perhaps because men are more vulnerable in general to performance pressures associated with sex on demand (Zilbergeld, 1992), sexual difficulties among men in treatment for infertility seem to occur most often with arousal pathways (e.g., erectile difficulties, difficulty with orgasm). Women in treatment appear to be more likely to experience problems with diminished sexual interest and desire (e.g., decreased lubrication, difficulty achieving orgasm). And, perhaps reflecting their greater sensitivity in general to relational disruptions, women are also more likely than men to report decreased satisfaction overall with their sexual relationship.

Gender Effects Reconsidered

These gender disparities tend to even out. Infertile men and women become more similar in their experiences over time, especially over several years. The news is not good, however. Over time, both husbands and wives in infertile couples become more likely to experience diminished self-worth and personal adequacy as well as declining marital satisfaction (Berg & Wilson, 1991).

There is a caveat to this bleak report that highlights an important methodological difficulty inherent in studies of infertility's impact on individuals: As every marital and family therapist knows, much of individual experience is mediated by the reciprocal influences of family members on one another. This seems to be no less true for couples struggling with infertility. For example, Andrews, Abbey, and Halman (1992) found that husbands' and wives' perceived quality of life influenced each other's quality-of-life experience. Subsequently, Meyers, Diamond, et al. (1995) wondered whether too much has been made of gender differences in how couples cope with infertility. These authors cited a body of recent work that suggests that, below the surface of self-report, men and women actually experience similar levels of emotional distress, role failure, self-esteem loss, and commitment to family building. Indeed, congruence within the couple may be the great, untold story of the infertility coping literature. An example of this newer wave of research is Peterson, Newton, and Rosen's (2003) study of marital adjustment and depression in infertile couples.

Peterson and his coauthors asked more than 500 infertile couples to complete a series of measures assessing their experience of infertility-related distress and depressive symptoms in general. They also gathered data about the couples' reported levels of marital satisfaction and adjustment. What they found was that couples with the highest mean levels of marital satisfaction and adjustment tended to show the most congruence (i.e., agreement between husband and wife) in their perceptions of infertility-related stress. Couples who had less congruence in their perceptions of social stress (e.g., sensitivity to reminders about infertility, infertility-related isolation from family and friends) were more likely to report marital adjustment difficulties. Men and women in couples congruent in terms of reported social stress also reported greater marital satisfaction. But that's not all. Incongruence within a couple, especially related to relationship concerns and the need for parenthood (e.g., attitudes about becoming a parent), correlated with depressive symptoms in women.

The latter finding suggests that incongruence between partners in these critical areas is particularly hard on women. Why might this be so? The authors speculated that divergent views between partners about how infertility affects their relationship or about the importance of having a family may "hinder positive communication or the sense that the partner empathizes with the other partner's point of view, which for women may lead to a feeling of isolation and depression" (Peterson et al., 2003, p. 66). Another explanation, one more consistent with findings in gender research, posits that women in general, because of their sex role training and socialization, tend to feel a greater sense of responsibility for their relationships than do men (Gilligan, 1982). Consequently, women are more likely than men to blame themselves when their relationships are not going well, which puts them at greater risk for depression.

All this makes the clinical picture of infertility more complicated than therapists who treat only individuals might assume. Clinical distress in couples facing infertility (especially women, as in the study discussed) is likely the result of a complex interplay of two types of forces: individual needs, expectations, and vulnerabilities (some of which may derive from gendered patterns of socialization), on the one hand, and dyadic or systemic processes (including communication and social support) on the other. This interplay of the individual and the system, of the subjective and the interpersonal, is fundamental to understanding how couples respond to infertility.

HOW COUPLES RESPOND TO INFERTILITY

Sharing the Labor

Infertility is not simply a condition; it's also a job—at least for those seeking a way to conceive a child. Just ask any of the couples who eventually make their way to a therapist's consulting room. The demands facing infertile couples, even those who do not yet know the cause of their infertility, are considerable—in some cases enormous and often prolonged. Like other chronic medical conditions, infertility obliges those receiving treatment to pay careful attention to their allocation of resources, as visits to doctors, clinics, and hospitals begin to multiply. One client couple referred to their extended enrollment in a medical regimen of daily blood draws, injections, and prescribed inseminations as "life under siege." Another couple in therapy likened their months in treatment to being dropped suddenly into a foreign country and having to make all the necessary arrangements for food, shelter, and medical care, enough to support a lengthy stay, all without speaking the native language. "It just commands all your attention and concentration. You feel like if you don't try to stay on top of everything, some critical detail will somehow get overlooked, and the whole project will be doomed."

Any couple receiving fertility treatment inevitably faces the need to redistribute responsibility for completing everyday life maintenance activities. Couples approach these task demands in a variety of ways, usually involving some combination of role sharing and division of labor. For some, this is no big deal; but for other couples, whose division of household labor reflects deeply held convictions about what constitutes men's versus women's work, this can produce considerable tension within the marriage.

One couple presented for therapy with a 5-year history of sporadic medical treatment for female-factor infertility. The couple resided at the outskirts of a large metropolitan area in a small religious community known for its conservative social values. The presenting problem was the wife's frequent crying and general withdrawal from household tasks and from her concerned husband. It became clear in the initial interview that there was much unresolved grief over their inability to conceive a child despite years of trying. Both expressed strong wishes to have a child, and both acknowledged that the prospect of living without parenthood was heartbreaking.

As the husband narrated the history of their efforts to become pregnant, including several unsuccessful treatments, each with a different doctor and clinic in the adjacent city, a critical issue emerged. When the therapist inquired about the frequent changing of doctors, the husband replied, "We just never got comfortable with what any of those doctors recommended—it all seemed like an awful lot of fuss and bother." At this point his wife spoke up and explained that every time they began a new treatment regimen, it wasn't long before her husband would complain about having to "change all around" their established ways of doing things, including household chores, food shopping, and meal preparations. He especially resented having to take on what he generally regarded as "women's work" on those days that his wife had a medical appointment in the city. Before long, he would announce his determination that they stop working with that doctor and try to find a different program. His wife would reluctantly agree, a new clinic would be found, and the cycle would commence again.

The therapist helped the couple talk together about the stress of undertaking medical procedures that require significant alterations in daily routines. The husband later admitted sheepishly that he had "lost sight of the big picture" in his refusal to make even temporary adjustments in his familiar routine. Subsequent sessions helped the couple share their grief over past failures while also exploring their previously unspoken feelings and attitudes about participating in medical treatment. They resolved to take a break from medical treatment for 3 months while they worked on clarifying their hopes and expectations about having a baby. Following this interval, they returned to treatment with the last doctor they had seen.

THE EXPLICIT MARRIAGE

In an influential book about how families cope with severe stress, Reiss (1981) advanced the concept of "the explicit family" to refer to a family's self-conscious response to the disorganizing effects of a stressful event. Borrowing from earlier writers on the organizational structure of everyday family life (e.g., Kantor & Lehr, 1975), Reiss argued that families in crisis lose "their most precious possession: an extended and dependable repertoire of background understandings, shared assumptions, traditions, rituals, and meaningful secrets that made it possible for them to function *implicitly*" (p. 178; emphasis added). To contend with this loss and restore a semblance of order and coherence to family life, besieged family members coalesce around a simple but explicit set of rules that govern everyday transactions within the family. The explicit family adapts to the increased demands placed on it by a stressful event (e.g., an unexpected death in the family, a catastrophic job loss, the diagnosis of a chronic illness) by becoming more organized, rule governed, and task focused. The explicit family thus preserves a sense of family order and unity, though often at the expense of flexibility and accommodation to any special needs of individual family members.

We can apply Reiss's family model to understand the response of married couples to the crisis of infertility. The defining conditions are all present in the case of infertility: (a) the unexpected threat of traumatic loss; (b) the sense of being under siege by conditions that are largely outside of one's direct control; (c) the impending threat of shattered dreams, wishes, and expectations for the future; and (d) the corresponding need (especially acute for couples in treatment) to accommodate unfamiliar, invasive, and generally disruptive alterations in everyday living. These four conditions give rise to the explicit marriage.

Recall that for many couples, infertility is the first major crisis of their marriage. Submerged in that crisis, infertile couples face new task demands that require a whole new kind of decision making. The options for medical treatment can be dizzying, and that may be only the beginning. Almost from the start, infertility forces couples to examine their fundamental assumptions, priorities, and expectations vis-à-vis parenthood. It requires them to consider more explicitly basic questions about the kind of family they would seek to build: how many children, when, how, and even why. Such considerations may occur privately at first, but over time they inevitably coalesce in shared communication between spouses, forming a kind of marital touchstone from which other decisions can be made (e.g., deciding upon a specific course of treatment or choosing among alternative family-building options). As they adapt to the task demands of their infertility, couples necessarily make explicit their marital aims and expectations. This in turn allows for more coordinated action in pursuit of those aims.

CONSERVING HOPE AND RESTORING MEANING

Creating an explicit marriage not only enables an infertile couple to navigate the minefield of decision making in the pursuit of family building, it also affords the couple an important means of sustaining togetherness in another task central to recovery and resolution. This is the task of conserving hope amidst loss.

Virtually all traumatic loss, whether real or anticipatory, produces a rupture in a person's implicit set of personal meanings, explanations, and understandings about self and life (what has been called one's personal cosmology or "assumptive world"; cf. Janoff-Bulman, 1992). These basic, orienting assumptions about the world confer coherence and predictability to lived experience. When disrupted or shattered by traumatic loss, survivors are driven to rebuild their basic assumptions, a process that takes time and also depends significantly on the support of others close to the survivors (Catherall, 1992; Figley, 1998).

People struggling with infertility face a similar rebuilding task, but here the focus is on *shared* meanings and assumptions (what Gilbert in chapter 1 of this volume calls the couple's "dyadic belief system"). The restoration of shared meaning helps to dispel the confusion, disorientation, and spiritual vacuum left in infertility's broad wake. In this respect, the emergence of the explicit marriage provides a couple with important leverage against confusion, pessimism, and despair.

THE THREE CRITICAL TASKS

Three critical tasks face infertile couples seeking to build a family:

1. Restoration of shared meaning and purpose
2. Restoration of collaborative agency
3. Restoration of connection

We have seen that the first task, the restoration of meaning, enables couples to conserve hope in their ongoing adaptation to loss. We have also seen that the restoration of collaborative agency ensures that couples will be able to carry out those tasks necessary for them to resolve their personal struggles with infertility. We turn now to the third task, the restoration of connection, which, it should be noted, supports and draws strength from the other two.

RESTORING CONNECTION: THE DANCE OF LOSS AND HOPE

There is no easy pathway for couples to restore the connection they enjoyed before infertility sundered their lives.

"We've been doing okay," said Justine in answer to my question. It was my third meeting with her and her husband, Richard. The answer somewhat surprised me, because only a week before they had received the crushing news that their latest cycle of in vitro fertilization (IVF) had failed. It was their third attempt, the one they had felt most confident about because all of the indicators (hormone levels, sperm viability, the presence of several "robust" embryos for implantation) had been positive. I knew that Justine and Richard prided themselves on their careful preparation for IVF. They studiously researched their options, thoughtfully selected the clinic and the doctor they wanted to perform the procedure, and seemingly left nothing to chance as they passed through the stages of the IVF cycle (ovarian stimulation, induced ovulation, fertilization, implantation, and the excruciating period of watchful waiting before the first pregnancy test). Of course, there is no such thing as leaving nothing to chance when it comes to infertility treatment. Indeed, infertility survivors could produce a thesis about the maddeningly elusive ways that chance governs their fate. What other condition binds its sufferers to the relentless passage of the calendar, through repeated cycles of hope and loss, in spite of everyone's very best efforts to achieve not perfection but simply normalcy? Knowing all this, I wondered about what might lie behind their tepid assertion that things were okay.

Taking a cue from Richard, who was smiling approvingly at his wife while she spoke, I inquired about their apparent consensus of feeling about this latest disappointment. There was a pause during which Richard's smile began to waver, and then Justine broke out, "I'm just trying to do the best I can with all this. He [meaning Richard] keeps telling me to keep my hopes up, but it's really hard, you know? I tried to talk to him about how bad I felt—I called him at work after the clinic called with the test results— and it seemed like he couldn't wait to get off the phone. I mean, I don't blame him. But, honey—" Justine turned to her husband, who looked like a deer in headlights, "we've hardly talked at all about anything since last week. I keep waiting for you to say something, anything, about what we just went through. And when I do, you just say something like, 'the odds are still in our favor,' and then you change the subject."

Working together to restore their connection is one of the most important tasks facing couples with infertility. Like Justine and Richard, partners who find their sense of togetherness blown apart by infertility's inescapable disappointments, failures, and losses begin to find their way back to each other by recognizing the gulf between them in how they experience and cope with their infertility. With recognition of their differences can come new ways of talking about them to each other, which in turn can yield a deeper appreciation of what each partner is struggling with, adapting to, and seeking to resolve. As Justine and Richard began to talk to one another about their separate experiences, Justine realized that Richard had been reacting less to their treatment failures and more to her. Like many husbands who, together with their wives, undergo extended courses of medical treatment for infertility, Richard had plugged into the familiar, male habit of suppressing his own feelings of disappointment and loss. But he had no idea what to do with his wife's strong feelings. From his vantage point, the best thing to do seemed to be to avoid saying anything that might add to her grief. So he said very little at all. Behind his silence, as they both discovered, he felt a very great deal: mostly confused, lost, hurt, and not a little ashamed at being unable to comfort his wife more successfully.

Communication opens doors for couples to reconnect. Rituals that support new ways of being together can supply the scaffolding needed for reconnection to be sustained. Some couples do this by ritualizing the time they spend together traveling to and from doctors' appointments. Others do this by planning getaway weekends in between treatment cycles. Justine and Richard made time to talk together on a regular basis by building this time around a daily activity (walking their Labrador) that they could perform together. Helping couples find and protect this kind of recuperative time together can be one of the most enduring contributions that therapists can make to improve the lives of their infertile clients.

DEFERRED GRIEF

Couples riding the roller coaster of fertility treatment face considerable pressure to guard their hope and defer their grief for as long as they can endure the ride. To meet these demands, husbands and wives often limit attention to their distress. This is partly due to the nature of infertility loss. As Rolland (1990), Boss (1999), and others have noted, when the loss in question is anticipatory or ambiguous, there is a corresponding tendency for families to disguise, suppress, or postpone grieving. Doka (1989) has named this sort of incomplete mourning *disenfranchised grief*, which is "grief that persons experience when they incur a loss that is not or cannot be openly acknowledged, publicly mourned, or socially supported" (p. 4). Blame, shame, and guilt undoubtedly play key roles in this process as well, discouraging the kind of face-to-face, sustained intimacy between husbands and wives that might otherwise ease the burden of infertility's ambiguous losses.

Some couples resolve matters by agreeing to table their grief in order to focus their energies on further treatment. Other couples take time off from their pursuit of pregnancy to mourn, however incompletely, both the real and the psychological losses they've endured so far. They may even commemorate the passage of these losses through ceremony and ritual, sometimes designing their own, personal tributes to the hoped-for children they have lost (Imber-Black, 1991; Meyers, Weinshel et al., 1995).

But many couples get snagged at this point, especially amid mounting losses and a growing need to conserve energy and hope. It is not an easy place to be. A recent study of infertile couples (Berghuis & Stanton, 2002) found that those who engaged in avoidant coping behaviors (e.g., Richard in the previous case example) also experience greater psychological distress compared to couples who engaged in emotional-approach coping. In other words, coping patterns that block emotional intimacy in infertile couples may exacerbate distress. Justine and Richard's situation illustrates what can happen to marital intimacy and communication at such an impasse. They eventually accepted the need to acknowledge their losses, and they spent time together talking more fully about what each failed treatment cycle meant to each of them. These proved to be difficult and painful conversations for both. Yet the process brought them closer to-gether, giving meaning to their experience and agency to their prepara-tions to face the future.

TREATING INFERTILE COUPLES

There is a growing literature on treating infertile couples in therapy. This section draws from much of this previously imparted wisdom in order to provide guidelines for the clinician. In addition to providing a di-gest of what has been written before for practitioners, the reader is invited to approach therapy with infertile couples from a perspective informed by the central themes of this chapter, namely, traumatic stress, ambiguous loss, and the restoration of meaning, agency, and connection in the process of recovery.

Encourage Communication

If there is a single, recurring directive in the treatment literature, it is that the therapist should encourage and maintain communication be-tween spouses. Benefits that open communication can bestow on couples struggling with infertility include (a) reducing isolation and disconnec-tion; (b) normalizing gender differences in how infertility is experienced, reacted to, and understood by each spouse; (c) reducing guilt, blame, and especially personal shame; (d) improving role sharing and the division of labor; and (e) making time together outside the immediate reach of infer-tility treatment regimens.

It is worth remembering that infertility is, in many respects, not so much an acute medical condition as a chronic one. Like other families with a chronic illness, infertile couples necessarily devote considerable at-tention to understanding their condition, a sometimes lonely exercise that can produce unhealthy amounts of guilt, shame, and guardedness for each spouse. Thus a central task for the therapist is to restore more func-tional patterns of communication, to supplant defensiveness and secrecy with candor and acceptance. Above all, as McDaniel et al. (1992) asserted in their definitive work on treating families with medical conditions, the therapist should endeavor to respect defenses, remove blame, and accept feelings previously regarded as unacceptable.

Get the Story

McDaniel et al. (1992) recommended that the therapist elicit each fam-ily member's unique illness story. By exchanging their stories, family members develop increased understanding and acceptance of differences in how they experience and adapt to the stresses imposed by the illness. They extended this recommendation to therapists treating couples with infertility. By making time to explore each partner's infertility story, therapists help promote empathy and reduce defensiveness in their beleaguered clients.

Getting clients to tell their stories also furthers the therapeutic restoration of meaning. Couples need to revisit their underlying reasons for wanting children, their personal identifications with parenthood, and the meaning and significance they invest in their current pursuit of pregnancy. Many clients find it helpful to reflect on the parenting legacies left by their own parents. For some, this may mean circling back over painful histories of childhood disappointment, loss, or trauma. Although the therapist should tread gently here, this kind of reflection can supply valuable grounding for the couple's subsequent efforts to restore purpose and meaning to their family-building effort. Finally, therapists should not neglect to ask couples about their past brushes with infertility, including past infertility experiences in previous relationships and families of origin (cf. Meyers, Weinshel et al., 1995, on the "problematic legacy" of past infertility).

Support Affect Regulation

One of the key findings of trauma research over the past decade is that trauma can produce long-term, negative effects on the survivor's ability to regulate affective experience. For example, van der Kolk (personal communication, October 3, 2003) has spoken of trauma having enduring, inhibitory effects on cortical processing of emotionally distressing events. Briere (1997), a prolific contributor to both the clinical and research literatures on trauma recovery, has made therapeutic support of affect regulation the cornerstone of his treatment model. Infertility also produces its share of affect dysregulation in those it touches. So it makes sense for therapists to attend to their clients' emotional states not only to reach a deeper understanding of their infertility experience, but also to help them regulate that experience, particularly the heightened affective arousal that accompanies that experience. For clients struggling with the traumatic repercussions of infertility, better affect regulation opens more possibilities for engaging in focused, collaborative problem solving with their partners.

How can we assist our clients to regulate their affective experience of infertility? A number of techniques currently used by practitioners who work in related ways with other trauma survivors can be adapted to use with infertile couples in therapy. These include relaxation exercises used in cognitive behavioral treatment of anxiety (cf. Barlow, 2001), mindfulness methods, guided imagery, and focusing techniques (e.g., Kabot-Zinn, 1994). These methods afford clients greater leverage over their trauma-engendered affective dysregulation than the kinds of palliative measures often recommended in the self-help literature for infertile couples (e.g., taking a warm bath, lighting candles, going for walks).

Educate and Advocate

Treating couples with infertility requires more from the therapist than a sympathetic ear. Clients need more than compassionate support because their difficulties involve more than disordered feelings. Consider the fact that medical treatment of infertility has grown substantially more complex. The sheer number of informed decisions the average couple seeking treatment needs to make before proceeding is staggering to the uninitiated. Hence, our infertile clients need significant educational and resource support as well. As with any other chronic illness, becoming a more informed patient often leads to better outcomes. McDaniel et al. (1992) noted that encouraging a couple's efforts to educate themselves about their infertility helps to "increase the couple's sense of agency," while supporting couples' efforts to understand the underlying biological factors of their infertility "often helps people depersonalize the problem and [reduces] the sense of failure and blame about something over which they have no control" (p. 172).

Therapists can support their clients' efforts in this regard by acquainting themselves with the infertility education, resource support, and advocacy networks of their local RESOLVE chapter (www.resolve.org). RESOLVE offers individuals and couples a number of different avenues for becoming better informed consumers and self-advocates. Some local RESOLVE chapters also offer ongoing peer discussion/support groups on selected topics of interest to the infertile community (e.g., considering donor and surrogacy; waiting to adopt; deciding when to stop treatment). In addition to serving as a forum for the exchange of resource information, groups also have enormous value as safe havens for participants to discuss personal infertility issues in a nonjudgmental arena. Participants tend to feel more empowered as well as less isolated from the infertile community (RESOLVE, 2002).

Stay Present with Loss and Grief

The losses that shadow every couple's brush with infertility can be enormously difficult to capture precisely in language alone. People often seem to wear their grief—or their effort to not grieve—on their sleeves, yet they can be stymied by the request to talk about their losses. They stammer and falter, strain and give up, deflect and withdraw, often without intending to resist. In order to assist couples in their efforts at managing infertility losses, both real and anticipatory, therapists need to do two things: support their clients' capacity to attend to and identify with the feelings that accompany their own and their partners' disclosures; and supply whatever scaffolding may be needed for couples to understand the psychological losses that underlie these feelings. The first task requires the therapist to be supportive in a directive way, and the second requires the therapist to be interpretive in a supportive way. McDaniel et al. (1992) referred to the therapist's willingness to stay with a couple's affective experience at its most intense and painful as "maintaining an empathic presence with the family" (p. 209). Creating a safe, therapeutic holding environment in this way allows couples to grieve in ways that restore connection, meaning, and collaborative healing.

It should be noted that one of the most painful decisions facing some infertile couples is the decision to stop medical treatment. For those who reach this point, stopping treatment means giving up the quest for biological parenthood. Although there are no reliable figures in the research literature, it is likely that a significant number of couples who seek therapy to better cope with their infertility do so in order to receive help with facing this terrible loss. The therapist may be called upon to help a couple decide when to take a break from treatment, as well as when to stop trying, and when to start mourning more fully the loss of their dreams of biological parenthood. It is generally agreed that mourning this loss should precede active pursuit of alternative methods of family building, such as adoption (Johnston, 1994; Kraft et al., 1980). However, many couples certainly forge ahead, at least in their consideration of alternatives, even with the understanding that there may be losses still to mourn. In any case, the therapist can assist his or her client couples in this grief work by making time for reflection and emotional repair within each session (see Carter & Carter, 1989, for suggestions to guide considerations about stopping treatment, living without parenting, etc.).

Create a New Frame for Play and Enjoyment

Infertility can be deadening to couples in a number of ways, as has been described. That's why any therapy that encourages couples to value and explore new ways of enlivening their relationship together provides welcome and much-needed relief from the chronic pain of infertility. First, help spouses separate infertility work from play in their ongoing relationship, especially in the bedroom (Salzer, 1991; Zoldbrod, 1997). By separating baby-making from lovemaking, couples can create a new balance between sexual work and play, even reinstating sexual intimacy for pleasure's sake.

Some couples may need guidance from the therapist about how to reconnect physically *without* intercourse (as Bruce and Elly did). In such cases, it is helpful for the therapist to discuss removing intercourse from its usual place at the center of the couple's sexual attention. Partners can be encouraged to rekindle their loving attention to one another through shared touching experiences and quiet holding. This also helps to dispel the intense goal directedness that often weighs down sexual intimacy for couples struggling with infertility.

Another helpful recommendation to both partners is to practice making reservations with each other for shared time together outside the envelope of infertility. The therapist can direct the couple's attention to (re)creating opportunities for respite, escape, play, and discovery—in other words, to finding stolen moments for being alive together.

Above all, the therapist should look for opportunities to improve the couple's experience of mutuality and connection, both in and out of the bedroom.

CONCLUSION: ADAPTING TO LOSS

Ultimately the process of living with infertility loss is ongoing. As with any chronic illness, the effects of infertility on marriage and family life are ongoing throughout the life cycles of the people it touches. Walsh and McGoldrick (1991) recognized that coping with loss is a process of adaptation, not resolution. McDaniel et al. (1992) echoed this sentiment when they encouraged therapists working with infertile couples to help them "develop a loving story" to tell present and future children about the role that their parents' infertility may have played in their lives (p. 182).

As therapists help their clients discover the deeper texture of infertility's imprint of loss on their lives, they will find as well much that affirms the human capacity for restoring meaningful agency and connection in the face of traumatic loss.

REFERENCES

Abbey, A., Halman, L. J., & Andrews, F. M. (1992). Psychosocial, treatment and demographic predictors of the stress associated with infertility. *Fertility and Sterility, 57,* 122–128.

Andrews, F. M., Abbey, A., & Halman, L. J. (1992). Is fertility-problem stress different? The dynamics of stress in fertile and infertile couples. *Fertility and Sterility, 57,* 1247–1253.

Barlow, D. H. (2001). *Anxiety and its disorders, 2nd ed.: The nature and treatment of anxiety and panic.* New York: Guilford Press.

Becker, G. (1990). *Healing the infertile family: Strengthening your relationship in the search for parenthood.* New York: Bantam Books.

Berg, B. J., & Wilson, J. F. (1991). Psychological functioning across stages of treatment for infertility. *Journal of Behavioral Medicine, 14,* 11–26.

Berghuis, J. P., & Stanton, A. L. (2002). Adjustment to a dyadic stressor: A longitudinal study of coping and depressive symptoms in infertile couples over an insemination attempt. *Journal of Consulting and Clinical Psychology, 70,* 433–438.

Boss, P. (1999). *Ambiguous loss.* Cambridge, MA: Harvard University Press.

Briere, J. (1997). Treating adults severely abused as children: The self-trauma model. In D. A. Wolfe, B. McMahon, & R. D. Peters (Eds.), *Child abuse: New directions in treatment and prevention across the lifespan* (pp. 177–204). Newbury Park, CA: Sage.

Catherall, D. R. (1992). *Back from the brink: A family guide to overcoming traumatic stress.* New York: Bantam Books.

Carter, J. W., & Carter, M. (1989). *Sweet grapes: How to stop being infertile and start living again.* Indianapolis, IN: Perspectives Press.

Doka, K. (1989). *Disenfranchised grief.* Lexington, MA: Lexington Books.

Figley, C. R. (1998). *The traumatology of grieving.* Philadelphia: Brunner/Mazel.

Freeman, E. W., Boxer, A. S., Rickels, K., Tureck, R., & Mastrioanni, L. (1985). Psychological evaluation and support in a program of in vitro fertilization and embryo transfer. *Fertility and Sterility, 43,* 48–53.

Galst, J. P. (1986). Stress and stress management for the infertile couple. *Infertility, 9,* 171–179.

Gilbert, K. A., & Smart, L. (1992). *Coping with fetal or infant loss: The couple's healing process.* New York: Brunner/Mazel.

Gilligan, C. (1982). *In a different voice: Psychological theory and women's development.* Cambridge, MA: Harvard University Press.

Herman, J. (1992). *Trauma and recovery.* New York: Basic Books.

Imber-Black, E. (1991). Rituals and the healing process. In F. Walsh & M. McGoldrick (Eds.), *Living beyond loss: Death in the family* (pp. 207–223). New York: W. W. Norton.

Janoff-Bulman, R. (1992). *Shattered assumptions: Towards a new psychology of trauma.* New York: The Free Press.

Johnston, P. I. (1994). *Taking charge of infertility.* Indianapolis, IN: Perspectives Press.

Kabot-Zinn, J. (1994). *Wherever you go, there you are.* New York: Hyperion.

Kantor, D., & Lehr, W. (1975). *Inside the family.* San Francisco: Jossey-Bass.

Kraft, A., Palombo, J., Mitchell, D., Dean, C., Meyers, S., & Schmidt, A. W. (1980). The psychological dimensions of infertility. *American Journal of Orthopsychiatry, 50,* 618–628.

McDaniel, S. H., Hepworth, J., & Doherty, W. J. (1992). *Medical family therapy.* New York: Basic Books.

Meyers, M., Diamond, R., Kezur, D., Scharf, C., Weinshel, M., & Rait, D. S. (1995). An infertility primer for family therapists: Medical, social and psychological dimensions. *Family Process, 34,* 219–229.

Meyers, M., Weinshel, M., Scharf, C., Kezur, D., Diamond, R., & Rait, D.S. (1995). An infertility primer for family therapists: Working with couples who struggle with infertility. *Family Process, 34,* 231–240.

Perry, B. D. (1994). Neurobiological sequelae of childhood trauma: PTSD in children. In M. M. Murburg (Ed.), *Catecholamine function in posttraumatic stress disorder: Emerging concepts* (pp. 233–255). Washington, DC: American Psychiatric Press.

Peterson, B. D., Newton, C. R., & Rosen, K. H. (2003). Examining congruence between partners' perceived infertility-related stress and its relationship to marital adjustment and depression in infertile couples. *Family Process, 42,* 59–70.

Reiss, D. (1981). *The family's construction of reality.* Cambridge, MA: Harvard University Press.

RESOLVE of Illinois (2002). *New member resource guide.* Chicago, IL: RESOLVE of Illinois, Inc.

Rolland, J. S. (1990). Anticipatory loss: A family systems developmental framework. *Family Process, 29,* 229–244.

Rothschild, B. (2000). *The body remembers: The psychophysiology of trauma and trauma treatment.* New York: W. W. Norton.

Salzer, L. P. (1991). *Surviving infertility: A comprehensive guide through the emotional crisis of infertility.* New York: Harper Collins.

Schnarch, D. (1997). *Passionate marriage.* New York: W. W. Norton.

Schnarch, D. (2002). *Resurrecting* sex. New York: Harper Collins.

Stammer, H., Wischmann, T., & Verres, R. (2002). Counseling and couple therapy for infertile couples. *Family Process, 41,* 111–122.

van der Kolk, B. A. (1994). The body keeps the score. *Harvard Review of Psychiatry, 1,* 253–265.

van der Kolk, B. A. (2002). The assessment and treatment of complex PTSD. In R. Yehuda (Ed.), *Treating trauma survivors with PTSD* (pp. 127–156). Washington, DC: American Psychiatric Press.

Walsh, F., & McGoldrick, M. (Eds.). (1991). *Living beyond loss: Death in the family.* New York: W. W. Norton.

Zilbergeld, B. (1992). *The new male sexuality: The truth about men, sex and pleasure.* New York: Bantam Books.

Zoldbrod, A. (1997). *Sex smart: How your childhood shaped your sexual life and what to do about it.* New York: New Harbinger.

7

When Parents Age: Unique Stressors of Adult Children

FREDA B. FRIEDMAN

Holidays in my family have their traditions: for Thanksgiving, the wonderful turkey smells, the grown-up kids gathering around the turkey bones in the kitchen and chatting while having a second meal of leftovers; for Fourth of July, the barbecue, the red, white, and blue decorations, and the younger kids doing their own parade. Always, the extra folding table and chairs and my mother making sure that everyone is having a good time. And then one year, my mother said she "wouldn't mind" if I took over the Thanksgiving ritual. That same year, my father handed over the turkey carving to my brother. I realized they were getting older and maybe, even, a little frail.

That was the year Susan Miller turned 48. Her mother had just turned 75, her father, 82. Her parents had always been active and involved, never asked for help and never complained about getting older. Susan always thought of her parents as kind of ageless . . . until that Thanksgiving. She began to notice that her mother's hands trembled a little, that her father had trouble catching his breath as he walked up the stairs. She noticed, but she didn't want to acknowledge the changes.

Bruce Dodd's parents are a bit younger. His father decided to accept a buyout package from his company and take an early retirement at age 64. His mom is still active in many community groups. Neither of his parents is ready to retire from life, and both want to take advantage of their health and energy to embark on some of the adventures they lacked time and money to pursue earlier in their lives.

> My parents act like they are in their early 20s. I'm delighted that they are having such a good time, but, to tell you the truth, my siblings and I are constantly worried about them. They are trekking in the Himalayas right now and next winter plan to rent a little camper trailer and drive through Mexico and Central America. It's great, but what happens if they get sick or stranded? My dad had a heart attack in his 40s and has been okay since, but you never know. . . . They call us every few weeks from wherever they are, but I know they would never admit to their kids that they are having any trouble. I did find out that on one of their trips to Africa last year, Mom had to be treated in the hospital for a few days for dehydration. They said they dealt with it and we couldn't have done anything anyway, so what would have been the point of telling us.

Alicia Santos's mother is widowed, lives alone in the same town as Alicia, and has diabetes, heart problems, and glaucoma. At 82, she still has a few friends living in the area, but many are dying off. She is fiercely independent and never wants to bother Alicia or her other children with her problems. She resents any interference from them and assures them constantly that she's doing "just fine."

> One morning, I called my mom and no one answered. I tried her all day and no answer. It was the winter and a cold snowy day. I didn't think she'd be out building a snow fort that day. When I stopped by her house on my way home from work, I found her collapsed on the floor. She had fallen, hit her head, and blacked out. When she came to, she said she couldn't get up. Despite her protests, I called 911. The ambulance came, the whole bit. She had broken a few ribs and her hip. One month later, mom is ready to be discharged from the rehab facility where she went after the hospital. She insists on going back to her house. This has opened up so many issues and problems I never dreamt of.

For most people in their late 30s to 60s, these stories have a familiar ring to them. Though Susan, Bruce, and Alicia have never met each other; live in different parts of the country; have different cultural and ethnic backgrounds, education, and economic levels; and have vastly different issues facing them professionally and personally, they share one thing that brings them together on common ground: worry about aging parents who are experiencing decrease in functioning, changing lifestyles, and/or varying degrees of acceptance or denial about their capacity to live independently. The onset of emotional, physical, vocational, and financial changes in elderly parents has been identified as one of the most pervasive health problems middle-aged people face today (Anderson, 2002; Rolland, 1999).

The U.S. Census Bureau (2000) reported that older adults—those aged 55 and older—numbered 25 million men and 31 million women in 2000; and more than three quarters of those 65 and older had at least one living child. Despite the assumption that children nowadays grow up, move far away from their parents, and seldom visit, national surveys reveal that 85 percent of the elderly with living children have at least one child who lives less than an hour away, and 66% of the elderly respondents had seen one of their children the very day they were interviewed or the day before (Silverstone & Hyman, 1989). Indeed, only 2% had not seen any of their children within the past year.

THE SANDWICH GENERATION

The adult children of the aging are often referred to as the *sandwich generation*. On one side are their younger children, careers, social and personal commitments, and desires; on the other side, their parents with their wide variety of physical and emotional issues. When an extra generation or two —older grandparents or even their own grandchildren—are added to the mix, there's often a triple or quadruple layer sandwich. These adult children, generally middle aged themselves, often find that dealing with all these layers of life is very stressful. Though they are usually motivated by concern and love, they are often also dealing with a sense of duty, guilt, and responsibility. Their emotions about their parents, their siblings, and themselves are likely to add several layers to an already complex situation.

That's the way life is these days for many people. Fifty years ago, it was unusual for one family to include living members of four and sometimes five generations. Now it's not only more usual, but part of most people's expected life pattern.

It is not the eventual death, but the illness and declining functioning of aging parents that affects adult children in profound and often unexpected ways. Furthermore, it often reactivates many old and sometimes dormant sibling relationships among the adult children of aging parents.

NEW SOCIAL TRENDS

The premature illness or death of a child, parent, or spouse garners a lot of attention because it is considered traumatic and unexpected. But the normal, even difficult, aging of an elderly parent is part of the expected life course. And just because it is expected, many people don't make plans or preparations. They often don't even think about it until they are flooded or engulfed by a problematic situation.

The biggest emerging factor is, of course, the ever-increasing number of older men and women in our society. Current trends and future projections include the following:

1. The population of aging parents is not only growing, but is changing in terms of longevity, health status, and needs. In the United States alone, there are 35 million people over the age of 65, and they will number 54 million by 2020. Projections suggest that a quarter of the population will be over 65 early in the next century.
2. The caregivers for the expanding senior population—their children and relatives primarily—range in age from 40 to 69; 72 percent of them are women (Berman & Shulman, 2001).
3. A baby-boom generation will soon arrive at *Golden Pond* or at the threshold of retirement.
4. There is an increasing geographical dispersion among family members.
5. Increasing numbers of programs, legislation, and expanded services and institutions will be required to meet the needs of the aging populace. These will offer many more options than in the past, which will have varying effects on the quality of life of the elderly and of their middle-aged children.
6. Families of the elderly will have many more options in their caretaker roles.
7. The traditional three-generation family, once rare, is almost ubiquitous these days, and the four-generation family no longer surprises anyone. Even the five-generation family is not uncommon, extending the family further and presenting problems almost unknown in the past. It is not unusual for middle-aged couples to have two generations of retirees ahead of them—parents in their 60s and 70s coping with their own aging while simultaneously trying to help their parents aged 80, 90, and even 100.
8. The prevalence of divorce and remarriage has produced a proliferation of step relationships—not only step-mothers, -fathers, -sisters, -brothers, -sons, and -daughters, but also step-grandmothers and step-grandfathers.
9. Family caregivers, formerly isolated with their own individual problems, are now receiving public recognition for the central role they play in the lives of their elderly relatives. Programs originally developed exclusively for the aged themselves are now being designed to assist, extend, and relieve the ongoing care provided by one or more family members.

10. Many old sibling patterns and experiences from childhood are reenacted and reexperienced as brothers and sisters deal with their aging parents. Stressors in sibling relationships that had been subtle or dormant since childhood are often reawakened

THE RANGE OF ISSUES FOR ADULT CHILDREN AND ELDERLY PARENTS

The problems that complicate life for the elderly (and for their adult children) are broad and can be overwhelming. These include the objective problems of aging—the normal physical, psychological, and social losses experienced by the elderly—as well as the range of responses and different ways the elderly learn to compensate for their losses. The objective problems are complicated by the emotional responses of both the elderly and their adult children. These emotions color the interactions between the generations, affect relationships between siblings, and help determine whether families work together or undermine each other. The solutions families find for the problems that arise between elderly parents and their adult children range from workable to untenable. It is often when their solutions have become untenable that families seek assistance and advice.

Until recently, there was little easily accessible assistance or information for the adult children of elderly parents. The past 20 years have seen an increasing attempt to fill that void, including organizations such as the Alliance for Children and Parents, the advent of a whole new profession of geriatric care managers to assist families with concrete services and resources, and self-help books on surviving an aging parent (Berman & Shulman, 2001; Silverstone & Hyman, 1989). Many of these books and other resources focus on strategies and techniques to deal with difficult situations, for example, plans for handling health care, money matters, and family issues; strategies for caring for an aging parent in their home (or one's own); and warning signs of cancer, Alzheimer's disease, heart attacks, and strokes.

These guidelines and guidebooks are helpful to educate, guide, and validate family members' concerns, particularly for family members who seek support and assistance. However, the more usual pattern is for adult children not to seek support until long after they have begun to face and feel stressed by the issues related to elderly parents. Or they seek medical help or emotional support for other, more apparent issues, such as depression, anxiety, fatigue, or physical problems. Thus, it is important for clinicians to be alert to the potential and actual stressors many middle-aged people experience related to their aging parents.

The professional literature offers some material to help guide clinicians and families, although there is surprisingly little research on the impact chronic illness in elderly parents can have on adult children. Most of the research has focused on the impact of caretaking (or lack thereof) on the elderly and on their formal and informal caretakers (usually children and relatives). Although much is known about confronting illness, disease, and disability, only recently have researchers and clinicians seriously examined chronic conditions in the context of adult children and aging parents (Bengston & Putney, 2000).

RESEARCH ON ADULT CHILDREN WITH AGING PARENTS

In the literature on aging parents and adult children, the research has focused predominantly on four main categories of variables:

- *Systemic relational impact*—the impact of declining functioning on the family systems of aging parents and adult children. These include the observable repercussions, such as changes in contact between parent and child and communication patterns among family members. They also include the covert repercussions, such as the emotional responses and stress level of family members.
- *Relationship status*—the impact on individual members of the family system with regard to such demographics as (a) whether parents are widowed, their level of physical and emotional functioning, place of residence (alone at home, assisted living, or in a nursing home, for example); (b) the marital status of adult children and their gender, geographical proximity, and health and socioeconomic status; and (c) the roles that various family members play, such as caregiver, financial coordinator, and driver.
- *Relationship quality*—the tenor of interactions and level of satisfaction family members experience about their relationships with each other.
- *Relationship behaviors*—such phenomena as attachment responses, hostile remarks, and critical or validating interactions.

These relationship variables are certainly not definitive or exhaustive, but merely reflect one way of categorizing the foci of research in this area, and they help clinicians better evaluate and understand the multifaceted issues that arise.

Systemic Impact

The gradual or sudden change in emotional and physical functioning of an elderly parent has repercussions that are not always immediately visible. However, therapists need to be aware of the potentially serious and far-reaching impact an aging parent can have on the rest of the family members. Often, adult children and other family members are not even aware or deny the significance of the impact an aging parent can have. Other times their issues related to aging parents may become the elephant in the room, not openly discussed yet an important factor in a family member's presenting problem.

For example, Joan, a 45-year-old married fifth-grade teacher presented with severe depression that was affecting all areas of her functioning. She and her husband attributed this to her lack of social life. Eventually, the therapist learned that the woman's elderly widowed mother, who lived in another state, was becoming an increasing source of constant worry, anxiety, and aggravation to her daughter. On further questioning, the therapist learned that Joan was feeling guilty about not visiting or phoning her mother more frequently and was concerned about the prospect of moving her mother to live with or near her. Although Joan had three siblings, she was the only daughter. Her family has a multigenerational pattern of daughters acting as primary caregivers to their aging parents. Joan felt that her own plate was more than full and dreaded the possibility of her mother moving closer. Because she and her mother had always had a good and close relationship, Joan was ashamed of her feelings and had not really discussed them with anyone. However, she was experiencing a great deal of emotional turmoil and dealing with it by becoming more withdrawn and isolative with her friends and family.

As in any situation involving trauma and change, the impact is not static; it changes over time. This is particularly true in the case of aging parents whose level of physical, emotional, and financial functioning is often on an inconsistent and unpredictable course toward an inevitable outcome. The experiences of family members can be very different at different stages of illness and disability in an elderly parent (Rolland, 1994).

Rolland (1994) discussed the tasks of families during different stages of an illness; some of these stages apply equally to the onset of illness in an elderly parent as they do to illness in a younger family member: When an elderly parent is first diagnosed and treatment is initiated, families must quickly gather their resources and reorganize to collect crucial information and make rapid decisions about treatment. Roles and responsibilities shift and are redistributed as the family organizes around the illness. Families who are close and can pull together often have an easier time than those whose members are less cohesive or more independent. However, when an ill parent enters a chronic phase where treatment may be long and drawn out, families must again organize for the long haul (Biank & Sori, 2003). This requires flexibility to make sure all family members have their own developmental needs met while ensuring that the sick member is cared for adequately.

A relapse or recurrence of a serious illness can often be even more devastating than the initial episode. Families who have bolstered up their resources and strength to deal with the original illness may feel more depleted and lagging in hope.

The lines of communication between an aging parent and adult children may be strained or ever shifting. Some family members may feel burdened by too much information; others may feel left out of the loop. Some of the adult children may feel too overwhelmed, preoccupied, or just uninformed about the serious and far-reaching implications of these events for their family.

Status and Roles of Family Members

The functioning of elderly people encompasses a broad range. At one extreme are the octogenarians who are still extremely competent in all areas of their lives; they work competently, drive safely, and effectively manage their own finances, meal preparation, and leisure time. A number of remarkable men and women chart new courses for their lives after they turn 70; they experience a rebirth by starting new businesses, returning to school, or embarking on new romantic relationships. These very able individuals function well, can make their own decisions, and decide what is best for them. When it comes to needing help, they usually know when they need it, what they need, and how much they need. Elderly parents who fall into this enviable group mostly need quiet support and acceptance for their choices and lifestyles.

At the other end of the continuum are elderly parents who truly cannot manage their basic needs. These elderly people pose a danger to themselves and others by attempting tasks that are beyond their abilities; they run the risk of setting fires in their kitchen or driving cars unsafely. These situations are even more tragic when elderly parents cannot or will not admit that their functioning is severely compromised as they insist on trying to do everything on their own just as they always have. These parents are an endless source of anxiety for their adult children. There are other variations that give adult children palpitations. Some elderly parents get along independently but in less acceptable, less socially approved ways. Some develop a lifestyle that is safe and satisfying for them, but that is embarrassing or foreign to their children. An elderly, widowed father may begin to pursue an active sex life with companions whom his children disapprove of or even despise. A mother may develop an obsession for some group or activity that consumes her time and resources.

The roles that parents have played throughout their younger life in the family may become more accentuated, such as the dictatorial father or the complaining or controlling mother. As youngsters, the children may have learned to tolerate, sidestep, or cater to the roles played by their parents, but as adults the children may no longer be willing or able to accommodate in the same way.

The adult children in the family also have their own styles of functioning and roles in their family of origin. Many adult children have formed their own family and disconnected from earlier roles in their family of origin. The baby brother of the family may now be a competent journalist and doting father and husband, but when he returns to the family fold, he is still treated as the youngest and perhaps the one most in need of coddling and least able to follow through on responsibilities.

Sibling Issues

Dealing with aging parents often brings siblings together on new terrain and highlights strengths and stressors of their relationships that have been subtle or dormant since childhood. How siblings come together and negotiate this new terrain is affected by many of the latent themes of childhood—a complex mixture of friendship and collaboration, rivalry, envy, and conspiracy around parental issues.

What adult children do for their aging parents and how they negotiate their behavior with siblings are salient personal issues for many people, affecting almost all siblings who have had, currently have, or may in the future have a parent who is elderly. It ultimately may concern all of us who have children and hope to grow old ourselves.

The earliest sibling bonds are usually formed in the context of their relationship to parents. As siblings grow into adulthood, the focus tends to move away from each other to their own children and to the sibling issues they have to deal with as parents. When siblings interact as adults, they are usually more able to relinquish the roles they enacted with each other as children. But as their parents age and they are caught in the sandwich generation, many adult siblings find themselves reconnecting on a new basis that often includes many old issues. Dealing with issues related to their aging parents often reactivates deep connections or reignites old fissures in their relationships.

How siblings reconnect in adulthood is part of the historical narrative of families. Some of the early sibling issues will have remained the same. But many new factors also emerge that have an ever-increasing influence on the way siblings deal with their aging parents and with each other (Friedman, 2002). Many old sibling patterns and experiences from childhood are reenacted and reexperienced as brothers and sisters deal with their aging parents. Subtle and dormant stressors and latent themes from their childhood relationships are reawakened.

Several issues can arise. The reenactments are frequently influenced by the idealization transference that siblings experience. And when the siblings begin to deal with each other around aging parent issues, there is a regressive pull to fall back into their childhood roles. Overall, the degree of differentiation in a family and among its individual members will parallel the degree of conflict between siblings as they deal with their aging parents. During this new stage of life, the attachment patterns developed in our earliest relationships heavily influence the way we renegotiate relationships with our siblings and aging parents.

In many families, there are countless stories that portray family members negatively, such as the irresponsible brother who is perennially getting himself into altercations or the intrusive sister who is continually offering unsolicited advice. These stories enhance our understanding of the sibling experience in adulthood and can help inform our approach to the actual and potential problems. For most adult siblings, the challenge in their relationship is not so much a matter of getting things done as it is preventing the resurgence of old conflicts.

Relational Patterns

Many theoretical paradigms lend themselves to better understanding the patterns that emerge when adult children deal with aging parents. Family systems theory underscores the importance of relationship patterns learned in the family of origin. Attachment theory helps us understand how early patterns of attachment are brought to adult relationships and affect the development of the family system. These, together with variables such as culture, ethnicity, multigenerational patterns, gender patterns, and cognitive and emotional styles of individuals affect the evolution of family issues as adult children deal with aging parents. The key is the *patterns* of the relationships that emerge (M. Reitz, personal communication, 2003).

Family members often assume that because they all are members of the same family, they all see the world in similar ways. On a rational level, they may realize that this assumption has not held true in thousands of situations, but people nevertheless cling to it, particularly during times of stress. Such faulty assumptions often play themselves out in terms of expectations and miscommunication, providing fertile ground for family conflict and trouble.

To summarize, chronic illness in aging parents influences relationships by altering relationship quality, roles, responsibilities, and social support. However, the onset and course of chronic illness and declining functionality in aging parents does not necessarily have a detrimental influence on the family relational system and individual relationships within the family. Although the issues facing adult children and aging parents can affect their relationships in a variety of ways, many are positive; astute clinicians can provide significant help so that families achieve more positive outcomes.

Attachment Patterns in the Context of Chronic Illness

Research on attachment has grown since Bowlby's (1980) seminal work. Some of the more recent research indicates that attachment behaviors play a central role in chronic illness (Maunder & Hunter, 2001). Specifically, it has been proposed that insecure attachment styles are associated with the onset and exacerbation of chronic health problems. Feeney (1998), for example, found that those with an anxious ambivalent attachment style reported significantly more physical symptoms and negative affect when compared with securely attached individuals. Avoidantly attached individuals also visited health professionals less often than did securely attached individuals. Research on defensiveness and repression (which create a presentation similar to an avoidant attachment style) indicates that individuals who repress negative emotions experience elevated levels of physiological arousal and multiple health problems (Esterling, Antoni, Kumar, & Schneiderman, 1993; Weinberger, 1998).

Studies on couples indicate that individuals with an avoidant attachment style are at risk for developing chronic illness and exacerbating health problems; in addition, they appear to be much less likely to access and use support (Kowal, Johnson, & Lee, 2003). Individuals with an avoidant attachment style had coping styles characterized by the suppression of negative affect and avoidance of support-seeking behavior (Kotler, Buzwell, Romeo, & Bowland, 1994). This fits with the results of studies linking insecure supports with higher levels of stress in the caregivers of people with chronic illness (Cicirelli, 1994).

It is not surprising, therefore, that chronic illness in elderly parents and attachment behaviors within the family appear to play central roles in the lives of adult children dealing with aging parents. The connection between stress and the attachment behaviors between adult children and parents with chronic illness appears to be mediated by stress regulation, affect regulation, and ability to engage in health-promoting behavior (Kowal et al., 2003).

IMPACT ON CAREGIVERS

This chapter touches on some of the issues related to the impact of aging parents on adult children. As aging parents face illness, retirement, the death of a spouse, and other enormous changes, their children face many questions about how involved they will become in their parents' lives. Many investigators have documented the negative biopsychological effects associated with aging parents and conceptualized those effects in various ways in the literature. Common concepts include caregiver burden (Zarit, Reever, & Bach-Peterson, 1980), caregiver strain (Archbold, Stewart, Greenlick, & Harvath, 1990), and caregiver stress (Nolan, Grant, & Ellis, 1990; Perrlin, Mullan, Semple, & Skaff, 1990). Other researchers have examined caregiving and dealing with aging parents from a more positive or neutral perspective. For example, positive aspects have been conceptualized as caregiver esteem (Given et al., 1992; Nijboer et al., 2000), caregiver satisfaction (Lawton, Moss, Kleban, Glicksman, & Rovine, 1991), and finding or making meaning through caregiving (Ayres, 2000; Farran, Miller, Kaufman, Donner, & Fogg, 1999; Folkman, 1997).

WORKING WITH FAMILIES FACING CHRONIC ILLNESS IN AGING PARENTS

Although a multitude of approaches have been developed for working with distressed families, relatively few have been specifically applied to individuals and families who are facing the chronic illness and declining function of elderly parents. (See appendix for suggested guidelines.) The majority of the research on the clinical efficacy of treatments is geared toward couples in which one or both partners are chronically ill. Many of these approaches hold considerable promise. Emotionally focused therapy (Kowal et al., 2003; Johnson, 1996; Johnson & Greenberg, 1985), existential therapy (Lantz, 1986), family systems therapy (Rolland, 1999), medical family therapy (McDaniel, Doherty, & Hepworth, 1992/1998), feminist collaborative therapy (Skerrett, 1996), and cognitive-behavioral therapy (Schmaling & Sher, 1997) have all been discussed in the context of chronic illness in couples.

An approach for working with individuals and families of elderly parents must focus on many of the basic issues facing them: communication, attachment, intense emotional reactions, grief, and intimacy. Emotionally focused therapy (EFT) is an integration of experiential and systemic approaches that focuses on intrapsychic processes (how individuals process emotional experiences), interpersonal processes (how family members organize their interactions into patterns and cycles), and attachment processes (how members' attachments may have been injured and require repair). As such, it addresses family members' experience of chronic illness as well as relationship dynamics. This focus is consistent with the work of Rolland (1994), McDaniel et al. (1992/1998), Kowal et al. (2003), Cohen and Ganz (1988), and Kirschner (1979).

A Case Example

In the following case, the applicability of using EFT for working with a family facing declining functioning in an elderly parent is illustrated.

Joanne had been working individually with a therapist for about 2 years, beginning when she began to experience some distress following the death of her father and some changes in her work situation. Joanne is an attractive woman of 54, with short light brown hair who sports stylish glasses and tailored clothing. She and her 60-year-old husband had recently moved to the area because of a job transfer for her husband. They had previously lived in New England, where she and her family had grown up and lived for most of her adult life.

During the first 2 years of therapy, Joanne focused on issues related to her relationship with her father, who had been a devoted husband but a somewhat emotionally distant father to her. He had died suddenly of a heart attack, and she felt there was much unfinished business in her relationship with him that she wanted to process. There were issues at work involving male authority figures that she was able to connect, in part, to her relationship with her father.

During the course of therapy, I learned a great deal about Joanne's family: She was the oldest of three children. She had two younger brothers, aged 50 and 47. The older brother, Michael, a successful lawyer, lived in Florida and had three children. His wife's parents, who lived near him, had been ailing during the past several years and Michael and his wife had spent a lot of time and effort seeing them through various illnesses, hospitalizations, and caretaking dilemmas. They were now settled in a nearby nursing home.

Her younger brother, Zach, lived in Virginia and was a struggling artist and graphic designer. He had always been considered the favorite child in the family according to Joanne and the one who was the least argumentative and assertive. His wife made most of the decisions in their family concerning their two children, ages 7 and 9, and all other matters. Zack went with the flow.

Joanne's two children, both in their 20s, had settled in two different parts of the country after graduating from college, and they were productively involved in launching their careers and romantic relationships. Joanne and her husband had warm and satisfying relationships with their children.

Over time, Joanne's mother increasingly became the focus of our sessions. Sally, Joanne's mother, was 77 and had recently moved to Florida, after the death of her husband. It was here that she had many friends and several relatives, including Joanne's brother Michael, who lived about 90 miles away from her.

According to Joanne, her mother had always been a difficult, narcissistic woman who was very competitive with Joanne in areas such as looks, achievement, career, and housekeeping. Sally was a strikingly attractive woman, always immaculately groomed and dressed, as well as an extremely gracious hostess for many gatherings for family and friends. However, in her own home, she was subject to frequent mood dysregulation and had a strong need to be in control. She particularly clashed with her husband, her middle child, and frequently with Joanne. She often held up her younger son as an example of "the kind of relationship a mother should have with her children." She had been healthy until several months after her husband died, when she began to develop myriad symptoms that were eventually diagnosed as Parkinson's disease.

Sally and her own parents had had a conflictual relationship that enmeshed her children's lives. Her parents were devoted grandparents and Joanne and her brothers adored them. Sally rather resented her parents' close relationship with her children, but appreciated their frequent babysitting and help. When their functioning began to decline from chronic illness, Sally had gone to great lengths to support her parents during the years of their illnesses. She drove them to their numerous appointments, took them shopping, and visited them often, first at their home and eventually in a nursing home in her neighborhood.

Despite the chronic nature of her illness, Sally initially was able to live a full and satisfying life that included many friends and leisure activities in her beautiful new Florida home. She denied any problems, but over time Sally's friends began telling Joanne and her siblings that Sally was experiencing fainting spells, dizziness, disorientation, and difficulty walking. Sally denied all these symptoms and hid them well when she was with her children. She even concealed two fender benders that Joanne only discovered when she was visiting her mother and went to pick up her mother's car at the local service station. Eventually it became clear that Sally was not taking medication consistently and was developing more and more difficulties with activities of daily living, even though she continuously denied this and became argumentative, belligerent, and increasingly vague in her discussions with Joanne and Michael.

Michael would occasionally get calls from neighbors and friends about disturbing things Sally was doing. Zach was the voice of optimism; he kept encouraging Sally to do her usual activities, and he minimized her difficulties. He made plane reservations for her to visit him and other distant friends and relatives, and these trips often had crisis episodes associated with them that involved falls, emergency room visits, and even a hospitalization. Joanne felt like a mediator trying to help ease the conflicts and lessen the tension between her two brothers, who were becoming increasingly polarized about Sally. Joanne's own feeling was that Sally could probably be kept in her own home with more full-time help, but Sally resisted having anyone in her house for more than an occasional cleaning.

I explored with Joanne how she experienced her relationship with Sally and her brothers at the present time. Joanne's focus was on her mother and brothers. She described her guilt over being so far away from her mother and also her relief that she was not closer. She worried greatly about Sally's emotional and physical well-being and about Michael's burden because he was the closest sibling to Sally. Joanne had numerous colds within the last few months and her blood pressure was up at her last checkup. She commented that she didn't know what to do with her mother anymore, because Sally resisted Joanne's attempts to implement measures that would make her mother safer and more comfortable. She also felt very frustrated with her brothers, who were each going off in their own direction with their assumptions and responses to Sally.

Joanne described the dynamics in the family and we began to see the reenactments and repetitious patterns that were occurring among the siblings and with Sally—the old triangle between Sally and Zach and the rest of the family, the insecure attachment issues that had characterized much of Joanne and Sally's relationship, and the assumptions and expectations about how elderly parents should be cared for.

After one weekend of visiting her mother, Joanne came to an appointment exasperated and weary. She had spent the weekend arguing with her mother endlessly about the driving issue, the condition of her house, the need for her to take medication more consistently, and her unrealistic plans for the following summer—a cruise to Greece with Elderhostel, with walks that were described as "moderately strenuous."

Much of Joanne's frustration had come to a head. She was ready to throw her hands up in defeat, but knew she couldn't.

It was time to radically focus on practical and emotional issues, including the emotions Joanne had about her mother and siblings as well as some of the still unprocessed feelings about her deceased father and beloved grandparents.

There were interpersonal issues between Joanne and her two brothers and each of them with Sally, regarding present and past issues. There were undercurrents of jealousy, sibling rivalry, old resentments, and a wish to work collaboratively. Unfortunately, they had some skill deficits about working collaboratively, given the modeling they had experienced with a very domineering mother and a passive-aggressive father. Finally, there were many concrete practical issues such as appropriate health care and living arrangements, financial planning, and division of labor for caretaking responsibilities.

Joanne and I made plans to have a conference call with her two brothers and to discuss issues that had been simmering below the surface for all of them. The plan was for the siblings to use their time talking together to voice their own feelings and, eventually, to develop a collaborative plan that would allow Sally to have a voice and for the adult children to establish their bottom lines regarding her safety.

Transcript of Conference   participants include
Therapist
Sally, the elderly mother
Joanne, the daughter
Michael, the older brother and primary caretaker
Zach, the younger brother

Therapist: Good morning, Sally, Michael, Zach. Joanne and I are here today so that all of us can talk together about some of the family issues that have been on your minds. I've had a chance to talk with each of you briefly in the last week about some of the issues you'd like to put on the table today and I'd like to outline them briefly today.

The first is the general issue of how each of you can support and help each other. Sally, you've said that you feel that you can manage in a lot of ways and that you think your adult children are trying to be controlling. Joanne, Michael, and Zach, you've all said that you want to support your mother to be as independent as she can be, but that you worry about her safety and well-being. So I am going to try to help you begin to talk together.

A family conference is an alternative to having one family member make the decisions, willingly or unwillingly. This technique may not work for all families, but when successful it provides the forum for open communication between all members, including the aging parent. The family conference does not have to be a formal affair; it can be a conference call if family members are geographically dispersed. Although some family members may not be willing to participate, the one member who is essential is the aging parent.

Therapist: I want to make sure everyone has a chance to talk today. To make this work well, I thought it would be helpful to lay out some ground rules; if anyone has any ideas that would help this work better, let's make sure we include them. So here are my ground rules: We all have a chance to speak and don't interrupt each other. We come up with an agenda at the beginning. I want everyone to feel that they have a chance to speak and that they won't be criticized in this discussion. And at the end, I'm going to summarize what we've talked about, and we'll follow up with a conference call again next week.

Family members have not usually been accustomed to discussing difficult and toxic matters in an organized and supportive manner with each other. Including the elderly parent is critical; otherwise carefully discussed plans made without that parent are likely to fail. If an elderly parent is unable to participate in the family conference, they should be informed about the discussion. Some semblance of cooperation and partnership can evolve in discussions like this if the therapist models for each family member an attitude of respect and validation for each person's opinions and point of view.

Therapist: Why don't we start with issues that each of you would like to address today and in future conference calls, and then we'll try to make an agenda. Let's start with you, Sally.

It is essential that all those participating in the discussion have a chance to speak their minds and to explain their own personal ideas, concerns, preferences, and suggestions. In the early sessions of a family conference, the therapist will probably have to play a more active role in order to keep the participation of each member somewhat balanced and the discussion focused. If tension starts to increase, the therapist can point out the increase in tension, normalize it, and facilitate discussion of what seems to be in the air. The therapist can also help to encourage and model comments so that there is a balance between acceptance and validation of all participants and support for change.

Sally: Well, I just want to say that I appreciate everyone getting together to talk like this. We usually don't get together at all like this and I think this is a good idea, but I want to make sure that you all pay attention to what I have to say and don't start ganging up on me the way you have in the past sometimes.

   Therapist: Sally, it sounds like you're a little worried about how things are going to go. My guess is that everyone is a little worried about that. I'm going to make sure that no one gangs up on anyone else and that everyone has a chance to voice their opinions and be heard by the others. What specifically do you want to bring up?

Establishing safety and normalizing the anxiety that family members may be feeling is helpful so that there is a communal sense of empathy that participants can feel for themselves and others.

> Sally: I want to bring up my driving. I think I should be allowed to drive; I haven't had any serious accidents and I really need my independence. I also need to discuss the help that is sufficient for me. We have had lots of arguments about that.
>
> Therapist: Okay, Sally. Those are two good issues to start with. Why don't we let each of your children express their feelings and concerns and ideas about how to resolve the issues and then we can move to some open discussion and develop a plan.

It is helpful to outline the plan of discussion and planning so that everyone knows in advance what to expect and where to focus the outcome. The family members each give their opinions and suggestions, and the therapist then summarizes each person's comments.

> The therapist then identifies the priority issues that family members have expressed: Sally's safety, the safety of other motorists and pedestrians when Sally is driving, Sally's need for independence, and the anxiety that the adult children are experiencing.

In conversations and conferences such as this, there are many obstacles along the way. Progress is rarely smooth, and it can take time to arrive at any kind of plan. Patience is critical; all family members should be warned of this and also commended for any little progress they do make, even if it is only their willingness not to interrupt each other as often as they might have done in the past.

Some of the usual roadblocks that can interfere with family communication such as this include

- Lack of candor and keeping family secrets
- Hiding feelings and saying what one thinks one *should* be saying, rather than what the person *wants* to be expressing
- Moving too quickly toward a unilateral fix-it solution in an effort to resolve the problem before it has been thoroughly discussed and everyone's opinions considered and aired
- Making promises that won't or can't be kept

Some of these roadblocks came up in the family conference with Sally.

> Michael: Mom, we really want you to continue driving and living in your own house. We know you love that house, and we have all loved coming to all the wonderful holiday dinners that you've

made for us. We really want you to stay there as long as you can. At the same time, we know that your two good friends are moving into Belden Gardens [the assisted living complex nearby], and we think you'd be really happy there, less lonely, and have more activities to enjoy there. Then you wouldn't have to drive so much, especially at night when it's difficult to see.

Sally: I know that Belden Gardens is lovely, but I'm not ready to go there. My two friends are going there because their children don't live anywhere near here, but I know that you are available to take me places when I need to go and really can't get there by myself.

There are several new developments that Michael is not telling Sally about. One of the things that Michael has not mentioned is that his wife is putting more pressure on him to get help for his mother. Her elderly parents have just moved to a nearby retirement community and are also beginning to require more help. Michael's teenage son had recently been suspended from high school because of drug and alcohol use and was participating in a rehab program that involves parental participation. Sally does not know about her grandson's difficulties, and Michael is not eager to share that with his mother. Most of all, Sally's doctor has told the family that Sally should no longer be climbing stairs in her house because of the decreasing mobility related to Parkinson's disease. As long as these secrets are not aired, there will continue to be a stalemate, with Sally seeing no reason to make any changes in her life.

Therapist: Michael, and Sally, we need to discuss more fully the issue of how much you need Michael and how available Michael is. He is certainly willing and wanting to help you out, but he also has many other responsibilities and may not be as available as you need him to be all the time. I know it is probably difficult for Michael to juggle some of those responsibilities and to prioritize them all the time in a way that works for everyone, but that's something that I'm sure you know from your own life and raising children, Sally. Michael, what are some of the issues that are coming up for you that might interfere at times with your being able to come and see your mother and help her out as much as before? And Sally, what are some of the things that you are wanting Michael to do more of than before?

By introducing some of these questions, the therapist is helping both Michael and Sally to put their feelings and concerns on the table in a way that is more candid and direct.

As the discussion continues, there are likely to be many gridlocks and impasses. But these do not mean failure. For many families, the whole process of getting together and trying to talk openly about difficult issues may be a new experience. Learning how to be more open and honest with each other, to approach issues that were unacknowledged elephants in the room before, and to stop hiding behind old masks can be an uncomfortable and anxiety-provoking experience for many families. But it can also open up lines of communication and help family members learn a new language and ways of relating to each other. A family therapist may be able to help diffuse, or at least detonate and control, the grenades that family members have been avoiding for years.

Although family therapy was originally considered effective mainly for families dealing with difficulties concerning young and teenaged children or marital difficulties, it is now being used more frequently for extended families dealing with the issues of elderly parents. Of course, family therapy (or even individual therapy) with one member of the family is not a sure-fire solution to the many issues that can arise. Inevitably, sometimes even after all steps have been taken and all the traps dealt with, agreement still will not have been reached. But even when solutions cannot be found or agreed upon, there is always forward movement when a family can learn to communicate more openly and directly with each other.

CONCLUSION

Many adult children and their elderly parents avoid and deflect such discussions for years. Sometimes the discussions never happen or happen after years of avoidance. Families who are able to courageously work together, often with the help of a therapist, usually find that they can develop new and more effective ways of relating to each other rather than reenacting some of the more dysfunctional and damaging patterns of the past.

There is already enough sadness, guilt, and stress experienced by family members as elderly parents develop chronic illness or decreased functioning. There are basically two roads from which to choose: the road of avoidance and denial, which leads to unresolved and troubled feelings that live on long after the death of the parents, or the road of hard work and anxiety that involves facing the challenges with an opportunity for adult children to repair bridges and build stronger ties with both their parents and siblings.

REFERENCES

Anderson, R. N. (2002). Deaths: Leading causes for 2000. *National Vital Statistics Reports, 50,* 1–85.

Archbold, P., Stewart, B., Greenlick, M., & Harvath, T. (1990). Mutuality and preparedness as predictors of caregiver role strain. *Research in Nursing and Health, 13,* 375–384.

Ayers, L. (2000). Narratives of family caregiving: The process of making meaning. *Research in Nursing and Health, 23,* 677–685.

Bengston, V. L., & Putney, N. M. (2000). Who will care for tomorrow's elderly? Consequences of population aging East and West. In V. L. Bengston, K. D. Kim, G. C. Meyers, & K. S. Eun (Eds.), *Aging in East and West: Families, States and the Elderly* (pp. 263–285). New York: Springer.

Berman, R., & Shulman, B. (2001). *How to survive your aging parents.* Chicago, IL: Surrey Books.

Biank, N., & Sori, C. (2003). *The therapist's notebook for children, adolescents and families.* New York: Hawthorne Press.

Bowlby, J. (1980). *Attachment and loss, Vol. 3, Loss: Sadness and Depression.* London: Penguin Books.

Cicirelli, V. G. (1994). Sibling relationships in cross-cultural perspective. *Journal of Marriage and the Family, 56,* 7–20.

Cohen, S. Z., & Gans, B. M. (1988). *The other generation gap: The middle-aged and their aging parents.* New York: Dodd, Mead.

Esterling, B. A., Antoni, M. H., Kumar, M., & Schneiderman, N. (1993). Defensiveness, trait anxiety and Epstein Barr viral capsid antigen antibody titers in healthy college students. *Health Psychology, 12,* 132–139.

Farran, C., Miller, B., Kaufman, J., Donner, E., & Fogg, L. (1999). Finding meaning through caregiving: Development of an instrument for family caregivers. *Journal of Clinical Psychology, 55,* 1107–1125.

Feeney, J. A. (1998). Adult attachment and relationship-centered anxiety: Responses to physical and emotional distancing. In J. A. Simpson & W. S. Rholes (Eds.), *Attachment theory and close relationships* (pp. 189–218). New York: Guilford.

Folkman, S. (1997). Positive psychological states and coping with severe stress. *Social Science and Medicine, 45,* 1207–1221.

Friedman, F. B. (2002). *Adult sibling relations and aging parents.* Unpublished doctoral dissertation, Institute for Clinical Social Work, Chicago, IL.

Given, C., Given, B., Stommel, M., Collins, C., King, S., & Franklin S. (1992). The caregiver reaction assessment for caregivers to persons with chronic physical and mental impairments. *Research in Nursing and Health, 15,* 271–283.

Johnson, S. M., & Greenberg, L. S. (1995). The emotionally focused approach to problems in adult attachment. In N. S. Jacobson & A. S. Gurman (Eds.), *The clinical handbook of marital therapy, 2nd ed.* (pp. 121–141). New York: Guilford.

Kirschner, C. (1979). The aging family in crisis—a problem in family living. *Social Casework, 60* (April), 209–216.

Kotler, T., Buzwell, S., Romeo, Y., & Bowland, J. (1994). Avoidant attachment as a risk factor for health. *British Journal of Medical Psychology, 67,* 237–245.

Kowal, J., Johnson, S. M., & Lee, A. (2003). Chronic illness in couples: A case for emotionally focused therapy. *Journal of Marital and Family Therapy, 29,* 299–310.

Lantz, J. E. (1986). Family logotherapy. *Contemporary Family Therapy: An International Journal, 8*(2), 124–235.

Lawton, M. P., Moss, M. S., Kleban, M. H., Glicksman, A., & Rovine, M. (1991). A two-factor model of caregiving appraisal and psychological well-being. *Journal of Gerontology, 46,* 181–189.

Maunder, R., & Hunter, J. (2001). Attachment and psychosomatic medicine: Developmental contributions to stress and disease. *Psychosomatic Medicine, 63,* 556–567.

McDaniel, S., Doherty, W., & Hepworth, J. (1992/1998). *Medical family therapy: A biopsychosocial approach to families with health problems.* New York: Basic Books.

Nijboer, C., Triemstra, M., Tempelaar, R., Sanderman, R., & van den Bos, G. (1996). Determinants of caregiving experiences and mental health of partners of cancer patients. *Cancer, 86,* 577–88.

Nijboer, C., Triemstra, M., Tempelaar, R., Mulder, M., Sanderman, R., van den Bos, G. A. M. (2000). Patterns of caregiver experiences among partners of cancer patients. *Gerontologist, 40*, 738–746.

Nolan, M., Grant, G., & Ellis, N. (1990). Stress is in the eye of the beholder: Reconceptualizing the measurement of career burden. *Journal of Advanced Nursing, 15*, 544–555.

Perrlin, L., Mullan, J., Semple, S., & Skaff, M. (1990). Caregiving and the stress process: An overview of concepts and their measures. *The Gerontologist, 30*, 583–594.

Rolland, J. S. (1994). *Families, illness and disability: An integrative treatment model.* New York: Basic Books.

Rolland, J. S. (1999). Parental illness and disability: A family systems framework. *Journal of Family Therapy, 21*, 242–266.

Schmalling, K. B., & Sher, T. G. (1997). Physical health and relationships. In W. K. Halford & H. J. Markman (Eds.), *Clinical handbook of marriage and couples interventions* (pp. 323–345). Chichester, England: John Wiley & Sons.

Schmaling, K. B., & Sher, T. G. (2001). The psychology of couples and illness: Theory, research, and practice. Washington, DC: APA Books.

Silverstone, B., & Hyman, H. (1989). *You and your aging parent: A family guide to emotional, physical and financial problems* (3rd ed.). New York: Random House.

Skerrett, K. (1996). From isolation to mutuality: A feminist collaborative model of couples therapy. *Women & Therapy, 19*(3), 93–106.

U.S. Census Bureau. (2000). *Population profile. 2000 US Census Bureau,* 18–19.

Walsh, F. (1998). *Strengthening family resilience.* New York: Guilford.

Weinberger, D. (1998). Defenses, personality structure and development: Integrating psychodynamic theory into a typological approach to personality. *Journal of Personality, 66*, 1061–1080.

Zarit, S., Reever, K., & Bach-Peterson, J. (1980). Relatives of the impaired elderly: Correlates of feelings of burden. *The Gerontologist, 20*, 650–655.

APPENDIX
CLINICAL GUIDELINES FOR WORKING WITH ADULT CHILDREN
AND AGING PARENTS

The following guidelines are adapted from Silverstone and Hyman (1989):

Identify and evaluate the following:
- The specific problem(s) precisely to gain greater clarity
- Who is involved in the issue and who should be involved or excluded
- What the elderly parent has to say
- Who is willing to be committed and to what degree
- The priorities
- Functional and emotional status of each family member
- Finances and attitudes about money and intergenerational patterns of aging
- Character of the relationship each adult child had with the aging parent earlier in life and has at the time of the parent's decline in functioning
- Unique experiences of each adult child to prior experiences of chronic illness and death (e.g., of another parent, close relative, friend)
- The degree to which each elderly parent and each adult child is able to anticipate the loss of functioning of parent and the impact on themselves
- Misconceptions and misinformation about normal aging and the nature of the chronic illnesses involved
- The loss of familiar roles for elderly parents and reinstatement and/or reenactment of earlier roles for family members
- Past patterns of obstacles and impasses

Plan and implement a forum for family members (face-to-face meeting or conference call), identifying whom to include or exclude. Give everyone a chance to voice his or her opinions and feelings. Strive to reach an agreement and make plans for ongoing evaluation and revision.

Obstacles that may exist include the following:
- Family secrets
- Hidden feelings
- Hastily given promises
- Crisis mentality and desire to find a quick solution rather than long-term planning

8

When Terrorism Threatens Family Functioning

DON R. CATHERALL

Since the dramatic attacks of September 11, 2001, American families have been learning to live with the threat of terrorism. The unique nature of the attacks—using commercial airliners as bombs—pierced many people's assumptions of security and introduced a new source of fear and anxiety into their lives. The magnitude and severity of emotional difficulties following a terrorist attack are much greater when the incident involves large numbers of fatalities, especially when children are included and when the incident leads to a protracted rescue and recovery effort (Sitterle & Gurwitch, 1999). The attacks on the World Trade Center thus produced enormous emotional damage and challenged one of the basic functions of the family (and social structures in general), that is, to provide a sense of security to members and to help members manage fear and anxiety during times of crisis. The ways in which families cope with uncontrollable stressors, such as the threat of terrorism, can either amplify the anxieties and fears of family members or provide a sanctuary from the stress of those emotions.

LIVING WITH THE THREAT OF TERRORISM

The perception of a genuine possibility of terrorist attack has a pronounced impact on a society. In Israel, the time span from 1962 to 1975
showed a marked increase in the frequency of war and terrorist attacks.
Surveys conducted in 1962 and 1975 showed a pronounced shift in concerns on both the personal and national level (Kats, 1982). There was (a)
a drop in the general mood, (b) an increase in fears of war, terrorism, and
the destruction of the country, and (c) a shift in economic concerns from
a focus on increasing productivity to a focus on maintaining a standard
of living. However, it is interesting to note that the terrorists, who committed 271 acts of terrorism in 1979 alone, not only failed to produce sympathy for their cause, but through their actions actually contributed
toward a strengthening of existing antiterrorist attitudes (Friedland &
Merari, 1985).

MEDIA EXPOSURE

Mounting evidence shows that emotional reactions to terrorism can be
exacerbated and extended by media coverage. In a controlled experiment,
a group of Israeli citizens was exposed to television news clips of terrorism and threats to national security, while a control group saw clips unre-
lated to national danger situations. As expected, exposure to media focus
on terrorist danger induced significant levels of anxiety (Slone, 2000). In
the United States, surveys (Schuster et al., 2001; Schlenger et al., 2002)
found that the extent of posttraumatic stress symptoms following the
September 11, 2001, attacks showed a strong correlation with the amount
of televised coverage that individuals watched. A growing body of evidence is showing a relationship between increased media exposure and
posttraumatic difficulties among children (Pfefferbaum et al., 2001;
Pfefferbaum et al., 2003) as well as between media exposure and other difficulties, such as increased substance use, among adults (Creson, Schmitz,
Sayre, & Rhoades, 2003).

Of course, an increased focus on media coverage can reflect anxiety as
much as create it. In a study of children who lost a friend or acquaintance
in the Oklahoma City bombing, those children who lost a friend watched
significantly more bombing-related television than those who did not lose
a friend (Pfefferbaum et al., 2000).

There is at least one important difference between exposure to media
coverage of terrorist events and exposure to actual terrorist events.
Exposure to actual traumatic events sometimes lowers anxiety levels, presumably as individuals learn that they can indeed survive. In a study of
university students in Israel, having been exposed to one type of traumatic event was associated with an increase in distress, whereas having

been exposed to multiple types of traumatic terrorist events was associated with a reduction in distress (Amir & Sol, 1999). It appears that heightened media coverage may be more similar to the impact of being exposed to a single type of traumatic event—perhaps with the added effect of prolonging the fearful component—while not providing the survival lesson that exposure to multiple types of traumatic events can confer.

ACTIVELY COPING WITH UNCONTROLLABLE STRESSORS

An uncontrollable stressor is an event that produces stress, including fear or anxiety, and that cannot be controlled. For example, the acquisition of a fatal illness is usually a stressor that cannot be controlled. Many stressor events contain both controllable and uncontrollable elements. We cannot stop the hurricane from making landfall at our coastline, but we can board up our windows and move people and things to safer settings. But once we have decided to ride out the storm in our home, we cannot change the fact that there is a hurricane wailing outside.

The value of being able to take action in the face of a stressful situation (as opposed to remaining passive) is that the activity can provide a sense of mastery and control. Animal research suggests that active coping may actually reroute neural pathways in the amygdala, the brain region responsible for fear conditioning (LeDoux & Gorman, 2001; Amorapanth, LeDoux, & Nader, 2000). Thus, some form of active coping appears to be quite desirable.

We usually think of active coping as activity directed toward the source of the threat, such as boarding the windows against the hurricane. However, even activity that is not directly related to the source of the threat, such as playing games, can divert one's attention from the threat and provide a means of discharging energy. These are the conclusions reached by Gal and Lazarus (1975) when they reviewed the literature on coping with stressful events. The two different ways of actively coping are referred to as *problem-focused coping* and *emotion-focused coping*. In problem-focused coping, the activity is directed toward dealing with the threat itself, and in emotion-focused coping, the activity is directed toward dealing with the emotional reaction to the threat.

In 1984, Lazarus and Folkman proposed a goodness-of-fit model and performed research that emphasized the role of appraisal processes in the individual's choice of coping strategy. *Goodness-of-fit* refers to the fit between the coping strategy and the appraised controllability of the stressor. They found that people were less stressed when their use of the two coping strategies was guided by their appraisal of the controllability of the stressor. Lazarus and Folkman contended that problem-focused coping is more effective when the stressor is perceived to be controllable, and emotion-focused coping is more effective when the stressor is perceived to be uncontrollable. Most studies have shown at least moderate support for the goodness-of-fit model, especially with high magnitude threats (Conway & Terry, 1992; Marks, 2000; Park, Folkman, & Bostrom, 2001; Roesch & Weiner, 2001; Zakowski, Hall, Cousino Klein & Baum, 2001).

The downside of appraised controllability is that symptomatology increases when there is a poor fit between appraisals and coping (Forsythe & Compas, 1987). In situations perceived to be controllable, individuals are at greater risk for the negative effects of self-denigration because they are less able to denigrate themselves or feel guilty if they view the stressor as uncontrollable (Conway & Terry, 1992;). In general, it appears that women either use emotion-focused coping more than men or rate it as more effective than do men (Boyd-Wilson, Walkey, McClure, & Green, 2000; Marks, 2000).

Choice of Coping Strategy

Lazarus and Folkman (1984) theorized that both emotion-focused coping and denial might be preferable when the stressor is uncontrollable. They reasoned that because cognitions concerning adverse stimuli increase levels of anxiety, activities that discourage cognitions about the uncontrollable stressor should decrease anxiety. Several studies have examined this hypothesis.

Problem-focused coping, emotion-focused coping, and denial were assessed among Israeli bus commuters following several terrorist attacks on buses (Gidron, Gal, & Zahavi, 1999). Problem-focused coping was assessed on the basis of looking for suspicious objects beneath the seats and studying the faces and origin of the other commuters on the bus. Emotion-focused coping was assessed on the basis of perceptual distraction, manifested by reading or looking at the view, and cognitive distraction, manifested by thinking about pleasant things or people. Denial was assessed on the basis of a general reduced perception of vulnerability to attack. They found that the commuters who developed the fewest problems first used the problem-focused strategy of checking the bus and then engaged in distraction and denial-like behaviors to reduce anxiety.

Both the bus study and a study of children who endured the Scud missile attacks during the Gulf War found negative effects of overreliance on problem-focused coping with an uncontrollable stressor. In the missile attacks, the problem-focused coping was manifested in the form of checking behavior by children who were enclosed in sealed rooms during feared gas attacks. Those children who continued to check on the quality of their sealed environment had worse postwar reactions than the children who relied on avoidance and calming distractions (Weisenberg, Schwarzwald, Waysman, Solomon, & Klingman, 1993). Again, of course, this was a correlational study; it may have been the more anxious children who were unable to stop checking or it may have been those children with adult caretakers who were less effective at engaging the children in emotion-focused activities.

Reducing Danger Appraisals

A fair amount of evidence indicates that people adjust to fearful situations when they discover that the feared events fail to produce the feared outcomes. Fear and anxiety reactions diminished over time in adults in the Scud missile attacks, just as with the bus commuters and with people exposed to multiple types of trauma (Amir & Sol, 1999; Gal, 1994; Gidron, Gal, & Zahavi, 1999). The diminishment in adult fear reactions to the Scud attacks highly correlated with individuals' general appraisal of the situation. It appears that subjective appraisals of danger (and the associated fear and anxiety) decline with repeated exposure to the "danger situation"—as long as no actual trauma occurs.

Lazarus and Folkman (1984) hypothesized that, in addition to emotion-focused coping, "healthy denial" could be adaptive in situations involving uncontrollable stressors. The strongest evidence for healthy denial has come from studies of chronic and fatal illnesses, where the capacity to deny has been viewed by some as a form of resilience that can contribute to the patient's ability to persevere (Druss & Douglas, 1988). Similarly, patients with illnesses that can be exacerbated by anxiety, such as angina, have been shown to have better outcomes when they rely on denial at certain stages of their disease (Levenson, Kay, Monteferrante, & Herman, 1984).

However, it is essential to note that denial is only helpful with chronic and fatal illnesses at those stages where nothing more can be done. Patients resort to denial after exhausting the appropriate problem-focused strategies, such as making lifestyle adjustments and following treatment regimens. Problem-focused coping is appropriate as long as there are controllable stressors. The same is true with the threat of terrorism. In certain situations, such as when the bus commuters first get on the bus, the problem-focused strategy of vigilance can be highly adaptive (as opposed to the maladaptive nature of hypervigilance). Denial only becomes adaptive when there is literally nothing that can be done to change the appraisal of danger.

ANXIETY AND APPRAISALS OF CONTROLLABILITY

The individual's appraisal of the controllability of the stressor thus determines whether the chosen coping strategy increases or diminishes anxiety. Here are some examples utilizing the problem-focused strategy of vigilant scanning:

- When the stressor is perceived to be controllable, the appraisal of danger can be reduced through an active, problem-focused form of coping and anxiety will be reduced. (Example: Passengers in airliner scan their fellow passengers as they first enter the plane, looking for known terrorist characteristics.)
- If the stressor continues to appear controllable after initial problem-focused coping, then continued problem-focused coping reduces anxiety. (Example: Occupants in a building known to be a likely terrorist target either personally scan everyone who enters the building or ensure that a designated individual will guard the entrance and scan everyone who enters. Because people continue to enter the building throughout the day, continued scanning lowers anxiety.)
- When the stressor is not perceived to be controllable, problem-focused coping cannot reduce the appraisal of danger and continued problem-focused coping is likely to maintain or even elevate the anxiety. (Example: Airline passengers continue to scan fellow passengers when no additional terrorist characteristics can be ascertained, as with the checking behavior of the children in the sealed rooms. They remain anxious.)
- When the stressor is perceived to be uncontrollable, emotion-focused coping reduces the anxiety. (Example: Once the plane is in the air, reading, listening to music, or talking with one's neighbor takes a passenger's mind off the possibility of potential terrorism.)

Conflicting Appraisals of Controllability

The issue of managing anxiety through coping strategies becomes complicated in a group situation. Members of the group may have different preferences for how they choose to cope. Some individuals may rigidly adhere to a preferred coping style regardless of the controllability of the stressor. Furthermore, even if all members are flexible and able to apply different coping strategies according to the perceived controllability of the stressor, they still may differ in regard to their appraisals of the controllability of the stressor.

- When the stressor is perceived to be controllable by some but not others, emotion-focused coping or denial increases anxiety among those who view the stressor as controllable, and problem-focused coping increases anxiety among those who view the stressor as uncontrollable.

- When the perception of controllability is filtered through one member's denial, it will increase anxiety among those who seek a more objective appraisal through active scanning.
- In general, denial increases anxiety among those who are not in denial, and problem-focused coping increases anxiety among those in denial.

The importance of appraisals of controllability does not end with the qeestion of how the group will cope with the danger situation. Individuals who have experienced traumatic events often feel subsequent guilt because they believe they failed to actively deal with some controllable factor in the trauma. Cognitive restructuring treatment of posttraumatic stress disorder (PTSD) often focuses on modifying appraisals of controllability (Carroll & Foy, 1992). When group members continue to differ in their posttraumatic appraisals, the potential for blaming is vastly increased.

The issue of within-group differences in regard to approach to anxiety management, appraisals of controllability, and preferences in coping style produces the highest anxiety when the group must cope as a single unit. This often leads to conflicts over control of the group and pressure on members to conform their appraisals toward the group norm. These issues reach their greatest potential to produce anxiety when the group is rigidly unable to tolerate differences among members and members feel unable to operate independently. The combination of extreme dependence on the group and a high demand for conformity can produce tremendous levels of anxiety. This has powerful implications for families dealing with the threat of terrorism.

THE FAMILY'S USE OF COPING STRATEGIES

If all members of a family share the same appraisal of danger and the same preferences for coping, then the family may be able to operate as a unified group and choose coping strategies that would provide the maximum reduction in anxiety for all members. Unfortunately, it is seldom the case that any group of people shares the same appraisals of danger and preferences for style of coping. Instead, the differences in these appraisals and preferences are likely to generate additional anxiety, especially when the appraisals involve danger. Under conditions of threat, fear, and anxiety, decision makers tend to be "more urgent, less willing to consider opinions or alternatives, and driven to premature closure" (Hall, Norwood, Ursano, & Fullerton, 2003, p. 142).

Representatives of our government regularly argue these issues, each promoting their respective appraisals of the extent of danger and their respective solutions for coping with the danger. Groups that regularly deal with danger situations typically develop specialization and leadership hierarchies in order to minimize the destructive paralysis that can result from disagreement about the appraised danger and solutions. The best example is the military, which maintains a clear hierarchical organization, allowing the leader to make decisions and specifying who assumes leadership if something happens to the leader. Informal groups generally have leaders as well, but the lack of a formal structure increases the possibility of a breakdown in group decision making in situations.

These are some of the issues that confront the family in danger situations. The family may need to make group decisions that are based upon appraisals of danger and which involve choice of coping strategies. The way in which the decision making is accomplished will vary according to a number of variables, including the family's power structure, point of development in the family life cycle, age of children, and the ways in which individual members are valued. For example, couples with small children will usually keep the decision-making process within the marital dyad (though the two adults may still disagree), whereas families with grown children may find that decision-making patterns from the past are no longer viable.

Anxiety is a major factor leading to emotional disturbance among people who live in proximity of terrorist activities (Zuckerman-Bareli, 1982). Unfortunately, the family's anxiety is likely to increase when there are significant differences between family members in regard to their appraisals and preferred strategies for coping with the threat of terrorism. Children are affected when the coping strategies of adults clash (Handford et al., 1986), and, although they may not influence the coping strategies of the family, children have danger appraisals that must be respected. Often a child perceives danger and cannot be talked out of it. Efforts to talk a child out of feeling fearful seldom work well because of a fundamental difference between fear and anxiety.

THE NATURE OF FEAR AND ANXIETY

The primary difference between fear and anxiety lies in the location of the danger—generally, fear is a response to one's *perception* of a real external threat, whereas anxiety is a response to the *possibility* that something might happen—a distinction referred to as *conception versus perception* (Catherall, 2003). Both emotions involve the affect fear-terror and include a physiological state of arousal. Treatments for anxiety are often focused on lowering the arousal state. Although it is helpful to reduce the arousal level with both fear and anxiety, simply lowering arousal is insufficient to resolve fear. In the case of fear, we must address the perceived external stimulus provoking the fear.

> We may be able talk an individual into a less anxious state but we cannot talk someone out of feeling fearful. Sometimes we may be able to change an individual's perception ("That's not an alligator, it's just a log.") but if the perception does not change then we must address either the stimulus ("We will move the boat away from the alligator.") or the response (the conditioned fear). (Catherall, 2003, p. 87)

Fear and the Family System

Individually, the perception of threat is simply a fact to be addressed, but in families the perception itself can be a source of contention. The less the family is able to tolerate differences, the more they become invested in establishing a consensual agreement about the perception of threat. This need for agreement undermines the security of members with discordant perceptions. If they feel pressured to give up their discordant perceptions, they are likely to either withdraw and participate superficially or become rebellious and vulnerable to being scapegoated by the rest of the family.

It is imperative that the family be able to distinguish between fear and anxiety, especially among children. The anxious child is concerned about what *might* happen, often feeding that anxiety with additional apprehensive thoughts. But the fearful child (or adult) perceives the source of the fear to be present—either happening or about to happen. If an individual feels fear and there is no obvious reason for it, then he or she is likely to look for the external source—the threat. (This is probably what occurs when the victim of a panic attack concludes that his heart is beating irregularly.) Because fear is associated with the perception of an actual threat, family members must respond in a problem-focused manner. Bear in mind that the fear is real, even if the perception of threat is not accurate. To treat the fear as not legitimate because the perception of threat is incorrect will not only fail to extinguish the fear, it will erode the credibility of the other family members and increase the sufferer's anxiety about getting help when fearful.

Lenore Terr studied and treated a number of children from Chowchilla, California, who were kidnapped and buried alive in a bus in 1976 — certainly a terrorist event for those children and their families. After the traumatic event was past, the children were still fearful—their perception was that they were still in danger and unable to protect themselves. Terr taught them to tape a quarter inside their shoe so that they could use a pay phone. Furthermore, she did not simply check to see if they knew their phone number, she had them practice the entire procedure of dialing the number, speaking to an operator, and calling collect (Terr, 1990). Terr taught these children to employ problem-focused coping; she taught it thoroughly enough that they could feel truly confident that they knew they could do something to protect themselves.

Fear Contagion

"By Tina being calm, it helped us to be calm."

> Michael Benfante, company manager who helped carry
> wheelchair-bound Tina Hansen down the stairway
> of the World Trade Center shortly before it collapsed.
> (*People* magazine, Oct. 1, 2001, p. 22)

Terr described how other children, who were not involved in the event, picked up some of the affected children's behavioral reenactments of their trauma. She compared that behavioral contagion to the power to elicit fearfulness, as seen in the works of authors such as Stephen King and directors such as Alfred Hitchcock (both of whom apparently suffered powerful fears in childhood). Researchers at the University of Hawaii studied the phenomenon of *emotional contagion*, which begins with the tendency to mimic and synchronize facial expressions, vocalizations, postures, movements, and instrumental behaviors with those of another person. The mimicry and synchronization allow a feedback process to develop, in which subjective emotional experience is affected, and people tend to "catch" other people's emotions (Hatfield, Cacioppo, & Rapson, 1993, 1994).

Nowhere is the phenomenon of emotional contagion more crucial than when the emotion is fear. Families are necessarily invested in containing the fear of members because it can spread and disrupt the functioning of the entire family. When one member experiences fear, it usually becomes an immediate focus of the other family members. Their efforts to extinguish the fear may be in the form of empathic responses to the fearful member's discomfort or they may be control tactics designed to shut down the contagious effect of a fearful member.

Anxiety and the Family System

A certain amount of anxiety accompanies being part of a family. Murray Bowen (1978) observed that emotionally significant relationships juxtapose counterbalancing forces of individuality or autonomy versus togetherness or fusion. Negotiating these counterbalancing forces is anxiety laden—to ignore either force in favor of the other leads to feared outcomes. Too much togetherness can interfere with being a whole person, and too much autonomy can threaten one's relationships. Every family settles into some level of differentiation that is based on the differentiation of the various members, that is, from emotionally fused to more fully differentiated.

Most families establish a stable pattern that might comprise anything from constant conflict to an easy comfort with one another. But a family's level of differentiation is variable. The stability can be disrupted by developmental events in the family, such as the increased differentiation of a member (e.g., a child matures and leaves the family to live on her or his own) or the decreased differentiation of a member (e.g., a child grows up but fails to leave home and instead becomes more emotionally dependent). These kinds of changes increase the family's anxiety and require the entire system to recalibrate.

The family's stability also can be disrupted by external events, such as a change from a benign environment to an environment of terrorism. When a new source of anxiety enters the family environment, there is a tendency for the family to move toward a state of greater fusion and to operate from a more emotional, less objective perspective (Kerr & Bowen, 1982). When the family operates from a state of greater fusion, individuals are less able to manage their own anxiety without recruiting others to help them. This recruitment of help can be a direct request for support and additional solutions or it can take the form of a covert process, such as projective identification, that uses others without their awareness or consent. Covert recruitment processes generally lead to the kinds of secondary problems that dominate family life and contribute to dysfunctionality.

CONTAINMENT, PROJECTIVE IDENTIFICATION, AND THE FAMILY

In a threatening environment, the family's primary job is to help contain the anxiety of family members. To understand what this means, consider our use of the term with individuals. Individuals who have problems with affective regulation are sometimes described in terms of a difficulty with *containing* emotions, that is, being able to recognize and experience emotions without acting them out. A therapy client's capacity to contain his or her anxiety is often aided by the connection with the therapist; the therapist can function as a container for the client's anxiety as long as the therapist can effectively contain his or her own anxiety.

The container function is often associated with projective identification, in which the client projects onto the therapist and behaves in such a way as to stimulate the therapist's own anxiety. As the recipient of the projection, the therapist must contain his or her own anxiety (Catherall, 1992). But an additional aspect to the process of projective identification has major ramifications for families: After the projector stimulates the recipient's anxiety, he or she disavows his or her own anxiety and adopts a view of the recipient as different, that is, the recipient is anxious and the projector is not. This process is at the center of many conflictual interactions in families. The recipient of the projection has been *covertly recruited* to help manage the projector's anxiety and may then be treated as though something is wrong with him or her.

It is the projector's shift from manifesting his or her own anxiety to disavowing it and disconnecting from the recipient that creates the problem and leads to the conflict. The projector's disconnection takes the form of believing and communicating that he or she is not like this other person and cannot relate to what this other person is feeling. The harmful implication is that the other person is feeling anxious because of something inherently wrong with him- or herself. The problem with this process is not that the second person is left feeling anxious; the problem is the disconnection. In families, this process can take place among the entire group of family members and result in one individual (or sometimes a subgroup of individuals) being scapegoated and becoming disconnected from the family.

RELATIONAL TRAUMA

The damage that can result from disconnection is the most severe when the entire family disconnects and refuses to validate the experience of one family member. This can occur as a result of projective identification by other family members or even when one member is fearful or anxious and the other members are invested in denying their own fear or anxiety and insist something is wrong with the one member. Viewing that member as different allows the other family members to block their identification with the distressed member and thereby disown their own anxiety, a mechanism long observed in groups (Jacques, 1955). This process of refusing to validate one member's experience can produce a *relational trauma,* and the anxious or fearful member is left "feeling alienated, vulnerable, and personally damaged" (Catherall, 1995, p. 87).

A similar process can occur in therapy, whether the therapist is receiving a projective identification, engaged in emotional contagion, or simply listening empathically. If we fend off our own anxiety by refusing to identify or empathize with our clients' anxious thoughts—perhaps by insisting their thinking is wrong, by internally dismissing them (often by labeling their character) or by adopting a role and not being real ourselves—then our clients feel something is wrong with them (Catherall, 1991). On the other hand, if we can maintain our empathic connection with our clients and relate to their anxious thoughts while managing our own anxiety, then they feel understood and validated. I think the vast majority of mistakes I have made as a therapist were due to my failure to contain my own anxiety.

The Disconnected Family and the Threatening Environment

Once a relational trauma occurs within the family, performance of the most basic function of the family, the caretaking of family members, is compromised and the family may be characterized as dysfunctional (Catherall, 1997). An observer would notice a distinct change in the warmth, control, and consistency of parental caretaking (Cusinato, 1998). If the family remains dysfunctional, at least one of the parents becomes emotionally inaccessible, leading one or more children to step into the caretaking breach and assume the role of the parentified child (Stiver, 1990a, 1990b). The family members quit being genuine in their interactions with each other, and the family no longer operates as a group invested in what is best for each member. The relational trauma has disrupted the connections within the family.

When the family connections have broken, fear of the dissolution of the group becomes more intense. Individual needs, including the need for autonomy, are viewed as less important, and there is greater pressure on individuals to base their decisions on "what's best for the family." Typically, some members become spokespersons for individuality, and some become spokespersons for what's best for the family. Those members who are struggling for individuality often become disengaged from the other family members, whereas a core of those concerned about keeping the family together tend to become enmeshed. Anxiety accompanies both the disengaged and the enmeshed members, and neither group is able to use the family as a container.

THE FAMILY AS SANCTUARY

In order for the family to offer a sanctuary from the external sources of fear and anxiety, members must be able to contain the internal sources of fear and anxiety. To cope as a group, members must each have a voice and feel sufficiently confident in the family decision makers to tolerate differences in appraisals and coping styles. Morale among troops about to go into combat is related both to personal variables, such as confidence in leadership and unit cohesion, and strategic variables, such as evaluation of the enemy and familiarity with the mission (Gal, 1986). The equivalent in a family might be confidence in the family decision makers and sufficient acceptance of their appraisals and coping choices.

COPING WITH THE THREAT OF TERRORISM

The preceding discussion identifies the components of the family environment that must be addressed for the family to cope effectively with the threat of terrorism. Each family member must be free to express his or her personal appraisals of danger, opinions about the controllability of stressors, and preferences about coping style. They should also be free to express theib fears and anxieties, and not be treated as though something is wrong with them if their feelings, perceptions, opinions, preferences, and choices differ from those of other family members. Anxious members must be free to talk about their anxieties without others trying to control them, and without the anxious members resorting to covert recruitment. All members should be attuned to the special nature of fear and respond to fearful members appropriately. Finally, there needs to be an effective decision-making structure. Overall, the goal is for family members to maintain their connections with one another.

THERAPEUTIC INTERVENTION

In family therapy, the therapist intervenes on two levels: The first level is manifested in the structure of the therapeutic environment, that is, the therapist validates all family members by accepting their feelings as legitimate and ensuring each has a full voice in the sessions; and the second level refers to the patterns, roles, rules, and other behaviors that become the focus during sessions (Catherall, 1997). Simply by leading a discussion of the way individuals in the family cope with fear and anxiety, the therapist is giving everyone a voice and identifying coping patterns, degrees of emotional safety and emotional accessibility, rules regarding emotional expression, levels of contagion, and potential sources of anxiety if there are significant differences in appraisals or coping preferences.

Interventions we can apply with families affected by an environment of potential trauma fall in the categories of either psychoeducation or psychotherapy. Psychoeducational interventions are either (a) sharing information and knowledge that a family may not possess or (b) teaching skills that may not be part of a family's repertoire. Helpful information might include the deleterious effects of excessive television exposure, the advantages of using problem-focused coping with controllable stressors and emotion-focused coping with uncontrollable stressors, the differences between pure fear and anxiety, and the necessity of using problem-focused coping with fear (if the perception will not change). Skills that can be taught include techniques for anxiety reduction and strategies for emotion-focused coping.

In determining the focus of psychotherapy interventions, the therapist assesses three primary areas: (a) the danger appraisals of the various members, (b) the coping strategies pursued and preferred by the various members, and (c) the ways in which family members deal with fear and anxiety—both in themselves and in each other. If there are significant differences in appraisals, the therapist is interested in validating the different members and unearthing the control mechanisms that might be silencing some members. If there are conflicts over approaches to coping, the therapist should note how the different preferences are resolved and which members are likely to be anxious and unhappy with the coping strategies employed.

It is important to determine (a) whether the family distinguishes between fear and anxiety and responds appropriately to fearful members and (b) whether those family members who have difficulty containing their anxiety can acknowledge their problem and seek help directly as well as whether there are covert recruitment processes at work. Most importantly, can family members retain their connectedness to fearful or anxious members, or are such members being treated as though something is wrong with them?

Here are some assessment questions that can help determine whether a family is coping with external sources of fear and anxiety in a functional manner.

Appraisal Processes

- Are there differences in the appraisal of danger? Are such differences tolerated or do some members dismiss the concerns of others?
- Is there pressure on those with discordant appraisals to conform?
- Are the appraisals of children treated respectfully?

Coping Strategies

- Is there flexible application of coping strategies, particularly involving the use of problem-focused coping with controllable factors and emotion-focused coping with uncontrollable factors?
- If the family's use of coping strategies does not appear flexible, then what strategies predominate? Do individual members rigidly adhere to particular strategies?
- Does the family use denial to cope with the threat of danger? Is there denial of differences between members?
- Are there family members who are not personally in denial? Do they speak up to the others, cope in their own preferred style, or submit to the family norm?

Management of Anxiety

- Does the family distinguish between fear and anxiety and attend to each appropriately?

- Are fears taken seriously and the source of the fear addressed by the nonfearful or less fearful members? If perceptions of fear do not change, does the family employ problem-oriented coping?
- Are children taken seriously? Are their appraisals of danger addressed openly or are they dismissed?
- Do parents have an ample repertoire of emotion-focused coping techniques with which to engage children? Are adults able to contain their own anxiety and respond to children in a manner that validates the children's feelings?
- Are there processes of covert recruitment for anxiety management? Are there members who are viewed as different (something wrong with them) because they have anxieties or fears that the other members refuse to relate to?
- Do family members use disapproval, threat of abandonment, criticism, or distancing to control other members' expression of anxiety?

The family may not be able to remove one member's anxiety, but they can help him or her to contain it and prevent it from stirring up a host of secondary problems. Our primary intervention is to enhance or preserve the family's ability to deal with fear and anxiety without diminishing the connections between members.

CASE EXAMPLE

Mr. and Mrs. F were Americans who lived in West Africa with their three children. This was the second time they had lived abroad due to Mr. F's job. The country they lived in was stable, but there were several unstable countries in the region, including one that was on a nearby border. Acts of terrorism had occurred in these other countries for several years, but the country where the F family lived had been protected from such acts. This changed when a series of terrorist acts occurred in the region near the border. The terrorist acts included explosions and the ambushing of automobiles.

The F family lived in a community composed of Americans and other English-speaking foreigners who worked in the country. The community was fenced off and guarded by armed guards. The children attended school at a private school (grades K through 12) that was similarly protected. The terrorist incidents occurred over a hundred miles away, and nothing had occurred in the developed territory, but the entire American community became more anxious as these events began occurring.

Within the F family, there was considerable difference in exposure to terrorist events. Mr. F was required to travel to other countries as part of his job. Though he was not present during an act of terrorism (except for hearing the explosion of a bus bomb during a trip to Israel), he encountered the aftermath of terrorist incidents on several occasions. Mrs. F, on the other hand, had not been exposed to anything resembling terrorism and was relatively protected from such events because she seldom ever left the gated community. The two younger children were in the early grades and had not been exposed, but the eldest daughter, who was a senior, had been near a terrorist shooting at an airport in a neighboring country. She had attended school in Europe for a few years and had traveled alone a number of times.

The F family, along with the rest of the community, tolerated the intrusion of terrorist activity in the border region well enough. However, this changed after there were two bomb threats at the children's school. Neither thbeat led to anything, but problems developed in the family. Mrs. F was the most anxious and began to argue in favor of the family leaving the country and returning to the United States. Mr. F kept insisting that the threat was not as great as Mrs. F perceived it to be. He tried to calm her anxiety by convincing her that the threat was minimal. The eldest daughter heard a rumor that at least one of the bomb threats was a prank by a student and took a very strong stand about wanting to remain in the school until she graduated.

The situation worsened when the youngest daughter began to develop sleep problems and anxiety about separations from her mother. Mrs. F became more anxious herself and a physician placed her on antidepressant medication. Mrs. F and Mr. F began to fight, and Mrs. F complained of having no voice in the decision making. They also began to revisit some older issues in their relationship that had seemed to have been put to rest years earlier. Mrs. F and the eldest daughter began to get into frequent conflicts; the daughter accused her mother of being hysterical and letting her fear destroy the family's life. Finally, Mr. F agreed to return to the United States and he arranged a transfer with his company. They returned to the states, but the conflicts continued and eventually brought them into therapy.

After an attempt at family therapy with a therapist who focused on the relationship between Mrs. F and the eldest daughter, Mr. and Mrs. F sought couple therapy. The first issue confronted in the therapy was Mr. F's view that Mrs. F's anxiety in Africa was excessive and stemmed from her relationship with her mother. Though he acknowledged he had been anxious about the children's well-being, he had a way of conveying that it was really not that big a deal. He remained stuck in this point of view until a series of sessions that explored Mr. F's childhood feelings of safety when his father was home. His capacity to relate to Mrs. F's anxiety began to expand as he recalled the feelings in his home when his father would have to travel on business. Ironically (but not surprisingly), Mrs. F was better able to explore the roots of her anxiety (stemming from her relationship with her mother) as Mr. F became more validating of her feelings in Africa.

The conflict between the eldest daughter and Mrs. F did not fully resolve until after the daughter had gone off to college (about 6 to 8 months after their return to the states). However, as Mr. F became more accepting of Mrs. F's reactions to the threat of terrorism, the daughter let go of the hysteria accusations, and their conflicts were more about the struggles of living together. Also, somewhere in the months after they had returned to the states, the youngest daughter's sleep and separation symptoms abated.

This case is an example of several of the points made in this chapter. Mr. F had been exposed to multiple terrorist events and hence had a very different appraisal of the extent of the danger from that of his wife. To a lesser degree, this appears to have been the case with the eldest daughter as well, although her reaction appeared to involve more denial. For that reason, it is possible that there was a projective identification process occurring between mother and daughter. The real damage occurred when father and daughter disconnected from mother and treated her anxiety reactions as though they were not valid. She then became the family scapegoat and, in a sense, may have carried the family's anxiety about the possibility of terrorism.

When Mr. F finally validated Mrs. F's anxiety (by revealing his own concern about what could happen if terrorists did indeed target the children's school), she felt immeasurably better. He had acknowledged this before, but it came across very differently when his words were supported by his affective state. It was true that Mrs. F's tendency to get anxious was higher than that of most people, but this did not change the legitimate nature of what she was concerned about. And Mr. F's resistance to validating her anxiety was a replication of her relationship with her mother. Yet these historical issues could not be examined or worked with until her perception of the terrorist threat (fear) was accepted as legitimate.

CONCLUDING REMARKS

One of the most basic and powerful ways that families help individual members manage emotional distress is simply by maintaining an emotional connection. Whenever people feel connected to others, especially to a group of others, their capacity to tolerate difficult emotion is enhanced. A powerful example of this phenomenon is the experience of the American POWs in the "Hanoi Hilton" during the Vietnam War. These men worked out a tap code that they used to communicate with each other from the isolation of their individual cells. These prisoners were not sharing state secrets; rather, the code allowed them to maintain a sense of connection with one another, and that made the grueling experience more bearable for each of them. Groups typically become more cohesive during periods of external threat. It also appears that individuals acquire a different perspective on their own problems. For example, the rate of suicides in Britain decreased during the month following the September 11 terrorist attacks in America (Salib, 2003).

The family is a group with an extensive history; it is part of a larger community, both current and historic. Feeling connected to the historical family and to the community in which the family resides strengthens individuals. For example, possessing knowledge of stories about grandparents or great-grandparents has been shown to predict lower sexual risk taking among women in a sexually transmitted disease clinic (Landau, Cole, Tuttle, Clements, & Stanton, 2000). When the family is part of a community that is dealing with the threat of terrorism, strengthening the connection with the community aids everyone (Catherall, 2002). The proliferation of flags and expressions of national solidarity in the wake of the terrorist attacks of September 11, 2001, is an example of a strengthening of the social network at the community level.

The worst damage that can be wrought by the threat of potential terrorism trauma is to disrupt our interpersonal connections. Our ability to maintain our connections—both within our families and within our communities—is our best sanctuary against external sources of danger. When intervening with families who are dealing with the threat of terrorism, the guiding principle should be to find ways to help them maintain and improve their connections with one another.

REFERENCES

Amir, M., & Sol, O. (1999). Psychological impact and prevalence of traumatic events in a student sample in Israel: The effect of multiple traumatic events and physical injury. *Journal of Traumatic Stress, 12,* 139–154.

Amorapanth, P., LeDoux, J. E., & Nader, K. (2000). Different lateral amygdala outputs mediate reactions and actions elicited by a fear-arousing stimulus. *Nature Neuroscience, 3,* 74–79.

Bowen, M. (1978). *Family therapy in clinical practice.* New York: Jason Aronson.

Boyd-Wilson, B. M., Walkey, F. H., McClure, J., & Green D. E. (2000). Do we need positive illusions to carry out plans? Illusion and instrumental coping. *Personality & Individual Differences, 29,* 1141–1152.

Carroll, E. M., & Foy, D. W. (1992). Assessment and treatment of combat-related posttraumatic stress disorder in a medical center setting. In D. W. Foy (Ed.), *Treating PTSD: Cognitive-behavioral strategies* (pp. 39–68). New York: Guilford.

Catherall, D. R. (1991). Aggression and projective identification in the treatment of victims. *Psychotherapy, Special Issue on Victimization, 28,* 145–149.

Catherall, D. R. (1992). Working with projective identification in couples. *Family Process, 31,* 355–367

Catherall, D. R. (1995). Coping with secondary traumatic stress: The importance of the therapist's professional peer group. In B. H. Stamm (Ed.), *Secondary traumatic stress: Self-care issues for clinicians, researchers, & educators* (pp. 80–92). Lutherville, MD: Sidran.

Catherall, D. R. (1997). Treating traumatized families. In C. R. Figley (Ed.), *Burnout in families: The systemic costs of caring* (pp. 187–215). Boca Raton, FL: CRC Press.

Catherall, D. R. (1999). Family as a group treatment for PTSD. In B. H. Young & D. D. Blake (Eds.), *Group treatment for posttraumatic stress disorders: Conceptualization, themes, and processes* (pp. 15–34). Philadelphia, PA: Brunner/Mazel.

Catherall, D. R. (2002). The power of community. *Family Process, 41,* 18–20.

Catherall, D. R. (2003). How fear differs from anxiety. *Traumatology, 9*(2), 76–92.

Conway, V. J., & Terry, D. J. (1992). Appraised controllability as a moderator of the effectiveness of different coping strategies: A test of the goodness of fit hypothesis. *Australian Journal of Psychology, 44,* 1–7.

Creson, D. L., Schmitz, J. M., Sayre, S. L., & Rhoades, H. M. (2003). Stress and behavior change in a substance-abusing population following September 11, 2001. *Addictive Disorders & Their Treatment, 2,* 59–61.

Cusinato, M. (1998). Parenting styles and psychopathology. In L. L'Abate (Ed.), *Family psychopathology: The relational roots of dysfunctional behavior* (pp. 158–179). New York: Guilford.

Druss, R. G., & Douglas, C. J. (1988). Adaptive responses to illness and disability: Healthy denial. *General Hospital Psychiatry, 10,* 163–168.

Forsythe, C. J., & Compass, B. E. (1987). Interaction of cognitive appraisals of stressful events and coping: Testing the goodness of fit hypothesis. *Cognitive Therapy and Research, 11,* 473–485.

Friedland, N., & Merari, A. (1985). The psychological impact of terrorism: A double-edged sword. *Political Psychology, 6,* 591–604.

Gal, R. (1986). Unit morale: From a theoretical puzzle to an empirical illustration: An Israeli example. *Journal of Applied Social Psychology, 16,* 549–564.

Gal, R. (1994). People under Scuds: Reactions of the Israeli population to the missile attacks during the Gulf War. [Hebrew]. *Psychologia: Israel Journal of Psychology, 4,* 182–192.

Gal, R., & Lazarus, R. S. (1975). The role of activity in anticipating and confronting stressful situations. *Journal of Human Stress, 1*(4), 4–20.

Gidron, Y., Gal, R., & Zahavi, S. (1999). Bus commuters' coping strategies and anxiety from terrorism: An example of the Israeli experience. *Journal of Traumatic Stress, 12,* 185–1)2.

Handford, H. A., Mayes, S. D., Mattison, R. E., Humphrey, F. J., Bagnato, S., Bixler et al. (1986). Child and parent reaction to the Three Mile Island nuclear accident. *Journal of the American Academy of Child Psychiatry, 25,* 346–356.

Hatfield, E., Cacioppo, J. T., & Rapson, R. L. (1993). Emotional contagion, *Current Directions in Psychological Science, 2*(3), 96–99.

Hatfield, E., Cacioppo, J. T., & Rapson, R. L. (1994). *Emotional contagion.* New York: Cambridge University Press.

Jacques, E. (1955). Social systems as defence against persecutory and depressive anxiety. In M. Klein (Ed.), *New direction in psychoanalysis.* New York: Basic Books.

Kats, R. (1982). Concerns of the Israeli: Change and stability from 1962 to 1975. *Human Relations, 35*(2), 83–100.

Kerr, M. E., & Bowen, M. (1998). *Family evaluation: An approach based on Bowen theory.* New York: W.W. Norton.

Landau, J., Cole, R. E., Tuttle, J., Clements, C. D., & Stanton, M. D. (2000). Family connectedness and women's sexual risk behaviors: Implications for the prevention/intervention of STD/HIV infection, *Family Process, 39,* 461–475.

Lazarus, R. S., & Folkman, S. (1984). *Stress, appraisal and coping.* New York: Springer.

LeDoux, J. E., & Gorman, J. M. (2001). A call to action: Overcoming anxiety through active coping. *American Journal of Psychiatry, 158,* 1953–1955.

Levenson, J. L., Kay, R., Monteferrante, J., & Herman, M. V. (1984). Denial predicts favorable outcome in unstable angina pectoris. *Psychosomatic Medicine, 46,* 25–32.

Marks, L. I. (2000). Perceived effectiveness of problem-focused and emotion-focused coping: The role of appraisal of event controllability and personality traits. Dissertation Abstracts International: Section B: the Sciences & Engineering, Vol. 61(1-B), 540, US: University Microfilms International.

Park, C. L., Folkman, S., & Bostrom, A. (2001). Appraisals of controllability and coping in caregivers and HIV+ men: Testing the goodness-of-fit hypothesis. *Journal of Consulting and Clinical Psychology, 69,* 481–488.

Pfefferbaum, B., Gurwitch, R. H., McDonald, N. B., Leftwich, M. J. T., Sconzo, G. M., Messenbaugh, A. K., & Schultz, R. A. (2000). Posttraumatic stress among young children after the death of a friend or acquaintance in a terrorist bombing, *Psychiatric Services, 51,* 386–388.

Pfefferbaum, B., Nixon, S. J., Tivis, R. D., Doughty, D. E., Pynoos, R. S., Gurwitch, R. H., and Foy, D. W. (2001). Television exposure in children after a terrorist incident. *Psychiatry, 64*(3), 202–211.

Pfefferbaum, B., Seale, T. W., Brandt, E. N. Jr., Pfefferbaum, R. L., Doughty, D. E., & Rainwater, S. M. (2003). Media exposure in children one hundred miles from a terrorist bombing. *Annals of Clinical Psychiatry, 15,* 1–8.

Roesch, S. C., & Weiner, B. (2001). A meta-analytic review of coping with illness: Do causal attributions matter? *Journal of Psychosomatic Research, 50,* 205–219.

Salib, E. (2003). Effect of 11 September 2001 on suicide and homicide in England and Wales. *British Journal of Psychiatry, 183,* 207–212.

Schlenger, W. E., Caddell, J. M., Ebert, L., Jordan, B. K., Rourke, K. M., Wilson, D. et al. (2002). Psychological reactions to terrorist attacks: Findings from the National Study of Americans' Reactions to September 11. *Journal of the American Medical Association, 288,* 581–588.

Schuster, M. A., Stein, B. D., Jaycox, L. H., Collins, R. L., Marshall, G. N., Elliott, M. N. et al. (2001). A national survey of stress reactions after the September 11, 2001, terrorist attacks. *New England Journal of Medicine, 345,* 1507–1512.

Sitterle, K. A., & Gurwitch, R. H. (1999). The terrorist bombing in Oklahoma City. In E. S. Zinner & M. B. Williams (Eds.), *When a community weeps: Case studies in group survivorship* (pp. 160–189), Philadelphia: Brunner/Mazel.

Slone, M. (2000). Responses to media coverage of terrorism. *Journal of Conflict Resolution, 44,* 508–522.

Stiver, I. P. (1990a). Dysfunctional families and wounded relationships—Part I. *Work in progress.* Wellesley, MA: Stone Center Working Paper Series.

Stiver, I. P. (1990b). Dysfunctional families and wounded relationships—Part II. *Work in progress.* Wellesley, MA: Stone Center Working Paper Series.

Terr, L. (1990). *Too scared to cry: Psychic trauma in childhood.* New York: Harper & Row.

Weisenberg, M., Schwarzwald, J., Waysman, M., Solomon, Z., & Klingman, A. (1993). Coping of school-age children in the sealed room during Scud missile bombardment and post-war stress reactions. *Journal of Consulting and Clinical Psychology, 61,* 462–467.

Zakowski, S. G., Hall, M. H., Cousino Klein, L., & Baum, A. (2001). Appraised control, coping, and stress in a community sample: A test of the goodness-of-fit hypothesis. *Annals of Behavioral Medicine, 23,* 158–165.

Zuckerman-Bareli, C. (1982). The effect of border tension on the adjustment of kibbutzim and moshavim on the northern border of Israel: A path analysis. *Series in Clinical & Community Psychology: Stress & Anxiety, 8,* 81–91.

Index

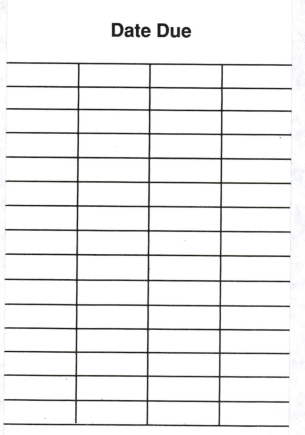

Date Due

BRODART, CO.   Cat. No. 23-233-003   Printed in U.S.A.